SARAH MARSHANK

being self*ish*

— AN UNORTHODOX MEMOIR —

MY JOURNEY FROM ESCORT TO MONK TO GRANDMOTHER

I dedicate this book to my beloved husband, Steven, whose fierce love

remains the cauldron within which I simmer...

the soil from which I blossom.

Appreciation

Writing a memoir is an exercise in truth telling. It's a confrontational reckoning with one's transgressions and triumphs...the stuff of every human life. Converting the narrative of my life into story, and polishing the many drafts into art, has stretched me to develop a new form of creative expression. This experience has shaped me into an emerging writer. The journey has been a stunning pilgrimage...nine years of unraveling, sorting, and crafting.

This book is a testimony to the virtue inherent in every life.

I could not have done it without the love and support of many.

My gratitude goes first to my mother. I must acknowledge her famously. It is through her womb that I was gestated into life, and through her generosity that I was raised in a home with plentiful food, clothing, educational opportunities, and love of the most rudimentary and exquisite sort: care. My representation of my mother in this book in less than wonderful light reflects my perception of her through the lens of who I was at the time and what I was capable of seeing. I trust you will take the journey with me as you read and discover how my perception of her changed because I changed—not because she did. What a deep lesson and teaching this has been for me.

Next, I take a deep respectful bow to my beautiful step-daughter. I entered her life when she was eight and still in the sweetness of childhood. Though I did not feel ready or capable of being a parent, even a "step" one, she showed me I was worthy, even if imperfect. Her sensitive and generous heart continues to spur my own heart's opening.

My father died while I was writing this book, but I still feel his presence, supporting my success in every aspect of my life. Thanks, Dad.

The journey with my siblings and their families has been difficult—evidence of the complexity of blood relations—and I am humbly grateful for their willingness to forgive and begin again. Especially my sister.

A special note of gratitude to my husband's family members, who have welcomed me fully into their hearts, especially my step-son and his wife, for their great kindness and love. And to Edie, Agnes, and Mae, because being Granni Sarah Rose is one of the most precious experiences of my life.

Many midwives helped me birth this book. For his steadfast support, creative talent, marketing genius and publicist powers, I'm fabulously grateful for my friend Paul West. The book cover is his creation. My astute and loving writing coach Edith Friesen, who helped me stay with it when I wanted to give up, masterfully guiding the process and the content. My editors, Marilyn Simmonds-Cole, Julie Akins, and Jennifer Margulis for their keen eyes and ability to call forth the perfect sentence or word. My readers and writing partners, Cat Gould, Marga Laube, Jill Chitra, Donna Zerner, and Leslie Caplan for their valuable suggestions and loving support. My picky picky picky copy-editor Deborah-Miriam Leff. My dear sister of the heart and soul, Erin, for her steady and supportive presence. And an especially rich debt of gratitude to Kathryn Thomas for being steadfast in her generosity and impeccability as friend and editor.

I am grateful to Sam…for providing me the opportunity to experience a decade of uninterrupted introspection, study, and devoted practice. His generosity was immense, and his injunction to sit down, shut up, and listen, has served me well.

I pay homage to all my teachers, some represented in this story, others unnamed. A special thank you to Jun Po and Marlies, dear friends and teachers who continue to be instrumental in the integration of my inner realization with my human life.

Finally, I extend my gratitude to you, the reader, for meeting me here, holding this book in your hand, ready to hear my story.

A Note to the Reader

An autobiography tells the story *of* a life,
memoir tells a story *from* a life.

All accounts in this memoir are true to my memory.
Some events and characters are a blend of more than one.
All names have been changed except for
Steven, Jun Po, and Edie.

Contents

broken

1

I'm pacing the perimeter of the abandoned tennis court behind my small secluded cottage in Bonny Doon, California. I'm alone, hunched over, looking down at the deteriorating concrete beneath my bare feet. I wonder how it is that things fall apart. How it is that I am falling apart. Walking in circles helps calm the incessant chatter in my head. The rhythm of my stride generates welcome space between my thoughts.

I take advantage of the opening and ask for help.

Who are you asking?

I can't say for sure. I only know that if angels or guardian spirits or even a God exists, this is the time for one of them to show up.

Don't you think they'd have shown up by now?

Maybe I'm not listening in the right way.

Or maybe you don't deserve their help.

Maybe you should shut up.

Are you going to have this baby or not?

I don't know!

Maybe you'd better decide.

I'd hate it if somebody else made this decision for me, but I'm not doing a very good job of making it for myself. Despite being raised in a traditional Jewish home, I don't believe in any particular religious code of ethics. I'm searching for my own sense of right and wrong.

A vision appears before me. It's a boy, roughly three years old, with skin the color of caramel. Golden curls frame his sweet face. He has my blue-green eyes. They're vivacious. I drop to my knees and reach for my child as he extends his arms towards me.

We're almost embracing when I notice his father, Malik, beside him. I freeze. Behind Malik stands his whole family. Strangers to me, they crowd together like an angry mob. They're African, wild and impossible for me to understand. I want to grab my son and run.

"GO AWAY!" I shout as I reach for my little boy. But they surround him and won't let me through.

I collapse beside the crumbling tennis court and cry. I wish my tears could wash away this entire mess and leave me free to get on with my life.

If only.

I roll onto my back and stare at the redwood forest surrounding me. This patch of land was cleared to build this tennis court almost forty years ago but the owners stopped maintaining it at some point. Now the forest is slowly reclaiming what was hers.

I roll onto my side.

I recognize the weed growing in front of my face.

"Plantain's great for skin irritations," my herbology teacher taught me. "Chew it to a pulp, then place it on inflamed areas."

I want to rip it from the earth and plaster it on my brain. Console the hysteria plaguing my psyche like a rash gone rogue.

Get up.

I stand, brush the dirt off my soft cotton dress, and redo my ponytail. I continue pacing.

If I don't have this baby, then I can just get on with my life, continue along the path I've been on.

And what path is that?

You know! The path I'm on. MY path. The path that doesn't have me birthing the child of some Rastafarian man I hardly know and certainly don't love. The path that doesn't have me living through another abortion. The path that leads me to fulfillment of my dreams, to a meaningful career, to my perfect mate, to happily-ever-after. THAT path.

Shit. You're starting to lose it. Relax. You can handle this. Neither decision is the end of the world. Do you hear me?

"Not the end of the world," I repeat like a mantra, planting one foot in front of the other.

Not the end of the world.

"Just the end of MY world," I shout, this time out loud.

Less than a year ago I had my first abortion. My boyfriend Mark and I had been practicing the rhythm method, exploring natural birth control as an alternative to latex or hormones. I took my temperature daily to track my ovulation. We abstained when I was fertile. The rest of the time he religiously pulled out. Until the time he didn't. Even though my temperature indicated we were safe, we weren't. I got pregnant.

Moving to California three years ago was supposed to satisfy my longing for a life eluding me in the Midwest. Even though I couldn't name precisely what I was yearning for, I could feel it. When I left the University of Michigan in the middle of my junior year and moved to Santa Cruz, my ideal future felt close. Until I got pregnant.

I'd been dating Mark longer than any other lover, but six months isn't enough of a foundation for marriage. Committing to him *and* a child felt scary and reckless. I was madly absorbed in my studies in Alternative Education at UCSC, enjoying my job at a popular restaurant on campus, and passionately involved in protests against the proliferation of nuclear power. The life I imagined for myself was materializing, but becoming a mother at twenty-two was never a part of my vision.

Terminating that first pregnancy was a relatively uncomplicated decision. After a very brief consideration to run away with Mark and become barefoot and pregnant for the next ten years, I chose the procedure confidently. Abortion isn't a big deal in my world. After all, it's the eighties. Roe v. Wade is ten years old. I knew two other girls who aborted their pregnancies. I viewed the undertaking as casually as having my wisdom teeth pulled; something I didn't need was going to be removed.

Simple.

Mark and I split up soon after. The abortion hit us harder than we imagined. Not knowing how to cope with our feelings, we each withdrew. Mark trekked off to India and I dove deeper into my studies at school. The decision to end both the pregnancy and the relationship was mutual. Still, I couldn't shake the feeling that somehow I'd failed. I was inconsolably sad. I tried therapy, which provided some support, but hiring a professional to ease my pain only succeeded in distracting me from it in the moment. As soon as a session ended I was buried under a certain bewildering sorrow.

Slowly suffocating.

I'm not the same person I was a year ago. I'm not sure who I am now. All I know is that having experienced one abortion, I can't so casually choose to have another. Not because I feel it's morally wrong, per se. It's more the uncertainty around knowing *how* to make this decision that troubles me. I'm not sure if I believe abortion is Wrong, capital W, or just wrong for me. I need more time to sort this out and time is something I don't have. I'm already three weeks pregnant. I'm afraid if I have this abortion and I realize afterward it was a mistake, I won't emotionally recover. I'm equally afraid if I have this baby out of fear of punishment or to avoid the psychological consequences, then I'll resent my child and be a horrible parent.

My philosophical reflection is overridden by my body's desperate plea.

"Not another one," it begs.

How will I ever reconcile these various parts of me?

Good question!

My attention is drawn to another hallucination.

Malik appears on the other side of the court walking towards me. He glides his small tight frame over to where I stand trembling and smiles at me with dazzling white teeth.

He looks so real.

His eyes are dark, like his skin, and angled, making him look part Asian. His matted black hair is bound up high in a tri-colored knitted cap with one long dreadlock hanging down his back.

"Leah." The ghost calls me by my Hebrew name.

I close my eyes and try to remember Malik's affection towards me. Memories of his kindness are fading.

"I don't think we should have this baby," I finally whisper to him. "I'm not ready to be a mom. There's so much I still need to learn. And, no offense, but you know I don't love you the way I want to love the man I marry and have kids with. Besides, you're a black man, and a Rastafarian. My family would freak out."

I'm scratching the cuticle of my thumb raw with my index finger.

"I understand," Malik says in his Jamaican-British hybrid accent. "But there's another alternative. You can give birth to our child and then give him to me."

I open my eyes and turn away from the vision, feeling unhinged. The sun is low in the sky and a chill grabs me on the front of my neck. I start to walk fast again, trying to get warm.

Malik and I met shortly after Mark left for India. My friend Laura introduced us. Malik is her boyfriend. I met Laura in a World Religion class last semester. I came to class curious about how other religions view death and find meaning in life, whereas Laura had already found her answers. Through Malik and Rastafarianism.

Malik suggested we have sex. He said having sex would erase my body's memory of Mark and help liberate the grief from the abortion. Laura said it was okay with her. She agreed that making love might heal my soul. I was willing to give it a try.

Malik and I did it only once.

The sex was awkward. Forced. I closed my eyes when Malik entered me, hoping his thrust would break through my sadness and make me feel happy again. But my body remained tight, my hope for even the tiniest amount of pleasure thwarted by his instantaneous ejaculation.

When Malik rolled off me, we discovered the tear in the condom.

It wasn't your fault.

I wish I would've used my diaphragm for added protection.

Wishing won't change a fucking thing.

"I can't have this child and then just give it away," I decide aloud, imagining a life separated from the child conceived in my body.

If I birth it, I raise it.

Malik's invisible presence still hovers above me.

"GO AWAY!" I scream as I swat furiously into the sky.

"I warn you, Leah," the voice is loud. "If you kill our child, you'll go to hell."

I begin to run, rattled by this curse. His condemnation infiltrates my psyche and lodges in the cracks forming there.

I'm familiar with Malik's moral beliefs because I've been studying his religion for months now. Rastafarians claim to be the lost tribe of Israel and the carriers of the authentic messianic teachings of Judaism. I began re-reading the Old Testament with Malik. Malik's interpretations of the Biblical stories offered me a whole new perspective on being a Jew. I was an eager student. Malik and I covered a lot of topics during our studies together. But he never mentioned hell.

The sun has dropped behind the trees and I feel painfully cold. Wholly abandoned.

"*You're* to blame," I cry out to Malik, wherever he is. "*You're* the one who should go to hell. It was *your* bad idea, *your* stupid penis, and *your* defective condom that caused this."

But the aftermath of those irreversible ten seconds lives in *my* body now. It doesn't matter how it got here or who the father is. I am pregnant.

Whether I have this baby or not, I am ruined.

You should've known better.

I brace against my inevitable breakdown, desperate for a clear and confident decision to miraculously appear. But I'm tumbling fast with nothing to hold onto.

2

My brother Jacob turns up on my doorstep the next morning uninvited and unannounced. Although I'm startled, I'm not surprised he's here. Showing up for one another began when we were little. Once when he was two I accidentally locked him in the bathroom. I stayed home from kindergarten that day and sat outside the bathroom door, my eye glued to the keyhole so I could see him. I told him stories until the fireman arrived to break the lock.

"You okay?" he asks me now as he drops his backpack on the floor and pulls me in for a hug.

"No," I admit. "I'm a mess."

"I had a feeling," he says. "I've tried calling you a hundred times with no answer, so I hopped on a plane last night."

It was just a week ago when I saw Jacob in Detroit while visiting our family for Passover. I wish I hadn't gone. I'd discovered my pregnancy only days before and wasn't planning on telling my family until after I'd decided what I was going to do. But I caved and told my mom while we were preparing a *matzah brie* together. Being in my childhood home must have lulled me into believing it was a good idea to share it with her.

I broke the unleavened bread into bite-sized pieces and dropped them into a bowl of cracked eggs. Then, as if I'd been held under water and finally surfaced, I blurted out the news in a gasp. As if confession was like breathing, natural and unfettered, freeing me from the burden of a secret. Instantly I knew it was a mistake. My mother would-not-could-not understand.

But it was too late.

I stood at the kitchen counter coming undone, one part of me reeling with shame for being unintentionally pregnant again and another part frozen behind a stifled panic. I watched my mother fold into herself. Her long fingers wrapped tightly around the bowl as she slid it closer to her.

My mother doesn't care much for discussing inner struggles. Her own or anybody else's. She's built for operational tasks, like shopping and laundry. Though small in stature, she easily gave birth five times and cared for a growing family while working as a first-grade teacher. She was highly praised for her performance at school. Hundreds of former students still pay homage to my mom for the impact she had on their lives.

They got a piece of her you never did.

"Well," she said, carefully pouring the raw egg mixture into a sizzling frying pan. I stared at the back of her neck, imagining the look on her face. "I know a doctor who can probably get you in for a procedure right away."

She didn't ask how I was feeling, how it happened, or even who the father was. I walked over to face her, searched for sympathy behind her malachite eyes, and attempted to embrace her unyielding body. Then I went to my bedroom and had a total melt down, crying for the mother I didn't get in this life, sobbing into the belly of my tattered Raggedy Ann doll.

I slept fitfully, unable to get comfortable in my childhood twin bed. I rose before dawn and called a cab, hoping it would arrive before anybody woke up. When my father heard the car, he ran barefoot into the driveway to stop me. His striped cotton pajamas and disheveled gray hair made me think of Albert Einstein.

If only your dad had Einstein's wisdom.

"Lis, baby," my father pleaded, his brow tight above worried blue eyes, "Why not stay a few more days? Let us help you sort this out."

"I can't, Dad," I said coldly, handing my suitcase to the taxi driver. "I need to go. I'll figure this out on my own."

"Let us help you do what's right," he begged as I settled into the back seat and closed the door.

I looked away from his hand pressing on the window, imagining him coercing me into a decision born solely out of his standards of right and wrong.

You and mom have no idea who I am. Or what's best for me.

But as we pulled away, I secretly hoped for him to stop the taxi, rescue me, and make all my trouble go away.

That's not his job.

I turn to my younger brother now. I notice a hint of my former self in his presence. My together self. Jacob's cobalt blue eyes shine like star sapphires. Clear and vibrant. Ready for an adventure. Mine are heavy and blood shot.

"I think I might be going insane," I confess. "I feel pummeled, like I've been wrung through one of those bathing-suit dryers we used after swimming lessons when we were kids. Remember those? With the rubber rollers?"

Jacob nods.

"My love of life has been squeezed out of me. And I feel scared," I admit.

He touches my hand. Says nothing.

I hope he can handle this.

"I can't believe I got myself into this mess. I can't fucking believe it."

Believe it already! Just make a decision, for God's sake.

"How can I help?" Jacob asks.

I have no answer.

He surveys my tiny kitchen for something to eat, but my cupboards are empty.

"How 'bout we get some food?" he suggests.

I haven't eaten in two days.

We drive to my favorite pizza place downtown. I slide into the booth across from Jacob, sinking into the corner, hoping I won't see anybody I know. We order a large cheese pie and two sodas.

"Lisa." Jacob reaches across the table to hold my hand.

Because Malik and Laura have been calling me by my Hebrew name, hearing Jacob say "Lisa" jostles me from a stupor. I take a deep breath to reorient my sense of self.

I wonder if I'm psychotic.

I take Jacob's hand in mine.

"Why don't you just have another abortion?" he asks, leaning his upper body towards the table. His voice tugs at my heart.

"I'm not sure. I think I might be afraid I'll go to hell," I say.

Jacob raises his eyebrows. "Hell?"

"Yeah. Malik says that's what'll happen if I abort. I don't believe in a literal hell, but something's got a grip on me. Since aborting my pregnancy with Mark I've been living in *some* sort of hell."

Jacob is silent. He looks at me with softening eyes.

"I asked Dad what Judaism's stance is on abortions," I continue, "and if I would get into some sort of Jewish trouble for having one."

"Really?" Jacob lights up. "What did he say?"

"He said that in the future when I do have a child, there would be a consequence only if it's a boy. My son wouldn't be entitled to receive the *pideon haben* blessing for a firstborn boy, because he technically wouldn't be first-born."

"That's it?"

"Yep."

"Okay, so no hell," Jacob seems relieved. "And as for that blessing, who cares?"

"Yeah, but what if it's not true?" I counter. "What if Dad just doesn't know, like so many other things about life he doesn't know. Or maybe he knows but didn't want to tell me because he never liked Mark and didn't want me to have Mark's baby. And forget about Malik. I can't imagine Dad would ever support me to have a child with a black man. Not *his* daughter."

I pause to consider my own prejudice, tucked away somewhere.

Is this why I don't want to have this baby? Does Malik's dark skin trigger my father's discomfort, or am I the one who has the issue with it?

How can you know the difference?

A chubby waitress in tight jeans places a steaming round pizza on the table. The cheese is perfectly golden. Jacob slides a slice onto a plate and hands it to me. I blow on it, then fold and bite. The calories go right to my brain. I feel suddenly sturdier. Jacob silently scarfs down his piece.

"Do *you* think hell exists?" I ask.

"I dunno, Lis," he answers with his mouth full. "But if I were you I wouldn't worry about it." Jacob slides another slice of pizza onto his plate. "Since you already had one abortion, you've already earned a sentence to hell if that's what happens. So, if you have another abortion, d'ya think God's gonna make you serve two terms back to back?"

"Maybe," I chuckle nervously at the absurdity.

"Well, then, who cares? You're screwed no matter what."

I hate this.

Jacob looks up and smiles at me. His love touches the edges of my emptiness.

"But what if you're not going to hell?" Jacob continues. "What if there's a way to get through this and move on? Don't you think it makes sense to take a chance? Having a baby right now seems like it could be too much for you to handle and unfair to the kid. And to Malik."

I nod.

"You can have children later, Lis, with somebody you love," he says. "You'll survive this. You'll figure things out. If anybody can do it, it's you."

I draw a long sip of Sprite through the straw until I'm sucking air between melting ice cubes. I'm not so sure Jacob is right about me.

"And here's what little I do know about souls," Jacob adds. "It seems like every religion has a way of fixing 'em."

"Such as accepting Jesus as my savior?" I say sarcastically.

"Who knows?" Jacob is optimistic. "Try to stay positive. Be open. Life is full of possibilities."

I push away the thought of becoming a Christian and for a moment envision a life even better than any I've ever dreamed of. I can't see the details, but I'm charged with a wave of pure hope.

Suddenly my thought stream gets hijacked and I perceive a different outcome. I see a frazzled woman leaning against a pole in an airport. She's waving goodbye to a young child with wild curly hair. The child's boarding a plane by himself. He's off to spend Christmas in Jamaica with his dad.

I feel suddenly nauseous, like I might not be able to keep down this pizza.

I lean into the booth and rest the back of my head on the seat. I close my eyes. Indecision surfaces for the millionth time.

I'm completely drained.

It's time to act.

I surrender to the most sensible choice.

Before I change my mind, I tell Jacob, the one man I'm certain loves me unconditionally, "I'll have the abortion."

"Okay," he says, "I'll arrange everything. Don't worry."

The waitress sets our bill on the table.

We stand to leave.

I reach for the ground beneath my feet.

It drops.

3

Jacob and I catch a red-eye that night and land at Detroit Metro Airport early on a humid Sunday morning. Our parents meet us at baggage claim. I feel so humiliated I can barely look at them.

I wish I had my shit together.

I hate that my parents are involved in this. I should be able to handle life on my own, without their help.

We drive in silence from the airport to a brick office building. The parking lot is deserted except for one silver Mercedes. A man gets out. He's short and stocky with a receding blond hairline. He takes off his sunglasses to greet us.

Dr. Levine is here to repay a favor to my mom.

My family waits in the car while Dr. Levine leads me into the empty building, turning on lights as we go. He takes me to a treatment room and starts arranging objects on a surgical tray. I can't bear to look. I'm concentrating intently on getting through this. I feel like I'm underground, waiting for this whole thing to be over so I can dig myself out and find my way back to the living.

I undress from the waist down and get on the table. I know the routine. I place my feet in the cold metal stirrups.

I close my eyes, vowing to hold my tears for later.

Not the end of the world.

"I'm going to numb the surface area and then insert something into your cervix to dilate it a bit before I proceed." He speaks to me but I'm barely listening. I'm holding my legs steady and whispering a desperate plea to whomever or whatever is listening that I'll be okay when this is over, that I'm not fucking up my life forever.

Dr. Levine drags a wheeled gadget close to us. It looks like a small portable vacuum. The air is stifling. He inserts a wand-like object into my vagina and flips a switch. The machine's whizzing sound startles me and I grip the sides of the table.

In less than three minutes it's over.

My second child is gone.

Both the man who fertilized my egg and the man who just sucked the fetus out of me have dramatically impacted my life. Meanwhile their lives go on as usual.

This pisses me off.

You have no idea what Malik is feeling.

Dr. Levine hands me a maxi pad and a prescription for Vicodin, then leaves me alone in the room to dress. As I step into my underpants I reel from a chilling wave of dread.

What have I done?

The irreversibility of the last ten minutes overtakes me. I confront the reality that, in my efforts to clean up the mess I got myself into, I've just made it worse. Like washing my mistake away with a dirty sponge.

I place the pad in my crotch and begin to weep quietly.

Dr. Levine escorts me back to the parking lot mumbling something about "Michigan weather" and "enjoy your visit." I want to smack him.

What if I were your daughter?

He reaches out to shake my father's hand, then hugs my mother.

She thanks him for his kindness.

I lie down in the back seat of the car and rest my head in Jacob's lap. He strokes my hair as I dream of Vicodin and sleeping for as long as possible.

As night arrives I'm awake in bed with a deep ache in my pelvis. The house is quiet. My parents are in their bedroom watching TV. Jacob is out with friends. My older brother David is away at college. My sister Ellen, a junior in high school, can't be bothered with family drama. She's spending the night at her best friend's house. My youngest brother Adam, an eighth grader stumbling his way through puberty, is holed up in his room. I'm not sure he even knows what just happened to me. We sat together earlier at the dinner table and spoke about nothing real.

Just like old times.

My mom made her signature chicken soup. I sipped from my bowl, hoping for comfort, but my stomach refused it.

See, nothing she gives you ends up being what you need.

I look around my old bedroom. It's still decorated lemon yellow from my adolescence. Books I devoured as a young girl are stacked neatly on the shelves: *The Happy Hollisters*, *Anne of Green Gables*, *Nancy Drew*. A pink jewelry box with a ballerina who twirls to music when the lid is open sits on the dresser next to my seventh-grade science fair award.

This place is haunted.

Memories begin to unfurl in my mind. When I turned eleven Peter moved in across the street. I had a huge crush on him. He played baseball with my brothers every afternoon in the summer. I would take them cold drinks, then stay for a while and watch them play. I'd wait for Peter to take an interest in me, but he never did. I stood at the curb feeling invisible, unattractive. Then in sixth grade my mom forced me to wear polyester pants to school when everybody else was wearing Levis. When I heard kids making fun of me I wanted to punch my mother, force her to let me shop for myself, find my own style. But my parents had opinions about proper school attire. So I ignored the remarks of my peers and pretended their comments didn't bother me. I acted as if I didn't care.

I'm tormented now by the many ways I never fit in.

No wonder you left Michigan. You don't belong here. You never did.

I heave myself out of bed and stumble down the hall to the bathroom, the pad in my underpants heavy with blood. I sit on the toilet, elbows on my thighs, forehead cradled in my hands, and close my eyes.

Another memory appears. I am nine years old. I'm sitting on this same toilet and it's the middle of the night. It's the end of summer. Eleven Israeli Olympians have just been assassinated in Munich by the Palestinian terrorist group, Black September. My parents were talking about this at dinner. A lot of people are upset.

I don't understand humans.

We recently moved into this new house in an undeveloped suburban neighborhood. The shag carpet still smells like rubber cement. I raise the blind on the window next to me. Without the glow of street lamps or city lights, the darkness is thick. I'm intrigued. I open the window and invite the darkness in. I stick my head out and stare at the sky. I've never seen so many stars.

If nobody were here to see them, would the stars still exist?

I sit pondering for some time.

My adult body shivers now. The time and space between that moment and this one contract like plastic wrap too close to a flame. The question about the stars and their observers imbedded itself into my psyche that night. I remember trying to imagine myself not existing, stretching to imagine *nothing* existing.

Now, sitting in the same spot fourteen years later, I open the window again. I peer into the night. I'm filled with wonder. Inhaling the gentle spring breeze, I invite the curiosity of my nine-year-old self to return to me.

The question arises again. Same, but different.

If there's no God to see my sins, do my sins still exist?

I feel suddenly inspired. Imagining a Godless world tickles some place inside of me. I sense the answer to my question might be so near that all I have to do is reach out and grab it.

Blood leaves my body and lands in the toilet, steady like a metronome. Drip. Drip. Drip. I feel my life force pouring out of me, hear the drops splashing, but can't feel what bleeds. I want to touch my wound, comfort it. After all, I caused it. I imagine it would be easier to suffer the horror of my torn-up uterus than face my despair. I will never know if this is true.

Despair wins.

4

Four days later, I'm getting ready to leave my parents' house. I shove my anxiety into a suitcase along with my toothbrush. I'll unpack it later. I take a stuffed animal from my closet, a pink dog with floppy ears I named Fluffy as a child. Though he's ragged and missing an eye, I knight him as my Patron of Hope and put him in my carry-on bag. My plan is to return to Santa Cruz and complete my last month of school. Once I finish, I'll have a degree in Alternative Education and a K-12 teaching credential. After graduation I don't know where I'll go or what I'll do. It hurts to think about it. So I don't.

My dad drives me to the airport. As we get into the car, I stare for a moment at this man who raised me. I feel overwhelmed with love. And disdain. We haven't spoken much over the past few days.

When I was a child I confided in my dad. He was the person I turned to for advice, and for love. He always made time for us to be together. When I was seven and returned home after four weeks in the hospital with rheumatic fever, my dad doted on me. For months, promptly at midnight, my daddy brought me six baby aspirin, one 500mg tablet of penicillin, a glass of orange juice, and a Ritz cracker. He sat on the edge of my bed watching me swallow my pills. Then he'd stay until I fell asleep again. When I was nine and sometimes lazy about brushing my hair, letting it get all knotted, my dad was the one who would sit with me for hours untangling it, talking to me about school and friends.

But when I left the private Hebrew day school I attended through eighth grade and entered a public high school at age fourteen, things changed between my dad and me. I no longer needed his help with my hair, and I found his traditional values beginning to clash with my own developing beliefs. My dad wanted to maintain our family ritual of being home together on Friday nights for the Sabbath, but I wanted to go to football games and parties with my friends. He listened thoughtfully as I presented my case for doing things differently. "I don't live in a Jewish world," I appealed to him. "A lot of fun things happen on Friday nights and I want to be a part of them."

In the end, we agreed I would eat dinner at home, and *then* go out with my friends. We compromised. But the negotiation strained us.

As my dad pulls out of the driveway, we make eye contact briefly and I notice how the skin around his eyes has wrinkled. I wonder who's looking at me through those eyes. He averts his gaze to watch the road. I say nothing. I stare out the window, listening to the BBC.

I remember the first time I saw my dad cry. I was five years old.

It was a warm summer day and I was riding my new gold bike with the tiny banana seat. I rode for hours, back and forth on the sidewalk of our city street, because I wasn't allowed to cross over to another block. It was 1968 and I was told black and white people were fighting nearby. I had heard the word *riot* on TV and imagined a monster of fire roaming our neighborhood. I watched out for it.

I rode until I heard Irene call my name. Irene was our maid. She wore comfortable shoes and a pressed white dress over her dark skin. She was soft and smelled like Ivory soap.

My parents came home just as Irene was tucking me in. My daddy sat down heavily on the edge of the bed. He was crying. I watched, curious. He gently moved a strand of hair out of my eyes and told me that his only brother, my uncle Buddy, had died that afternoon.

Uncle Buddy was born with Marphan's Syndrome, his genetic makeup determining that he would grow and age nearly twice as fast as a normal person. By the time he was twelve he stood over six feet tall. When he went in for surgery at age thirty-six, he had the heart of an old man. My father made it his mission early on to look out for his little brother, but there's only so much a big brother can do.

"Where's Buddy now?" I'd asked.

"He's dead, baby. You'll never see him again."

I squirmed out from under the sheets and climbed into my daddy's lap.

"Why can't he just wake up?" I questioned, imagining my uncle sleeping.

"Because his body doesn't work anymore."

"Why not?"

"Because that's what happens when people die."

"Why?"

My father paused.

"Because that's how God wants it," he explained.

What kind of God would want that?

"Why, Daddy?" I pressed.

"He just does," he said as he cradled me and kissed my forehead.

"But we can pray for Buddy's soul," he added, as if I knew what that was.

As if he *knew what that was.*

"What's a soul?" I asked.

My father hesitated.

"It's the part of us that goes back to God when we die."

"Where is it?" I asked.

"It's inside us."

"Where?"

"In our hearts."

I closed my eyes to find mine.

I touched my chest.

I felt sad for my dad, and for my uncle Buddy.

My heart felt like a fresh scraped knee.

"Dad?" I address him now, almost twenty years later, feeling again my broken heart.

"Yeah, baby," he replies without looking away from the road.

I still love it when he calls me baby.

"Remember when Buddy died?"

"Of course."

"Did you feel responsible for his death?" I ask.

"I did," he admits.

"How did you get over it?"

He considers.

"I'm not sure I have," he answers. "But, I guess, time."

"Dad?" I turn down the radio, shifting my body to face him. "I'm not sure I'll ever get over this," I say, my voice catching.

"Oh baby, of course you will," he places his hand on my knee.

I'm silent.

"I wish there was more I could do," he offers.

"Me, too," I say.

Give some guidance. It's not too late.

"Maybe you should never have moved to California in the first place," my father finally says, removing his hand from my leg. "Maybe if you'd stayed close to home none of this would have happened."

I swivel my body to face forward again, letting his judgment enter me sideways.

I pretend it doesn't hurt.

"You may want to talk to a rabbi," he adds, as if the idea just came to him. "Maybe a rabbi could help."

Are you kidding me? A rabbi?

I want to throw up.

5

I slog through my final weeks of school, my body mired in a stifling dread. Malik and Laura aren't speaking to me. I've been damned to hell. Most mornings, I can barely get out of bed, let alone dressed. One day, riding on a spurt of energy, I drag my sorry ass to the bookstore in my pajamas and buy a bunch of self-help books, including *The Road Less Traveled* and *Handbook to Higher Consciousness*. I hide out in my cottage between classes, randomly pulling titles from the stack. Reading gradually consoles me. I know something is shifting because the clenched muscles in my calves begin to relax.

I'm considering a strategy for my life-after-graduation when I get a call from a friend of my dad's, an Orthodox Jewish woman. Uninvited, she assures me that Judaism has the answers to my questions about life, death, and the consequences of having two abortions. I don't have the energy to interrupt her. I let her make her case.

"You won't find what you're looking for in the Judaism you were raised with, Leah," she tells me when I gently challenge her conviction. "You need to study the teachings in the Kabbalah, the esoteric branch of our religion. And you would need to start living a religious life."

You must be joking.

I politely thank her for her interest in me and hang up. Then I search for a book from my World Religion class. *Kabbalah* by Gershom Sholem sits, not yet opened, on a bookshelf next to William James' *Varieties of Religious Experiences.* I take Sholem's book off the shelf and get into bed to read. Despite years of private religious school, a bat mitzvah, fluency in the Hebrew language, and a summer in Israel, the mystical branch of Judaism has successfully remained hidden from me. After hours of reading, I set the book on my nightstand and close my eyes. The cosmological details of the Kabbalah don't interest me, but *something* does. A subtle tugging sensation deep in my belly tells me I may be onto something.

One week after graduation I leave the shadow of my abortions on the West Coast and move to upstate New York to study Kabbalah in Kol Neshama yeshiva, a school for secular Jewish women who are consider- ing becoming religious. I'm here because I'm not sure where else to go. I don't feel psychologically ready to take on a full-time job and the yeshiva has offered me room and board in exchange for working in the kitchen. Plus I can tutor part-time. I figure Judaism deserves another look. Maybe my dad's advice wasn't so ridiculous after all. According to his friend, Kol Neshama is the best institution in the U.S. for women to study the deeper teachings of our religion. Within a month I begin to morph into a dutiful Jew, seeking solace in my ancestral roots.

Religious Jews adhere to a very specific code of conduct called *hala- cha,* which literally means "the Way." Taken from the Torah, received by Moses on Mount Sinai, the Way was transmitted orally until 70 CE when it was written down in the Talmud. In the mid-nineteenth century, many Jews began reinterpreting the Way, attempting to adapt it to modern cul- ture and thinking. Nowadays there's a broad range of Ways to be Jewish.

Immersing myself in the Orthodox Way becomes a touchstone for my desperate self. Whereas those from other branches of Judaism may follow few, if any, of the ancient guidelines, Orthodox Jews follow more than 250 of the original 613 commandments. The rules provide welcome structure to my days. There's a prayer to acknowledge God for every aspect of life, including taking one's first breath in the morning, the sighting of a rainbow, and successfully completing each visit to the toilet.

Soon I begin to appreciate how the commandments provide me the opportunity to slow down and become mindful of my actions. I notice substantial benefits. I think less about my future and enjoy the simplicity of the moment. Some days I feel happy. But many of the directives seem slightly ridiculous to me. Such as being forbidden to drink milk at the same meal where I'm eating meat. And then there are laws I consider outrageously offensive. For example, when I'm married, I'll be obligated to show a rabbi my menstrual rag so he can determine if I'm "clean." This is because, as a married woman, I'm forbidden to have sex when I'm menstruating, and apparently I'm not able to determine for myself the status of my cleanliness.

Though here at the yeshiva I'm being taught some of the philosophical and theological tenets surrounding this strict lifestyle, mostly I'm being told to act and not question. I find this insulting. When I do push back, it's suggested that my psychological state of rebellion is directly related to being out of alignment with the Way. I need to trust the rabbis, I'm told. I acquiesce, determined to give this path a fair chance. However, after eight months, I reach the limit of my tolerance and start to recoil.

Today I can barely restrain myself from interrupting the rabbi who's teaching the morning lesson. Each week on the Sabbath, a section of the Torah is read aloud in synagogue until the whole book is finished. This process takes exactly one year. During the week, rabbis offer their insights and inspirations from the portion of the Torah being read that Sabbath. We've just celebrated the Jewish New Year and are starting to read the Torah from the beginning again. So today our rabbi is offering commentary on Genesis, the first chapter in the first book of the holiest text belonging to the Jewish people.

This passage is where the whole lie started.

As the rabbi speaks, my hostility towards Judaism starts to heat up. Out of respect, I hold my agitation in check and listen very carefully, just in case I'm missing something. I let the rabbi finish his exegesis before responding. I look around the room, checking to see if anybody else is uncomfortable with what he's saying. The room is windowless with individual desks arranged in tidy rows. There are twelve other women in class today. They all appear receptive.

Submissive.

I raise my hand. The rabbi points to me.

"If I understand you correctly, Rabbi," I begin, adjusting myself in my seat, "you're saying the Adam and Eve story is essentially God's blueprint for all human life."

"Yes, Leah," he says, glancing at his watch.

"Are you saying that God *intentionally* made us sin?" I ask.

The rabbi nods.

This is insane.

"So, because of the predestined act of eating from the Tree of Knowledge…or wait, Rabbi, let me be clear here." My tone changes. I press into him with what just might be lifetimes of repulsion. "Because of *Eve's* sin of eating the apple and seducing Adam, even though she had *no choice* in the matter, all of us are now born sinners until we follow the rules outlined in the Torah, supposedly written by God Himself, in order to redeem ourselves so we can return to the Garden of Eden, where God will reward us because we've played the game so well."

I catch my breath after that run-on sentence.

What I really want to say is, "Are you fucking kidding me? GOD SET IT UP THIS WAY? Why would any merciful God, which you claim He is, intentionally create such a convoluted mess?"

I can't believe the rabbi doesn't see how screwed up this whole story is.

I feel like puking.

You should.

I look around the room again. One woman, my new friend Reva, is looking at me with a knowing smile.

I turn to face the rabbi, waiting for him to explain himself. Explain God.

His long sideburns are neatly tucked under his skullcap and a graying beard rests on his fat belly. His shin-length black coat gives him an air of grandeur. Self-importance drips off him like sap from a tree.

"Yes, Leah," he replies, unaffected. "But you shouldn't be so concerned. It's beyond our human capacity to comprehend the will of God."

Was that part of His plan, too? Making us stupid?

"We mustn't question it," the rabbi raises his voice, as if pressing his words into my face.

I stay silent, knowing my rebuttal would not be welcome.

I need a moment with this God.

After class I walk slowly to the dining hall, my shin length gray dress weighing heavily on my skin. Pondering the gravity of what I just heard, I serve the lunch I helped prepare earlier today. What I really want to do is disappear. Instead, I set bowls of tuna salad, mixed greens, and hummus on the buffet table, along with plates of bread and sliced cheese. Once I set out the drinks, I'm free to go. When I notice Reva sitting alone at a corner table, I put some salad on a plate and join her. We bless the food.

"Am I the only one here who finds God's plan offensive?" I say to Reva, looking around to make sure nobody else is listening. "It was God's plan all along for us to sin and suffer? Really? Plus, He set it up for Eve to take the blame!"

Reva is a petite blond from Baltimore, raised in a Conservative Jewish family like mine. She has the kind of radiant blemish-free skin I envy, along with light blue eyes that reflect depth beyond her twenty-three years. I'm eager to hear her thoughts.

"Well, you might be missing the point of the story." She speaks like she knows something I don't. "Truth has many layers, Leah. The rabbi's not interested in satisfying your intellectual doubts. From his perspective, the best thing he can do is guide you to observe the commandments. And get you married."

I turn my chair so my whole body faces Reva.

"But how could God have intentionally orchestrated life this way? It's so…" I search for the right word. "Unfair."

"God is not unfair, Leah," she promises me.

"Where is the fairness in blatantly tricking the entire human race?"

"Stop trying to figure it out rationally." Reva's tone is compassionate but strong. "The Torah comes from God, regardless of whether you're convinced or not. You need to have faith. Stop questioning."

Sounds like you drank the Kool-Aid, sister.

I push my plate aside and lay my head in my arms on top of the table, feeling defeated.

"I wish it were so easy," I mutter.

"Oh, stop acting like a victim, Leah," Reva says. "Just follow the commandments and it'll all work out. You'll see. You *are* Jewish, after all. This *is* your path."

"How do you know I'm Jewish?" I lift my head to challenge her. "Maybe I'm really something else? Maybe that's my problem. Maybe I don't belong here."

"You belong," she assures me. "You were born from a Jewish mother. You know that's how it works."

That's a ridiculous way to determine a person's religion.

"What if she lied? What if I'm adopted?"

"Oh, Leah," she pleads. "Why must you make things so difficult?"

She places her hand on my back. Her touch feels warm.

"I'm not *trying* to make it hard," I say. "Something just doesn't feel right."

Trust that feeling.

Reva tries a different approach. "Is there any part of being here that *does* feels right?"

"Of course there is."

"Like what?"

Yeah, like what?

"Like the Sabbath." I sit up and close my eyes, imagining the peace that approaches when I light the candles on Friday nights. "I love it that the whole community stops and turns inward."

You now love the same Friday night ritual you rejected when you were in high school?

"Me too," Reva says quietly. "What else?"

"I love learning philosophy and theology, and I love the Hebrew language. As for this place in particular," I add, "mostly I love working in the kitchen cooking for all of us."

Reva smiles at me, then lifts her empty plate and stands. "Maybe you just need to give it more time, Leah."

"I don't know how much more time I want to give it," I say as I stand with her.

"Why not?"

"Because none of the things I like about being here are exclusive to Judaism. And a lot about this place really bothers me."

I skip the next class and spend the rest of the afternoon in town wandering aimlessly through shops. I stare at Orthodox women with their head coverings, clothed from neck to ankle, strolling with their toddlers in hand or infants in buggies.

That'll be you in a few years if you're not careful.

I step into an antique store and disappear into aisles of old stuff. It smells like must and sweat and moth balls. I purchase a small enamel box the size of my palm. The lid is the color of a clear blue sky. I return to the apartment I share with five other young women being groomed for Orthodoxy and marriage.

I put the box on the shelf behind my bed. I pretend it holds my future. I lie down and close my eyes to imagine it.

You've got to get out of here.

6

I'm dozing in my deck chair letting the sun tan my face when the phone rings. I linger in the scent of budding flowers and fresh spring air before I run inside to answer the call. It's Batya. We worked together in the kitchen at the Yeshiva. We haven't spoken since I left New York and moved back to Michigan more than a year ago. I'm surprised to hear her voice.

"Hi Batya. How are you?"

"I'm wonderful, Leah, thanks for asking. Life is good, thank God."

I don't know what to say. I'm wondering about the purpose of this call.

"And how are you?" Batya fills the gap. "How is it in Michigan? I know our community here wasn't the best fit for you. How is the community there?"

She's referring to the Orthodox Jewish community thirty miles away. The one I deliberately chose not to live in.

"I'm good, Batya," I lie. "I'm teaching fifth grade, and in grad school. The community here is nice. I don't live there, but I do study the Kabbalah weekly with my friend, Shoshana, and spend occasional Sabbaths with her family."

I decide not to tell Batya about the Native American teachings I'm exploring, the Eastern philosophy books I'm reading, or the human sexuality workshops I'm attending. I also don't mention my persistent depression and how I self-medicate with food, sleep, and movies.

"Wonderful, Leah. I'm so glad. Listen, I'm calling because I have a guy I think you should meet."

So that's it!

"Thanks for thinking of me, Batya, even after all this time," I say, "but…"

"I've thought of you many times, Leah," she interrupts. "I know you need a very special guy if you are going to remain faithful to Judaism, and I think Jeremy could be that guy."

I'm not dating. Especially not religious Jews. Since leaving the yeshiva I've been slowly acclimating into a more "normal" life. I have a job and an apartment. I'm going to school. This is enough for me to handle.

"Well, Batya, honestly, I'm not dating, and I'm not very religious anymore."

"That's okay," she replies. Her tone is soft, as if she's eavesdropping on my volatile inner landscape.

"It doesn't matter," she reassures me. "God looks into your heart for your devotion to Him."

My heart is devoid of love for your God. Every time I've asked Him for help, He hasn't shown up.

"Well, I'm working on that," I say quietly.

"Of course, sweetheart, we all are. But listen, Jeremy's a deep guy. He spent years meditating and studying Eastern religions. He's more worldly and older than the other guys you dated when you were here. I think it's worth at least talking to him. You know I wouldn't call you for just any man."

I recall the two dates I agreed to go on before I left the yeshiva. One with a light-haired man sporting a scruffy beard who smelled like bourbon and avoided my gaze. The other candidate was spindly and clean shaven except for long brown sideburns. He fidgeted in his dark suit the whole time we were together and then told the rabbi's wife that I wore an inappropriate dress, too conforming to my figure.

I can't imagine this guy Jeremy being much better.

I'm about to refuse Batya's offer when I wonder if there might yet be a place for me in Judaism, one not quite so extreme. Maybe with Jeremy.

Why is it when a guy enters the picture things begin to shift for you?

My body slumps with the acknowledgement of this pattern and I know I'd be smart to hang up. But I don't.

Idiot.

"Okay," I say. "You can have Jeremy call me."

I'm grading math tests when the phone rings.

"Hello, Leah?"

"Yes."

"This is Jeremy. Batya gave me your number."

"Hi Jeremy." The sound of his voice pokes at my loneliness. My belly quivers.

"How are you?" I ask.

"I'm well, thank God," he answers. "I just got back from my rabbi's. I live with my elderly mom during the week, in the town where I have my business. But I spend the weekends with my rabbi, studying and observing the Sabbath."

I can't bear to lead him on or make small talk. I know my directness has gotten me into trouble in the past, but I can't help myself. I *am* direct. If he doesn't like it, then he can decide now to not waste his time with me.

"Jeremy, did Batya tell you I'm not really religious anymore?"

"Yes, she did," he replies, "but why don't *you* tell me about it. I'm curious."

I'm taken by his openness. It presses into my ache for a man.

You've barely spoken twelve words to the guy!

"Well, when my life fell apart a few years ago," I begin, sparing him the details, "I decided to look to Judaism for help. That's when I went to the yeshiva. I eventually left because it wasn't quite right for me. I got a lot out of my time there, much of which I'm still exploring in my own way, but most of it felt way too chauvinistic and outdated."

I wait for his rejection.

"I understand," he says. "Orthodox Judaism is very difficult to settle into for many reasons. I studied Zen Buddhism and martial arts for eight years, thinking I would never leave those traditions. In fact, I was totally shocked when it happened."

"How *did* it happen?" I'm curious.

This ought to be interesting.

"One day a rabbi came to give a talk at the monastery..." Jeremy's tone is soft as he describes the moment the rabbi walked into the room and how, simply via the rabbi's presence, something woke up in Jeremy's heart. Everything the rabbi said was essentially what Jeremy was discovering in Buddhism but, when the rabbi spoke, it touched some place in him where Buddhism couldn't reach. It actually brought him to tears.

"I couldn't deny something significant was happening," Jeremy continues. "I decided to talk more with the rabbi on my own, and then I began to study with him. I don't know how else to say it: the Jewish way of life just felt like home to me in a way Buddhism never did. So I left the monastery and went to Jerusalem to study for two years. That was four years ago."

Oh, how I yearn for that feeling of home.

My ache for belonging lures me to consider the possibility that Judaism might still be my path.

You're pathetic.

"Why would you choose to live fully as an Orthodox Jew?" I question. "Why not just take what works from Judaism and leave the rest?"

"Judaism is not a cut and paste approach." Jeremy is taking a stand. "It's a complete system that works only when you follow the whole thing. It's the perfect antidote to life's miseries, Leah, if you're a Jew. Buddhism would be perfect if you were a Buddhist."

Maybe I am a Buddhist.

"We're born broken, Leah. The Torah is our fix. It's that simple."

His certainty irks me.

"I'm afraid I may be *extremely* broken," I say.

"Nobody is unredeemable," Jeremy says with a tone of authority. "God is infinitely merciful."

Not that line again.

"I cannot speak to this," I say.

"Listen," he offers. "Why don't we continue to talk on the phone over the next week and then plan to meet in person?"

I pull back. It's so fast, this Orthodox Jewish dating scene.

"You know, Jeremy, I've been through some tough years. I'm still sorting things out, trying to trust my process. I'm not really certain about anything."

"I understand," he says. "But I promise, it's all here in Judaism, everything you're searching for. I'll show you."

His voice is tender.

I want to trust him. To let him show me how Judaism is the Way.

Of course you do.

"Okay," I give in. "As long as you don't expect anything from me."

How can you be so naive?

"Just a willingness to get to know one another." Jeremy's voice is steady. "I'll check my schedule and call you soon to arrange things."

"Jeremy?" I feel tears welling.

"Yes, Leah."

What I want to say is, "Wait! Can't you feel how lost I am? Do you really want to meet somebody as messed up as I am?"

Instead I say, "Thank you. It's nice to talk to you."

I hang up the phone and walk slowly out to my deck. I feel the weight of my incomprehensible yearning as I fold myself into my favorite chair and pray.

"Hello, God?" I whisper.

Silence.

"Where are you?" I plead.

Silence.

See, God doesn't answer you. He never does.

I wait.

I rock.

I cry.

I give up.

I draw a hot bath. Anxious to be held, I let the water engulf me. I shake off God's avoidance, turn away from fantasies about Jeremy, and imagine being in class tomorrow with Diana. Diana is my teacher in the Native American ways. I've already attended a number of her evening talks on the basic fundamentals of Native American philosophy. I like her. She's intelligent and kind. Something about the way she carries herself attracts me. The topic for this month's series of talks is sexuality. This new series is for women only and will be the perfect complement to the co-ed human sexuality workshops I've been attending.

There's no way Jeremy will fit into this part of your life.

I light a candle and sink deeper into the tub as I close my eyes. I disappear into the warm wetness, letting it console me.

So easy: Body. Bath. Warmth. Surrender.

This simple formula reminds me of the four elements in the Native American tradition: Earth, Water, Fire, and Air. According to Diana, these four principles are the primary manifestations of Divinity. The purity of the Native American lineage appeals to me. Diana never tells people what to do, because there are no rules in the system she teaches. She encourages me to do what feels nourishing: to rest outdoors, to pray as if speaking to a friend, and to connect to a deeper knowing through my body.

Diana is like the ideal mother who comes to me sometimes in my dreams. When I'm in her presence, I relax my fear of being unfixable or doing life completely wrong.

7

Diana's house is filled with the sound of women's chattering voices. I hang my coat in the closet and set my tray of lasagna in the kitchen for the potluck. I enter the living room where the dark wood floor is strewn with multicolored pillows. An elderly woman is sitting in a corner playing a bamboo flute. I sit on a blue pillow next to a high school friend named Angela and greet her with a long hug. Within minutes Diana takes her seat and calls us to order through the soft playing of her hand drum.

Diana is in her thirties, married, and pregnant with her first child. She's tall and lean with long dark hair. At seven months, her belly looks like a basketball glued onto a surfboard. She discarded her Italian Catholic roots thirteen years ago and began studying under her teacher, White Owl, whose Cherokee and Scottish heritages blend in these Native American teachings.

"Sexual energy is a gateway to our personal freedom," Diana begins.

Or a portal to hell.

"Let's begin with the Medicine Wheel," she says.

The Medicine Wheel is a map in the shape of a circle with eight points. Each point corresponds to a compass direction. Though this particular class revolves around sexuality, Medicine Wheels are used to teach everything. There's a Wheel for mapping plants, animals, the systems of our bodies, unseen energies, and phases of life.

Diana places a large round poster board on the floor in the center of the room. It's divided like a pie into eight slices. Each slice has the name of a sexual mask written on it.

"A mask is the way we present ourselves in the world," Diana says, "as a persona or an identity."

On the poster, different colors and different styles of handwriting express the uniqueness of each mask.

"These masks represent the varieties of sexual personalities within each of us," Diana continues. "When we're sexual, we engage a very potent part of ourselves. When we suppress this energy through denying aspects of our sexuality, we obstruct the realization of our full human potential."

Diana walks around the room, hips swaying, belly rocking.

I stare at Diana's belly and feel my pelvis expand, as if my uterus is ready to welcome an upload of its inherent wholeness.

I try to remember when I had my last orgasm as Diana reads aloud from the handout she prepared describing the masks.

Innocent: explores with childlike curiosity
Explorer: experiments with the unusual, bizarre, and extreme
Unbridled: expresses the lusty, promiscuous, and voyeuristic
Tyrant: consciously enters the sadomasochistic realm
Professional: makes clear contracts for sex
Healer: uses orgasmic energy to heal self and others
Priestess: attains full enlightenment through celibacy
Conditioned: conforms to cultural sexual norms

Diana tells us that children in White Owl's community are given these sexual teachings at a young age and initiated into their sexuality at puberty by an elder of the opposite sex. The elder shares the traditional knowledge, instructs them in anatomy and physiology, then shows them how to pleasure themselves and their future partners. Intercourse is reserved for their first mutual encounter. The results, Diana says, are low rates of sexual dysfunction, few sex-related crimes, and rare instances of broken marriages.

I don't know if I believe this.

"Stand in the direction where you feel most uncomfortable," Diana says.

The fifteen of us shuffle through the room emitting nervous giggles.

I stand in the Northwest section of the wheel where the Tyrant lives. Healer is my second choice because I have no idea what healing with sex might look like. I notice a light flutter in my chest when I even consider it.

The room divides fairly equally among all eight directions, with only one direction empty: Conditioned.

It figures.

I can't decide if I want to laugh or cry.

Conforming is safe.

Conforming is boring.

If you'd accepted the social conditioning, you'd probably be married with a few kids by now; no abortions or fractured psyche to deal with.

Maybe not fractured, just brainwashed.

How can you be so sure?

I wasn't born to conform.

"When you cultivate an accepting relationship with each mask and recognize it as essential to your well-being, then you'll express it in whatever way feels right for you," Diana explains.

I've only recently begun to deeply consider what sex and relationships might be intended for, beyond fulfilling the romantic notion of love and marriage. I'm now deliberately examining how to relate sex and love to my spirituality, wishing I would've considered these things before I got pregnant the first time. My whole life I've fumbled through sex and relationships carelessly, having been taught by soap operas, the uninformed actions of my friends, and the unconscious behaviors of adults.

I consider the insanity of my upbringing. I wonder if I'd be sitting here in front of Diana, had somebody talked straight to me about sex early on.

"Now, take a moment," Diana instructs us, "and close your eyes."

The room gets quiet.

"Identify precisely what is uncomfortable about the mask you've chosen. What drew you there?"

I search for the Tyrant's tale in me and recall having sex with a guy named Scott in my freshman year in college. Scott had thick red hair and a hard body from years of playing rugby. He was outgoing and smart. Scott and I met through mutual friends while playing ultimate frisbee on a perfect fall afternoon. One night he showed up at the end of my waitressing shift offering to walk me back to the dorm. It was after midnight when we arrived at my room, where he began to kiss me. I let him. I liked it. But when he slid his hand under my shirt, I pulled away, feeling ambivalent. I was tired and had an early class the next morning. I liked Scott but wasn't sure how much. He proceeded to tell me how much he liked me, wanted to date me, thought I was hot. The more I hedged, the more he pushed.

He threw me down on the bed and undressed me with force. All the while he laughed and played as if I wanted it rough. Part of me did. But only a part. I asked him to stop. Ignoring my resistance, he thrust his large erect penis inside me as if my "no" was simply me playing hard to get, a turn on. The strength he used to pin me down left me no option but to acquiesce. I didn't want to make a scene. I knew him, after all. I had invited him into my room.

I remember feeling both wet *and* violated, orgasmic *and* enraged. The experience left me confused. How could my body enjoy it when *I* didn't?

I never told anyone about that night. Scott never called to ask me out. When I saw him around campus he flashed a charming smile as if nothing had happened. I smiled back as if I was liberated enough to handle it, while my shoulders rounded under the weight of my hidden shame.

I wonder now if it was the Tyrant in me who was enjoying it, wanting to play rough, wanting to be taken. However, because I didn't have any consciousness about what was happening, I couldn't negotiate a mutual experience. Instead, I became another victim of date rape and Scott, another perp.

"When you feel complete with this inner exploration, open your eyes and let your body guide you to the direction it *wants* to experience." Diana's voice sounds far away.

I can still smell Scott in the room.

I shake my body and look around.

The group fills Priestess, Healer, and Unbridled evenly.

I take a deep breath and consider where I'm feeling drawn. Priestess stimulates the most excitation in my chest, Healer the most intrigue in mind, and Professional the most curiosity in my belly. I walk in the direction of the Priestess.

Instead of asking us to linger in this new direction, Diana drags in four large boxes filled with costumes and toys and all sorts of theatrical accessories. She has us dress up as the mask we've just chosen.

"Try them on," she commands.

We spend the rest of the afternoon play-acting all eight masks, performing skits for one another, giving voice to both healthy and unhealthy expressions of each mask. I haven't had this much fun with a group of women in a long time.

We share our potluck as the sun sets.

Driving home, I mull over Diana's teaching in my mind.

"The Innocent moves with trust. When suppressed, she's manipulative and coy, trying to get something for herself, or confused and disoriented, susceptible to manipulation by others."

I imagine myself seventeen years old again. A curious young virgin with a budding sexuality and no pressure to be sexually active.

I purposefully call my innocence back to me.

"The Explorer wants to try every configuration of sex imaginable."

I feel slightly aroused as I imagine being licked all over or having intercourse in unconventional positions. My body is ripe for such pleasure.

"The Unbridled one has no shame about her sexual appetite."

I'm now remembering my pubescent desire for sex, and the first time I had intercourse.

It happened on the night of my senior prom. I was seventeen years old. I wanted to have sex before I went off to college in the fall, but didn't currently have a boyfriend. Most of my friends had already "done it." I ached to feel sexually desirable. I needed to know what the big deal was about intercourse, and I wanted to get it over with. I decided to invite a guy to prom rather than wait and hope for someone to invite me. I chose an acquaintance named Jed.

I wasn't going to leave losing my virginity to chance.

I see myself dressing for the evening. I feel beautiful, sexy, and nervous. I imagine Jed kissing me. This thought sends a tingle up my inner thigh. I plan on fully giving myself to Jed, but I also feel a bit shy. I imagine him entering me for my first time. I wonder how much it will hurt.

Jed picks me up in a limousine. He looks hot in a tux. My parents take pictures. They don't object to us spending the night together at a hotel with a group of other kids. It's what happens in suburban Michigan on prom nights in 1980.

Jed and I are at the prom eating dinner and dancing. I look at the other couples on the dance floor and feel proud of my handsome date. Later at the hotel, Jed and I start drinking alcohol and smoking pot. The more Jed drinks the more distant I feel from him. I shrug it off. Carry on.

Suddenly, I'm under him, and he's forcing himself inside of me. It burns. Jed grunts. He doesn't even look at me.

When he's finished, Jed kisses me and cracks open another beer. Then he's gone, down the hall into another room to party with his friends. At dawn Jed returns to me, sleeping alone in our hotel room. He wakes me up and drives me home.

I find out later what the other kids at the hotel were saying about me.

"How could she be so loose? It was their first date."

"Slut."

That word overwhelms me now.

Slut.

The shame resurfaces.

"The suppression of the Unbridled mask can cause all kinds of physical and emotional disturbances."

"My sexual curiosity was healthy!" I scream into the car.

"My actions were not shameful!" I yell at those stupid kids who made fun of me, now grown up somewhere, probably just as fucked up as me.

"I didn't know any better," I say softly to myself.

I was curious.

You still are.

8

Jeremy takes a nonstop from Newark, arriving on a sunny Friday afternoon. I'm standing at the gate fidgeting with my car keys when the passengers deplane. I notice Jeremy before he sees me. He's a big man, wearing a long black coat, shiny black wingtips, and a large *yarmulke*. He stands apart from the crowd like a black hole among bright stars. My heart sinks. My hope that I might be attracted to him is shattered. He's plain looking. Padded around the midsection. Balding.

I wave.

"Hello," he says, greeting me with dark brown eyes. He smiles and they brighten.

"Hi! Welcome to Michigan," I say.

We plan to spend the weekend together, straining the Orthodox rules. Tonight we'll stay at Shoshana's for the Sabbath, but tomorrow night we'll sleep at my apartment. This is a huge no-no because unmarried religious men and women are forbidden to be alone together.

Good thing you're not religious.

The actual commandment forbids sex before marriage. The rabbis prohibit single men and women from being alone together in order to protect them from sexual temptation and thus from possibly breaking the commandment. This precaution is called a fence. Because Jeremy and I plan to find out if we want to be together, we've decided to step inside the fence.

Jeremy barely fits into my Chevy Sprint. He ducks his head to enter.

"My rabbi doesn't approve of you," he blurts as he buckles his seatbelt.

"What?" I say, feeling startled.

I start the engine.

"He says you're not committed enough to Judaism."

Fuck your rabbi.

"Do you believe everything your rabbi tells you?" I shove the stick shift into reverse and pull out of the space.

Jeremy smiles at me as though he enjoys my feistiness and I start to feel more attracted to him. Sitting close to him I feel drawn, like a free electron pulled towards a vacant atom.

"Yes. But that doesn't mean I wouldn't marry you."

"Really?" I test him.

"You may not be committed to Judaism enough for my rabbi," Jeremy explains. "But you might be for *me*."

"Define committed," I challenge.

"Clear that Judaism is your path, and willing to become more religious as time goes on," he says.

How can anyone know what the future will bring?

I merge onto the freeway, allowing the steady flow of traffic to suck us into its surge.

"What if I don't know, Jeremy? What if I can't know until *after* we're married?" I say, once I've crossed safely into the middle lane.

"We're not going to take that chance, Leah." His voice is emphatic.

My stomach clenches.

I'm not sure if I feel afraid or excited.

Or both.

I change the subject and ask him about his mother.

We stop at my favorite flower shop. The owner is an Armenian woman named Ani whose family emigrated to the U.S. during the Armenian genocide. When we first met and she told me her story, I felt ashamed that I didn't know about her people's history.

How had I grown up hearing about the six million Jews killed in the Holocaust of Nazi Germany and never heard about the millions of Armenians slaughtered in Turkey a few decades earlier?

Remorse over my ignorance rises in me as Ani helps me choose flowers for a Sabbath bouquet. I'm overwhelmed with sadness, feeling an unreasonable urge to apologize to her.

Nobody told me about your people. I'm so sorry.

I'm glad Jeremy is waiting in the car. In his Orthodox cloak, he's a living symbol of the Jewish separatism that I find repulsive.

I'm glad Ani didn't see him.

We arrive at Shoshana's just before sundown. She greets me with a hug but doesn't touch Jeremy. While she fills a vase with water for Ani's flowers, her eldest son shows Jeremy and me to our separate bedrooms. I'll be sleeping in a room with her two daughters. Jeremy will sleep in their basement guest room.

The whole family gathers to light the candles ushering in the Sabbath and then the men race off to synagogue. As the wax begins to melt I feel myself softening too. I still love the Sabbath. I sit in silence with Shoshana while she nurses her three-month-old baby.

When the men return from services, we eat dinner. Jeremy stays up late with Shoshana's husband, Shlomo, studying the Torah portion of the week while Shoshana and I discuss our lives over a pot of mint tea. Unlike every other Orthodox Jewish woman I know, Shoshana has never pushed me to get married. Tonight as she subtly questions me about my current stance with Judaism I sense her pressuring me regarding Jeremy. I feel betrayed.

Why must my life revolve around a man?

The next morning we all walk together to synagogue for prayers. After services, we sit around the large dining room table eating *cholent*, a classic meat and bean stew. I watch Shlomo ignite joy in his five children through stories and jokes. Their giggles tickle my heart.

I want children. A family.

Feeling a man, potentially *my* man, sitting next to me, activates my fantasy of a knight in shining armor. This time, he's wearing a *yarmulke*. I slide my chair closer to Jeremy and imagine what our Sabbath table might look like. Earthy ceramic plates. Fresh wild flowers. A giant salad.

After sundown, driving back to my apartment, I want to tell Jeremy I'm feeling uncomfortable being alone with him. Now that the Sabbath is over, I'm back in the secular world and feel unsure of how to behave.

I don't say anything.

Instead, I open the window to let fresh air into the space between us. It's a breezy night. I drive faster. I imagine asking Jeremy to hold me.

I haven't been with a man since Malik.

At my apartment, I open the futon in the living room. Together Jeremy and I put sheets on the bed. I accidentally brush up against him and we both pull back. We look into each other's eyes.

I look away.

Be a good girl. Don't tempt this man. Go to your room.

"Leah." He looks at me softly.

I begin to cry.

All I want is to settle in to something.

Jeremy reaches out and hugs me. I'm stunned. My face is on his chest. He smells like incense and sweat. He smells good.

He pulls us apart and plants me on the edge of the bed. He sits next to me. We are no longer touching.

"Leah, I feel torn," he begins. "Though I've been fixed up a number of times, you're the first woman I've felt connected with since I became Orthodox. I'm definitely attracted to you and want to move forward with our relationship. But I'm still concerned about your commitment to Judaism. I know how hard this path is, especially for women. I don't want to pressure you. I just wonder if you're capable of doing it."

Me, too.

I don't say a word.

JUST TAKE ME, I scream behind closed lips.

Slut.

"We can talk about this in the morning," he says calmly. "Let's call it a night."

I'm no longer listening. I'm touching his face.

My lips meet the softness of his, my fingers caress the stubble on his chin, my chest lunges forward.

We're hugging and kissing now. With abandon. Until he finally revolts.

He pushes me away. Firmly.

"Oh my. I'm so sorry, Jeremy. I just..." I fumble.

"I know," he interrupts, his body tense. He pulls his shoulders back and takes a long breath, then looks me in the eye.

"Goodnight, Leah." He turns his back to me.

I run into my bedroom and slam the door. I fall onto my bed shaking. I wait for Jeremy to open the door, turn me over, undress me, and make passionate love to me.

Ten minutes go by.

I hear Jeremy brushing his teeth.

And then it's dark.

I crawl under the sheets fully dressed.

I let my shame smother me to sleep.

I wake up in the morning to the whisper of Jeremy's voice reciting morning prayers. I comfort myself with the belief that we're both at fault for last night. It was a momentary lapse. We didn't, after all, break any rules. We just behaved like humans. Fallible ones. We touched. We kissed. Big deal. Nothing irreparable.

Maybe we can just pretend it didn't happen.

I dress quietly and head to the kitchen to make coffee. I say good morning when Jeremy walks in, but don't look at him.

"Good morning." His voice is gentle but distant. "How are you?"

I'm not sure how to answer. I want to say, "Confused. I feel ashamed and excited and lost and scared and hopeful and dirty. How about you?"

"Not great," is what I muster.

Before he responds, we hear a noise in the living room.

On the balcony staring at us through the sliding glass door is a raccoon. He's pressing up against the glass, scratching wildly. His eyes are wide, and he's making a high-pitched chirping sound. He sees us and runs away in a frenzy, knocking over the deck chair.

At first I'm struck by the raccoon's cuteness. I want to help him. I move towards the sliding glass door when Jeremy grabs my arm. His touch is like a lightening bolt striking my vagina.

"What do you think you're doing?" Jeremy snaps.

He looks at me like I'm an idiot. I'm certain it has nothing to do with the raccoon and everything to do with me throwing myself at him last night.

"What do you mean?" I ask, hoping he will address *us* and not the raccoon.

"That animal is scared. He must've climbed up there in the middle of the night and couldn't get down. He's clearly trapped and, trust me, you don't want to get near him. He'll attack you."

I realize Jeremy's probably right. The sound coming from the raccoon is definitely a distress call. It's daylight, and he's trapped in the sun, three stories up, desperate to get back to the dark. He's vulnerable and hating it.

I can relate.

"What should we do?" I ask.

"Call somebody to trap him."

"It's Sunday. Who can I call?"

"Start with your landlord. I'm going to take a shower."

"I'm sorry about last night," I blurt out.

"Don't be," he says.

"Why not?"

"Because now we know," he says flatly.

"Know what, Jeremy? What exactly do we know?"

"That you're not serious enough."

Fuck you.

"You mean, serious enough for *you*," I manage to say calmly.

"Yes, Leah," he agrees. "Serious enough for me."

"I'll take you to the airport when you're dressed," I say, tucking his rejection away.

At the airport curb Jeremy takes his suitcase from the trunk and turns to face me for the last time.

"I have a friend you might find interesting," he says. "His name is Sam. You should call him. I met him eight years ago at a Zen retreat. We hit it off and have been close friends ever since. He's devoted his life to answering the kinds of questions that consume people like you and me."

Jeremy smiles and hands me a piece of paper with Sam's number on it. I wonder when he wrote it. In the dark last night after our kiss? This morning in the bathroom washing off the residue from where we touched?

"Is Sam Jewish?" I ask, wanting to prevent any chance of me tempting another Orthodox man.

"He's Jewish by birth, but he doesn't practice Judaism," Jeremy explains. "He has his own way of being spiritual. Sam's eccentric. You should know that sometimes he doesn't speak for long periods of time. Plus, he doesn't have an answering machine. So when you call, if he doesn't answer, you'll have to try again."

"Thanks," I say, feeling intrigued by this gesture. "I'm sorry if you think I've wasted your time."

You don't need to apologize.

I search Jeremy's face for forgiveness.

"Not a waste of time, Leah," he says genuinely. "I now know what I want in a wife."

Is that an insult?

"And really," he stresses, "do yourself a favor. Call Sam. If Judaism isn't your path, which clearly it's not, Sam might be able to help you figure out what is."

Jeremy lifts his small suitcase and turns towards the airport entrance.

I'm relieved he's leaving. I get into the car and close my eyes. My body relaxes into the warm seat.

In my hand is a piece of paper with some guy named Sam's phone number on it.

I tuck the paper in my purse and drive home to a wild raccoon.

open

1

I purge Jeremy from my system through focusing on my relationship with myself. I begin going to regular yoga classes and start seeing a therapist. With her help I separate my identity from the religion of my ancestors once and for all. I won't let myself be tempted again into believing that Judaism can deliver what I need. Instead, I concentrate on the other beliefs and traditions I've been exploring.

I wake up extra early to get to Diana's on time. After many weeks of evening meetings, today is the first day-long class of this series. Twelve of us gather around Diana's hearth.

"Now that we've learned about the eight different vulva types, and I assume you've all done your self-exploration, it's time for Show and Tell."

Everyone gasps.

When Diana promised today might be the biggest stretch yet, I had no idea she would ask us to expose ourselves. Though the class is all women and we've been meeting together for several months now, I'm not so sure I want to show *anyone* my vagina in broad daylight.

Diana responds to the panic in the room by asking us to talk about our reaction to her invitation. One by one we begin to reveal the roots of our stifled panic.

"I think my negative feelings about my vagina might have started in fifth grade," I tell the group when it's my turn to share. "Our class took a field trip with the eighth graders, and one of the really cute older boys told me and my best friend that we smelled bad *down there.*"

I recall the boy's worn leather jacket. His dark curly hair and air of confidence.

"In the back of the bus he told us this news as if he were giving us top secret information. He told us we'd need to know how to get rid of this smell if we ever intended to have a boyfriend. He seemed to know what he was talking about."

He'd probably never seen a naked vagina. Let alone smelled one.

"I never knew what a vagina actually looked like," another woman admits, "until I had my son. And that wasn't because I'd seen my own but because in my Lamaze class I watched videos of other women giving birth. I was twenty-nine and had never looked at my own body!"

"I won't let my boyfriend give me oral sex," declares Marjory, a radiant hair stylist in her early thirties, "even though he assures me he really does enjoy it. I'm not sure why I refuse it. I guess I'm afraid he won't like *my* vagina, and then maybe won't like *me.* But after spending time looking at my vagina and touching myself for homework, I'm more willing to consider it now."

Around we go, sharing our stories, our anxieties, our disdain for our own bodies.

All because somebody else told us it was dirty down there.

"This is what we're going to change," Diana informs us, "because the only things stinky or shameful about your bodies are your negative thoughts. What if you could have a different experience, one that fully cel-ebrates you as a woman?"

There's a long pause.

"What do we have to lose?" shouts Melissa, a curvy, dark-haired beauty. "What the heck. I feel safe here. Besides, now that I've looked at mine, I'm sort of curious what yours look like." She smiles, stands up, and starts to take off her pants.

I feel shy and scared.

It's okay to leave.

I consider bolting but my curiosity is piqued. So I feign coolness and undress with the others.

We sit in a circle, each propped up with a pillow, legs spread. Then one at a time, we walk around looking at each other's vaginas.

Colors range from bright red to a pale salmon. Some have very thin inner lips, whereas others are large enough to overlap the outer ones. I'm amazed at the different sizes of clitorises, and even the mounds of hair come in a variety of colors and textures. The loveliness is startling.

And yet, I can't deny some discomfort.

What's so off-putting?

Not the smell. Not the visuals.

Just a thought. Not even my own. One instilled in me by numerous ignorant fools from both sexes.

Ugh.

I begin to weep. I let myself feel the deep ache I've been harboring from hating my body. I sense how furious I am about losing my virginity to a clueless jerk. I'm suddenly aware of the rage I carry due to allowing penises inside me when I didn't want them there. I feel an almost unbearable sorrow about letting two strange doctors scrape my womb raw. I cry for myself and for all the women in this circle, in the world, in all of time. I sob, too, for the men who could-not-would-not do things differently.

I place my hands on my vulva and ask forgiveness. The rest of the women envelop me in a group embrace. We take turns holding each woman in this way, as if a womb composed of real women might birth a different experience of our feminine selves.

At home I fill the bathtub and slide in.

I wish I had somebody here with me, to help me learn to love my body.

An almost infantile sadness overtakes me.

I want my mommy.

You can't be serious.

I close my eyes and remember my mom when I was a kid and she was young. I search for a memory of her holding me. I can't locate one.

When I was in high school, almost every night my mom would soak in a bath like this, read a book without getting it wet, crawl into bed with a bowl of rocky-road ice cream, and watch TV till she fell asleep.

It was her ritual.

I wonder if I've inherited my love of baths from my mom.

Maybe she did give me something of value.

From now on, I declare to the Universe, baths will be my symbolic Mother.

My womb.

I rest my finger on my clitoris and gently caress it until my body shivers. I sigh, then submerge my head so the water covers every bit of me.

2

I stare at the piece of paper with Sam's number on it. It's now wrinkled after months of handling. I'm still curious about this guy, so I dial the number for the fifth time.

If he doesn't pick up the phone, you're throwing his number away.

He actually answers. "Hello."

"Um. Hi," I stumble. "This is Leah. Jeremy's friend. He gave me your number."

"Yeah," Sam's voice is high-pitched and slightly grating. "What do you want?"

"Well, Jeremy said I should call you to talk about spirituality and stuff."

"Yeah," he replies. "What d'you want to know?"

He reminds me of a department store salesman, questioning me so he can let me know if he has in stock what I want.

"Well, I'm not exactly sure," I say. "Jeremy and I had a nice connection. We had some amazing conversations. About everything. When it became clear I wasn't doing the Jewish thing, he said we could no longer be friends. He suggested I call you. He said you would be someone I could talk to."

"Yeah. So ask a question."

I imagine him twiddling his thumbs.

I still have so many questions.

I begin somewhere. "What's the point of life?"

"There is no point," he answers without pausing to consider.

"What do you mean, no point?" I fire back, feeling offended, but not certain why.

"God, or whatever you want to call it, created this world for no particular reason, other than, you could say, his enjoyment," Sam declares. "That's what I mean by no point. No lofty purpose. No right or wrong way to be. No commandments to follow. No spiritually righteous way to eat or have sex or make money. No heaven or hell."

"But there has to be *some* point?" I protest. "Without a purpose, how do I know what to do? How do I make decisions?"

This is the essential question. How do I discern right from wrong?

"My advice is to decide to stop playing the game entirely."

I'm totally confused.

"Do you mean commit suicide?"

I'm not sure if I like this guy.

"Not literally, but spiritually."

Sam goes on to explain, in simple terms, his understanding of Buddhism and karma. He describes karma as the law of cause and effect, set in motion when the Universe came into existence.

"Buddhism teaches that the source of human suffering is desire," Sam tells me. "So if we remove all desires, including the desire to live, then karma ceases. Without desires to fuel it, the game of life ends. And so does our suffering."

I turn off the lights in my living room and light a candle. Then I nestle into my comfy chair so I can concentrate on what Sam's saying.

"It's pretty straightforward," Sam adds with certainty.

I begin to cross-examine him. "How do you know for sure what you say is true?"

"Because I've spent a lot of time studying and contemplating this stuff, that's how. But don't believe me. Don't believe anybody, actually. Find out for yourself."

He's challenging me.

"I'm working on it, thank you," I say defensively.

"Well, the only way I know to find out for certain is to spend some time alone with these questions. Sit down, shut up, and listen for a while. Find out for yourself what the truth is."

His tone is confident. I find this both comforting and unsettling. He knows something I need to know but am not sure I really want to face.

"Listen, Detroit," he continues.

"Detroit?" I interrupt.

"Yeah. Detroit," he repeats. "That's your name as far as I'm concerned. When Jeremy told me about you, he referred to you as 'the girl from Detroit.' It stuck."

"Uh, okay," I say.

I kinda like it, actually.

"Listen, Detroit," he picks up where he left off. "If you're really serious about this stuff, you can't expect to arrive at any clarity overnight. Discovering the truth doesn't happen without major effort. And it definitely won't happen if you think somebody else is gonna give you all the answers. Including me. You may not believe what I just said is the ultimate truth. Which is good, because beliefs alone are useless. But if you sincerely commit to the quest, I guarantee you'll get your answers."

"That makes sense," I say. "I don't have any problem with that. But giving the quest my full attention is not as easy as it seems."

"Understatement, Detroit," he's laughing now. "Huge stinkin' understatement!"

I'm laughing now, too.

Seven hours later Sam and I finally hang up, not because we want to, but because it's after midnight and I have to teach in the morning. Otherwise we would surely carry on into daylight, continuing to explore topics ranging from the origin of the word *soul* to the impact of psychedelics on consciousness.

Talking with Sam is easy, like catching up with an old friend. Our backgrounds are similar enough that we could've grown up in the same neighborhood. If he weren't seven years older than I am, we might've even hung out with the same crowd.

Something about Sam feels like home.

I brush my teeth and get into bed, curling up under the warmth of my down comforter. Sam is loaded with the kind of information I'm interested in, and I'm slightly overwhelmed from the depth and breadth of the conversation. I hope my mind will stop buzzing so I can sleep for a few hours.

I toss and turn, thinking of what I want to explore on our next call. Sam seemed to genuinely enjoy talking with me, and I know he thought highly of my questions because he told me so. Not only did he value my theoretical concerns, he also took interest in my personal process. I feel somehow comforted by this attention, his curiosity about the details of my life and the particulars of my quest. I feel enlivened by our connection, even though we just met. I want more of him.

I roll onto my back with my arms at my side and turn my palms to face the ceiling like I do in *savasana*, the corpse pose, the final posture of almost every yoga class I've taken. One of my teachers said savasana looks like the easiest pose but is actually the most difficult.

"It's a momentary death," the teacher told us. "An opportunity to empty yourself of everything."

I wonder if this is the kind of death Sam is talking about.

My whole body is humming. I breathe slowly, watching my breath, longing for sleep. I'm almost there when a thought catches me.

I wonder if Sam has a girlfriend?

3

Jeremy was right. Sam is completely devoted to discovering the ultimate truth. His passion is so intense, it verges on obsession. We've talked most evenings for the past month and I'm dazzled by how much he knows. I eagerly absorb the information streaming out of Sam. He shares his hard earned knowledge generously, until he deems it wise to caution me.

"Intellectual understanding is only one element of finding the truth," Sam says. "Universities are filled with people who only think and talk about this stuff. Whereas religions are filled with people who don't think critically enough. They just blindly follow. This is why personal practice is essential. It's the only way to reliably develop your own knowing."

Based upon Sam's suggestion, I make a reading list and begin to study in earnest. But more important, I start meditating. Having trained in the Zen tradition, Sam calls meditating "sitting."

Sam instructs me. "Sit without moving and become aware of what arises."

"*Everything* that arises?" I ask.

"Yes," he answers. "Your thoughts, emotional feelings, and physical sensations."

"What for?" I ask. "How will that help me?"

"You're trying to separate the observer from the objects of aware-ness," he explains. "Over time you'll eventually become firmly identified as the one who is watching yourself."

"And then what?" I'm searching for a good reason to force myself to sit still.

"Find out," Sam replies.

Three mornings a week I wrap myself in a blanket and sit cross-legged on a firm pillow in the corner of my bedroom. I set a timer for fifteen minutes, close my eyes, and attempt to observe. Sam says observing the breath is a good place to start.

"The breath is a reliable place to focus because breathing's always happening, and you won't lose yourself in it."

I'm not certain what he means by "losing myself" but I imagine I'll find out.

I'm pleasantly surprised to discover that I'm able to sit still and not fidget too much. But I'm not very good at observing. Mostly, I'm thinking. I might catch a glimpse of my breath every now and then.

Sam promises me I'll get better with practice.

"If it were easy to acquire a stable witness consciousness, many more people would be meditating," he says. "Too bad people aren't willing to put in the effort, because the ability to detach from one's thoughts and feelings is a very handy skill to have. You'll see."

I persevere.

I decide to spend one day a week alone and silent. On Saturdays, I turn off the ringer on my phone, unplug the TV, and keep holy com-pany with myself. I slow down. I read from my reading list, sit, and prac-tice observing myself doing things such as laundry. It's my own personal

Sabbath. Sam says silence is one of the greatest teachers. After experiencing my first silent Sabbath, I think he could be right. Being quiet brings me great relief. It creates space in my mind.

Soon, I incorporate a walking meditation into my schedule. I mindfully hike the path around the lake, where the quiet of nature replaces the buzz of humanity. I slow my steps, watch my feet, and contemplate my path.

"Man lives his life in sleep, and in sleep he dies," Sam reads aloud to me during one of our calls. "This is a quote from Gurdjieff, a radical teacher you should study at some point."

I always have a notepad next to me when I talk to Sam. I jot down "Gurdjieff."

"Gurdjieff says 'People in their typical state function as unconscious automatons governed by outside influences and unconscious behaviors. But it's possible to *wake up* and become a different sort of human being altogether.'"

Is this the path I'm on?

Sam fasts regularly. He fasts with the same intensity as he meditates. He's hard-core. Once he water fasted for three days of every week for an entire year.

"Fasting challenges my mind *and* body," Sam explains. "I notice the beliefs and habits that tug at me regarding food and survival. I don't give in to them. I simply observe. Then, through not acting on the physical, emotional, and mental demands to eat, I strengthen my will *and* the witness consciousness."

Sam says austerities, over time, build the strongest observer—one who is not governed by internal and external forces. Eventually we're able to mindfully choose which impulses and desires to act on. I suspect his austere practices contribute to how steady Sam feels to me.

"Once the witness is strong, many things are possible," Sam assures me.

This is what I'm hungry for.

I dedicate one day a month to not eating, which I swiftly regret.

Fasting is one of the hardest things I've ever done. Within hours, my blood sugar plummets. I succumb to a cranky fatigue and feel utterly miserable. All I want to do is curl up in a ball and sleep until it's over. Then gorge myself on Oreo cookies and milk.

Why would you want to remove desires? You love Oreos.

I tell Sam I'm proud of myself because instead of copping out I meet the misery with courage.

Quitting is not an option.

Sam is impressed.

Spring break is coming up and I invite Sam to Michigan for a visit. He agrees to stay for four days. After five months of talking on the phone I can hardly wait to see him in person. With the exception of the picture on his driver's license, Sam doesn't allow photos to be taken of himself. I have no idea what he looks like. And he won't tell me.

"I'm not interested in giving attention to what I look like," Sam tells me when I ask for a description. "And I don't allow photos to be taken because, when I die, I want to leave no trace."

I drive to the airport to pick Sam up on a sunny Friday afternoon. The daffodils have burst through the hardened winter ground and spring feels imminent. I'm wearing a simple white cotton dress, and my long wavy hair is pulled back in a loose headband. A hint of makeup brightens my face.

Sam may not care what *he* looks like, but I care what *I* look like.

And he may care, too.

When Sam walks out of the jetway, I recognize him immediately. Though he's relatively small in stature, maybe five-foot eight, his presence is large. There's something about him. Seeing him sends a surge of energy through my body.

Sam's wearing crisp Levis, a black, long-sleeved, slightly worn T-shirt, and Converse sneakers. His hair is thick and straight, as dark as his shirt, and hangs loosely to his shoulders.

We make eye contact. Sam grins. His teeth are straight and white, his smile framed by a full black beard. I blush.

I walk over to him. His eyes are a muddy blue, speckled with brown and gray flecks of darkness. He drops his shoulder bag and hugs me. For a long time. Right in the middle of the crowd. His lean, fit body merges easily with mine.

I'm totally attracted to this man.

We drive to my apartment talking like two giddy kids on a play date.

"I'm surprised at my attraction to you," I share easily.

"Why?" he asks.

"I dunno. I guess it's the sound of your voice. I pictured it being attached to a different looking person. A less attractive one."

"That's what you get for making assumptions," he says.

I smile.

Sam's been celibate for nearly five years, since his last relationship ended. When he mentioned this, it intrigued me. It didn't occur to me that I might actually be motivated to influence his decision.

"Sam," I venture, "do you think you'll ever have sex again?"

Like, maybe, with me?

"I have no idea," he replies. "I was told to become celibate, and if I'm told to have sex again, I will."

Sam receives his guidance from an internal knowing that he's been cultivating since he was in his late teens. He speaks of this guiding voice in third person. At thirty-six years old, his connection to this inner compass is strong.

I envy it.

"What if I offered you a compelling reason to change course?" I wink.

"Sorry, Detroit." He is unruffled. "Unlike other men, I'm not seducible. It won't happen. You can wish for it all you want."

I'm not interested in wishing for it. I'm interested in jumping your bones when we get to my apartment.

"Well, would you ever consider changing course for the right person?" I say, half joking.

You're an idiot.

"Detroit, why are you even going there?" He seems agitated. Or am I making that up? "What difference does it make if I want to or not? If I get told to have sex again, it won't matter whether I *want* to. I'll do it. What does it matter to you? Our relationship isn't about sex. It's about something way more important."

Maybe he's not attracted to you.

"Besides," he adds, "even if I do get told, you probably wouldn't be the one I'd be told to have sex with."

Ouch.

"Why not?"

"Because it would have to be with somebody fully committed to removing all desires and attachments to sex, with no intention of falling into any sort of romantic relationship."

I could be that woman.

"And you're definitely not that woman," he looks right into me.

I shut up and drive.

At the time I began studying with Diana, I was also attending workshops called "Sex, Love, and Intimacy." Over many weekends, through masterful facilitation, participants examined all three subjects in the title. We explored how our life experiences differ from what we were taught by our parents, religion, peers, and society. Sam's view on relationships lines up with what I've discovered in these workshops: Sex, love, and intimacy are each distinct experiences and don't always show up together in a single relationship. And they don't need to.

This goes against everything I've been taught but matches precisely what I've experienced.

"We don't need to have sex in order to be intimate," Sam says as he lays his hand on my shoulder. "This belief has messed you up."

"I know, Sam," I look over at him. "But it feels like sex and intimacy *want* to go together. At least, in me they do."

Are you certain this is so?

"Look carefully at this, Detroit. What's the actual feeling? Where does it come from? What's it telling you?"

I don't want to "look" at my feeling, you idiot. I want to act on it.

I pull into my apartment complex.

"It's not that you *shouldn't* want sex, love, and intimacy together. It's that they don't *have* to go together," Sam clarifies, as we walk up the steps to my apartment. "We miss out on significant relationships when we demand all three elements be squeezed into one person."

"So stop trying to squeeze you?" I ask as I slide the key into the lock.

"It'll only cause you suffering." His face is so close to mine I almost kiss him.

I hate that he's right.

"I guess I like to suffer," I say as I turn the knob and walk inside.

"Guess you do," he says, dropping his bag on the couch.

Sam and I take a silent walk around the lake, practicing mindfulness together. We've talked so often over the past months, it's nice to simply be together and not say anything. I like the feeling of him next to me. Sam takes my hand as we walk. My mind races, but I plant my awareness into my feet.

One foot in front of the other.

Before going out to dinner we head to my parents' house for a short visit. I want Sam to meet them. He's indifferent about the meeting because he's not interested in spending time with people who aren't devoted to a quest for truth. But I want Sam to put faces to my roots. I assure him that, besides Jacob, he won't have to meet my other siblings. My sister Ellen is away at college and my youngest brother Adam, now a high school senior, is in Florida with his friends for spring break, probably getting drunk as we speak.

My mother is in the kitchen spooning matzah balls into bowls of homemade chicken soup. She turns to give me a hug. We casually embrace as I kiss her cheek. Nothing has changed between my mom and me. We remain distant. Though she's never mentioned the abortions, she did manage to express how hurt she was by my involvement with Orthodox Judaism. She said she was insulted because, if I had married, her grandchildren wouldn't have been allowed to eat in her kitchen. Though she keeps kosher to the degree my Dad asks of her, it would not have been kosher enough for an Orthodox Jew.

It's all about her.

"Mom, meet Sam," I say.

"Hello," she says, and smiles.

"Hello," Sam says as he shakes her hand without returning her smile. It's not because he's rude, it's because a genuine smile doesn't arise. Though they stand less than three feet apart, the distance between my mother and Sam is vast. I'm embarrassed by who she is.

My dad is in the family room, relaxing in his chair watching CNN. He sips on a glass of Southern Comfort.

"Hello son," he says, standing to greet Sam. "Nice to meet you."

They shake hands. They're the same height.

"Hi," Sam says.

"How was your flight?"

"Fine." Sam is curt.

This is a big mistake.

"Wonderful." My dad is sussing Sam out. "Nice weather we're having. Don't you think? Why don't you kids sit down?"

Sam and I sit on the couch as my Dad turns down the TV.

"What kind of work do you do out there in Oregon, Sam?"

So predictable.

"I build furniture," Sam answers.

"Very nice. What kind of furniture?"

"Fine furniture. From exotic woods."

"Great," he says unconvincingly.

Sam is silent. Calm.

I wish my dad would ask something meaningful.

In the background, the CNN broadcaster is interviewing experts about the culpability of the police officers who beat up Rodney King last week in LA.

In the foreground, my father's interrogating Sam, to see if he's "good enough" for his daughter.

I hate that he does this.

"How are things going with you, Dad?" I derail him. "How's work going?"

Before he can answer, my mother calls from the kitchen that it's time to light the candles for the Sabbath.

I'm relieved.

"I'm good, baby. I'm good," my Dad says as we head towards the dining room. Sam walks behind me.

Sam probably hates you now.

"*Baruch Atta Adonai...*" my mother begins the prayer over the candles as she covers her eyes. I know I'm expected to join her, as I have in the past, as I always did growing up. But I don't feel connected to Judaism anymore.

My father joins her and gives me a look of dissatisfaction for remaining silent. I ignore him and move closer to Sam.

4

I wake up rested and excited to spend the day with Sam. He's still asleep on the futon in the living room when I go to him. Our plan is to start each morning meditating together. Before I wake him, I stand for a moment staring at his hands. They seem too delicate for a carpenter.

Who is this man?

He stirs and opens his eyes.

"Morning," he smiles. "You're up early."

"Not really. You're just on West Coast time."

"Right," he says and steps out of bed naked. "Let's sit."

I gaze at his sinewy body as he slips into gym shorts. He's covered with hair in all the places men can have it.

He grabs the blanket off of the bed.

I follow him into my bedroom and hand him a pillow to sit on. I wrap myself in a cotton shawl and sit in my usual spot. Sam places his pillow against the wall a few feet away. I set the alarm for twenty minutes and close my eyes.

Keeping my spine straight and steady, I observe my breath filling my torso. My belly rises and falls in waves distinct from the rhythm of my beating heart, yet somehow in sync with it. Cool air brushes the tip of my nose.

Then everything slows down. The space inside me expands. A thick energy fills the space around me and inside of me. I feel like I've entered an echo chamber and the only thing reverberating is the barely audible whisper of my own breath. Everything is completely still.

I feel frozen and stabilized by the silence.

The alarm rings.

I slide off the pillow and lay my upper body over my legs to stretch my back. Sam is still sitting.

"Did you feel how quiet that was?" he says in a whisper.

"Yeah," I reply. "That was amazing."

Even more amazing that we both had the same experience.

"Most sits aren't like that," Sam informs me.

"What did we do that made it so quiet?" I wonder.

"Nothing." He smiles. "It was grace."

Something you could use more of.

"Does the deep quiet come more often after you've been meditating for a long time?"

"Not necessarily." Sam seems distant. "Grace isn't in our control. All we can do is show up and sit. However, a regular disciplined sitting practice certainly creates more opportunities for grace to appear."

"What else happens after years of sitting?" I ask.

"A lot of boredom." Sam answers, smiling. "Which is actually a valuable challenge. But that's a conversation for another time." Sam pauses to consider. "And, every once in a while, some really weird stuff."

"What sort of weird?" I laugh.

"Once, every day for three months, I heard a voice describing in detail how to build a windmill."

"A windmill?" I look at him funny.

"Yep," he says. "I've never built a windmill, have no desire to build one, and have never seen any plans on how to build one. And yet, during every sit, I heard a voice giving a very clear description of how to build a windmill. Step by step."

"What did you make of that? Did you think you were being *told* to go build one?" I ask, wondering if it was the voice of his internal guidance at work.

"No. I viewed it as just another worthless voice in my head," Sam says sliding off the pillow and landing right next to me. "There's only one voice worth following, Detroit. The one committed to waking up to the truth."

I sit up straight and twist my torso to the left. Wringing myself out.

"Eventually the windmill voice stopped talking to you?"

"Yep."

"So, if I listen to the voice that wants to wake up, then the others will fall away?"

"Yep."

"What about the voice that tells me to eat. Or pee?" I twist my body to the other side.

"Those voices are different," Sam says. "They're not really desires in the way we're talking about. They're biological needs. I'm talking about the voices that want to run your life. The ones that tell you to behave like your friends, find the perfect guy, get your parents to love you. The voices that judge, cajole, fantasize, and… You fill in the blank."

"Follow *none* of them?"

"None of them," he says seriously. "Unless they support the one who wants to wake up."

"How will I know which is which?"

"Trial and error."

"And then what? What happens when all the other voices are gone?" I'm trying to grasp the big picture.

"Then you jump into the Abyss."

"The Abyss?"

"Yes. The Abyss. But we'll also save that conversation for another time. Meanwhile, keep sitting. Meditate as if your life depends on it."

Because it does.

Sam stands and folds his torso over his legs. He groans as he alternately bends and straightens his knees, lengthening his hamstrings. Then he straightens up and raises his arms.

"Right now," he says, "let's go eat bagels."

Jacob has worked in this bagel shop since high school. When Sam and I enter, a teenage girl is behind the counter filling plastic containers with cream cheese. Baskets of warm bagels crowd the display case. The smell is irresistible. Through a partitioned window, I see Jacob standing in front of a large oven, flipping bagels with a wooden paddle. He sees me and gestures for us to come back.

Sam grew up in New York. I tell Sam that Jacob's bagels are as good as New York bagels because they're boiled and not steamed. Sam is doubtful they're anywhere close to being as good as New York bagels.

"Hey," Jacob says, closing the oven door. He takes off his oven mitts to give me a hearty hug.

"You must be Sam," he says. "Glad to meet you. My sister says great things about you."

"And your sister says you make decent bagels," Sam remarks.

"Help yourself."

Despite all the flavor options, Sam takes two plain bagels.

I grab a warm sesame bagel and a cup of coffee. Jacob takes lox and cream cheese out of the cooler and the three of us walk out into the sunshine. We sit on a picnic bench in front of the store.

Sam doesn't bother with any of the fixings. He takes a bite. I hear a crunch, which is the mark of a good bagel, I'm told. It means it has the perfect crust, unlike steamed ones. Sam chews and considers.

"Okay," he smiles. "Not bad. Not bad at all."

"Glad you approve," Jacob gives him a nod.

This is when I know they like each other.

I feel happy about this.

It's Sam's last day in Michigan. We're cuddling on the futon, discussing his visit. I'll be taking him to the airport soon.

"Why don't you come to Oregon for a while?" Sam suggests.

"What's a while?" I ask.

"How about for the summer?"

"The whole summer?"

"Why not? You have it off."

"I know, but three months is a long time. What if I don't like Oregon?"

What if you do?

"What wouldn't you like?" Sam asks.

Meditating, fasting, challenging my beliefs, restraining my desires. What's not to like?

"I don't know," I say. "Your life is pretty austere. I might be uncomfortable. Where would I sleep? Would I even have a bed?"

"Relax, Princess Detroit. You'll be fine."

"Sam?" I'm curious. "How do you afford to live the way you do, meditating, studying, and talking to people like me all the time?"

This is the question my father wanted to ask.

I probe. "Do you make enough money building furniture?"

"No way," he laughs. "I make furniture as a spiritual practice. I help manage a family business for money."

"What does that involve?"

"It involves phone calls and trips to New York, when needed. The business gives me enough income to live my simple life and devote my time to what really matters. So what d'ya say? You coming?"

I roll out of his embrace and onto my back. I rest my head in my hands and close my eyes to think. I've just had four days of the deepest intimacy I've ever experienced with a man. And we never even kissed. We've seen each other naked but haven't engaged in any sexual activity. We hold hands, lie in bed together, talk about everything. I find this both encouraging and uncomfortable.

I sit up and turn to him.

"Sam, I have to ask you something."

"Anything."

"Are you attracted to me?"

"This again?" He rolls his eyes.

Yeah, this again?

"I want to know," I insist.

"Why? What difference does it make?"

"It's weird. That's why. I'm totally attracted to you. Emotionally, spiritually, *and* physically. I feel closer to you than I ever have with anybody. And I wonder. I know you're celibate but, is it me? Is there something about me that keeps you from wanting to have sex with me?"

"Detroit." Sam sits up to face me. He grabs me and slides me closer, so that I'm practically in his lap.

"I'm a guy," he begins. "Guys will have sex with pretty much anybody, or anything. And if women would tell the truth about their sexual appetites, they would say the same."

I squirm, not liking where he's going with this.

It's not about you.

"If I were sexually active, I would gladly have sex with you. You're an attractive woman. It would be easy."

That's not the answer I'm looking for.

"But do you *want* to?" I press. "Not, would you be *willing*?"

I want you to want me.

"I want to wake up, Detroit. Other desires don't matter to me."

"How can that be, Sam?" I'm unsettled by his declaration. It's so final. "How can it be that nothing else matters? What about love? What about what's happening between us?"

"What's happening between us is a deep connection around a mutual desire to realize truth. Don't confuse it with a romantic fantasy about love and all that crap. That's what's screwed you up in the past. I'm about *un*screwing you up."

He's not your guy.

I fall back on the bed exasperated.

I'm afraid I might be falling in love with a celibate monk.

Forget the love part. Just do the spiritual stuff with him.

Sam sits stoically, his hand resting on my back. After a few minutes I pull away from him and get up.

"We better get ready to go to the airport," I say.

"What about spending the summer in Oregon?" he asks without moving from the bed.

"I'll think about it."

5

I fill a cardboard box with the paperback books I collected for my students. I reminisce about the time spent in this classroom. Two days ago I finished my second, and last, year of teaching fifth grade at this private Hebrew Day School. While chatting with a recently hired male teacher, I discovered an egregious pay discrepancy in our salaries. When I confronted the headmaster with the blatant discrimination, he refused to give me a pay increase, citing "school board policy" and other "budget limitations." I politely told the headmaster how despicable his behavior was. Then I resigned.

Today I'm clearing out the last of my supplies.

I feel tender. I've gained confidence teaching at this school, being intimately involved in the lives of the young people who sat at these desks. I've also been reminded of what I consider to be my greatest shortcoming, a lack of authentic wisdom. Though I'm great at teaching kids academic subjects like math and science, I fall short when it comes to guiding their moral development. I can't handle getting it wrong. I froze when ten-year-old Hannah asked me if I thought God was real.

I'm still figuring these things out for myself.

They don't pay you enough to teach that stuff.

I put the last box into my car. The parking lot is empty and the warm weather is here. I lean against the car facing the sun. My plan for the summer is to find another job for the fall, finish writing my master's thesis, and spend the month of August in Oregon with Sam.

It's late Wednesday afternoon and I'm at my kitchen table working on the final edits of my thesis. I'm determined to finish today because on Monday I leave for Oregon.

Completing this degree in History and Philosophy of Education has deepened my love of teaching. I'm humbled by how much power teachers have to change lives. My study of Rudolf Steiner, the topic of my thesis, has been so transformational to my thinking that I'm considering training as a Waldorf instructor. In Steiner's opinion, spiritual development is integral to everything we do as human beings. Anthroposophy, the spiritual movement founded by Steiner, was born out of the belief that children's creative, spiritual, and moral dimensions need as much attention as their intellectual ones. In my thesis I postulate that this statement is not solely a belief, but a fact. Without including spiritual and moral education in the classroom, young people are destined to struggle later in life. I use my personal story as evidence.

I'm thinking about Gurdjieff's philosophy, wondering if he and Steiner ever crossed paths, when the phone rings. It's the director of a private alternative school in Ann Arbor. I applied for a position there and interviewed with the director last week. She wants to hire me. I'd be one of three teachers working with teenagers in an ungraded, unstructured classroom environment. I'll be encouraged to implement aspects of the work and philosophy of Rudolf Steiner. The director says the reason she chose me for the job is because I embody a "contagious enthusiasm for doing right by the kids."

This is so perfect.

I'll teach the way I wish *I'd* been taught.

I tell her I'll take the job.

I've never been on an airplane this small. It has propellers and only forty seats. As we begin our descent into the Medford airport, the aircraft wobbles and my stomach lurches. I lean towards the window and scan the landscape below. A river winds gracefully through large green fields. Two flattop mesas stand like guardians at the edge of the valley. Strip malls and neighborhoods appear as we get close to landing.

I exit the plane directly onto the tarmac. The smell of freshly cut wood from nearby lumber mills fills the air.

Suddenly I feel nervous.

Sam and his friend Robert from California are waiting for me at the curb in Sam's yellow Corolla. Last week Sam told me Robert would also be visiting in August. I was surprised that I wasn't the only expected visitor. Sam says Robert visits whenever he can get away.

I walk up to the car as Robert gets out of the passenger side, then slides the seat forward so I can get in the back.

"Hi," he says.

Robert looks somewhat like Sam. Same dark hair, dark skin, and build. But he *feels* very different. Whereas Sam is bold and intense, Robert seems awkward and slightly nerdy.

"Hi," I say, waiting to see if Robert hugs me or tries to shake my hand. He makes no move towards me.

I throw my suitcase in the back seat and hop in.

"Hi," Sam says.

"Hi," I reply, meeting his eyes in the rearview mirror.

"Oregon's beautiful!" I say, staring at a snow capped mountain in the distance.

"Are you hungry?" Sam asks.

"Sort of."

We drive to downtown Medford and pull into a HomeTown Buffet, one of Sam's favorite places to eat.

"Pay attention to how unconscious people behave when it comes to food," Sam instructs Robert and me as we wait in line for a table. "Notice how many obese people there are in here, count how many times they go back for refills, watch how high they pile food on their plates, and see how much gets thrown away."

I feel sick already.

"Then, observe how much *you* eat, " Sam says, "what you eat, why you eat it, and how it feels in your body. This exercise is about mindfulness and becoming aware of your habitual patterns. It's not about being healthy or eating well."

Sam, Robert, and I head to the different food stations. I look around, scanning my options before loading up my plate. There are two warm food bars filled with entrées and steaming side dishes, a station where a man wearing a chef's hat is slicing slabs of various meats, and an enormous salad bar with an array of fresh fruits, vegetables, and toppings.

My sudden awakening to the number of options available paralyzes my ability to choose. I stand for a moment watching. Then I slowly build a large green salad, impulsively adding a scoop of potato salad at the end. Sam is already eating lasagna when I join him at our table.

"What questions do you have for me?" Sam asks.

He doesn't do small talk, does he?

Robert sets down a plate with three small piles of food on it. He sits and begins to eat methodically, like a bird.

At Sam's suggestion I've been studying the works of Carlos Castenada, a controversial anthropologist turned shaman, trained by a Toltec master in Oaxaca. Sam believes Castaneda holds views identical to his about how to end the cycle of rebirth and free oneself from the suffering of being human.

"I've been thinking a lot about recapitulation," I say.

In *The Eagle's Gift*, the fifth book in his series, Castenada talks about recapitulation. It's a method of releasing behavioral patterns and beliefs from our past. Recapitulation works by capturing memories, then visualizing them as you breathe in a specific pattern. Recapitulation changes habitual perceptions, allowing the practitioner to perceive each moment clearly, unfiltered by the past.

"What about recapitulation?" Sam is enthusiastic.

"I'm not even sure what questions I have yet," I say. "But I do know I want to experiment with recapitulating while I'm here this month."

"What are you imagining?" Sam asks.

"I was thinking about doing a sexual recapitulation."

"Why sexual?" Robert asks.

He speaks!

"I'm putting a lot of focus on my sexuality these days," I tell Robert, "identifying and discarding the moral and psychological garbage trapped in my body and psyche."

I finish my salad and am ready for my next plate of food.

"Why recapitulation?" Robert asks.

"Well, first off, I'm intrigued by the practice and I want to try it. Recapitulating my entire life, like Castenada did, would be too much to tackle in this short visit, but focusing on my sex life seems doable. In theory, recapitulating my sexual encounters will create more spaciousness in how I'm engaging sexually. And I'm curious about what my sexuality has to do with my spirituality."

"You address *that* one, Goldberg," Sam says, looking at Robert, calling him by his last name. "I'm going to get more food."

I look at Robert expectantly.

"The short answer is your sexuality has everything to do with your spirituality," Robert says, finishing his last bite of food. "I'm sure we'll talk a lot about this while you're here. And I'm hoping you'll consider having sex with me as part of your experiment."

I'm taken aback.

Robert looks at me hesitantly, as if he's scared I might say no, but also nervous I might say yes.

I'm not completely surprised by his request. After all, this is the way things roll with Sam. Everything's fair game, which means every aspect of life must be examined when it comes to seeking the truth. There are no restrictions put on the experiments we come up with. Still, Robert's suggestion feels a bit forward.

"I'll think about it," I reply as I stand to get more food.

"Great." Robert smiles.

I load my plate with a roasted chicken breast, a small portion of lasagna and a spoonful of candied yams.

As I turn to head back to our table, I brush up against a young woman who's probably also in her twenties. She's my height, but twice my size. She smiles at me. Her cheeks are flushed. I feel warmth towards her. And loathing. I critique her thighs and her eating habits as she piles on enough mashed potatoes to feed a family of three.

I turn away, embarrassed by my negative judgment.

You don't even know her story.

"I'm feeling ill," I say to the guys as I sit down.

"Eat too much?" Sam asks, smiling.

"No. At least, not yet." I stare at my plate.

"I'm sick from *seeing* too much," I say.

"Good," Sam says. "Now, let's eat the rest of the meal in silence so you can give feeling sick your full attention."

As I chew the chicken, I consider how eating is normally a social activity. I feel awkward eating with Robert and Sam while not engaging in conversation. I want to ask Robert a bunch of questions about himself.

I slow down and pretend I'm meditating. My anxiety lessens. I watch myself chew.

By being quiet I do find it easier to observe what's going on in my head and what's going into my mouth.

Just because you see it doesn't mean you can change it.

Though I'm full, right before we leave I stuff a piece of chocolate cake and a scoop of vanilla ice cream into my reluctant belly.

Sam's home is fifteen minutes out of town along a beautiful winding mountain road. We turn onto his street just as it's getting dark. In a few hundred feet we veer onto a driveway, stopping at a metal gate. Robert gets out, opens the gate, then closes it behind us and walks the rest of the way to the house. Sam and I park next to a white stucco house shaped like a double wide mobile home. It has a flat silver roof and a large screened-in porch.

Sam grabs my suitcase and I follow him to the entrance. The front door is an abstract collage made from exotic woods. It's gorgeous.

"Wow!" I exclaim. "Did you make this?"

Sam nods. He unlocks the door and we walk into the living room, a carpeted, rectangular space, empty except for a wall of books and one brown chair.

"Follow me," Sam says, leading me through a small kitchen and dining area into the other side of the house. We walk past another room with a beautiful door, obviously made by Sam, and into a room with a stunning cherry wood floor.

"This is where we'll do yoga," Sam says. "And where you'll sleep."

Sam drops my suitcase on a double bed nestled into a nook at the far end of the room. Across from my bed is a giant picture window facing the hills beyond Sam's property.

Robert is staying in the guest house, a two-room structure located a few hundred feet from here. We'll all share the one bathroom in the main house. Sam sleeps in a tiny room adjacent to the living room. He builds furniture in his shop along the back side of the house. The whole house smells pleasantly of sawdust.

I unpack my suitcase and join the guys already sitting on the screened porch.

I plop down between Sam and Robert on a tattered old couch. We listen to the crickets until the sound of a car on the road interrupts our peace.

"How do you two know each other?" I ask.

"We met at summer camp when we were ten," Robert answers.

Robert tells me about his friendship with Sam as adolescents, both of them baffled by girls and passionate about sports. I learn that Robert studied electrical engineering in college and now works for a tech company in Silicon Valley. Robert tells me he's followed Sam's interest in spirituality since they were in their early twenties.

I stare at Robert, considering whether I like him or not. He has a weird upper lip and a lisp. Robert's eyes are dull and bulge out of his head behind his glasses. I wonder what having sex with him might be like.

"We start sitting at 5:45 tomorrow morning," Sam says. "You may not want to stay up too much longer tonight."

"What time *is* it?" I ask, having lost track.

Robert looks at his watch. "Almost 9:30."

"That's well past midnight for me," I say. "I guess I'll turn in."

I stand, feeling suddenly disoriented. I walk to the bathroom, leaving Sam and Robert sitting on the porch.

The house feels stark and cold.

Or is it Sam who feels stark and cold?

I brush my teeth and crawl into bed.

6

The alarm buzzes at 5:35 am. I grumble, fumble, then turn it off. I reluctantly roll out of bed and into the meditation room. The room is tiny, maybe seven by seven, and dark, except for filtered light entering through a small window facing the woods. Sam's already here, wrapped in a brown crocheted blanket, sitting tall on his zafu, a Japanese style meditation cushion. Robert and I arrive at the same time. I take my seat on a small square pillow across from Sam, and Robert sits to my left. I wrap a blanket around me, close my eyes and turn my attention inward.

A timer goes off after fifty minutes and not a moment too soon. I've never sat for this long. My leg is so prickly it's giving me the heebie jeebies. It was all I could do to not fidget or scream.

I ease off the pillow and, as soon as fresh blood flows into my feet, I make my way to standing. I follow Sam and Robert into the yoga room. Robert hands me a purple yoga mat.

I've been studying yoga on and off since college. Sam's been practicing daily for five years and Robert regularly takes classes in the Bay Area. Sam hands me *Light on Yoga,* the source text of the Iyengar Yoga tradition. For the next ninety minutes, we take turns selecting poses for all three of us to do. Sam chooses a twisty arm balance, which I strain to hold because my upper body is so weak. I suggest a deep forward bend. I easily melt into the pose and watch Robert's hamstrings revolt. To counterbalance, Robert opts for a long stay in dog pose. My whole body shakes.

This is intense.

After yoga, we return to the meditation room. Again, we sit for fifty minutes. My body's a bit more willing to be still, now that it's been stretched, but my mind has already begun its rebellion. It fires anxious thoughts about what I'm getting myself into here in Oregon with Sam. I question Robert's sexual motives and cast doubt on the benefits of meditating.

I start to hope for more pins and needles, which might be easier to cope with than managing the challenging voices in my head.

You're supposed to be focusing on your breath.

My breathing is erratic, so I opt to focus on a phrase from Judaism which mysteriously pops into my head: *Hear oh Israel the Lord our God the Lord is One.*

I speak it internally in Hebrew: *Shema Yisrael Adonai Elohenu Adonai Echad.*

My breath begins to calm down.

Who is this God?

I'm still listening for an answer. Even after all these years.

Shema Yisrael Adonai…

Now I'm thinking about Sam's chest and how I want to touch it.

Elohenu…

Now I'm thinking about The Great Spirit that Diana speaks of and wondering if It knows this God of Judaism.

Adonai Echad…

Now I'm thinking about how much I'm thinking.

When the timer goes off, instead of leaping up, I pause in the space between being still and moving again. I decide to explore the transition a bit. It's similar to the brief interval between an exhale and an inhale. Suspended and timeless.

I like it.

I follow the guys to the kitchen for food.

After breakfast Sam and I take a hike while Robert stays at the house to read. We walk along the gravel street just past the neighbor's gate where it turns into an old logging road. We hike deep into the forest. Sam tells me this land belongs to one of the largest property owners in the Rogue Valley, the Brookings family. They were some of the first Oregon settlers.

"They mined it for gold," Sam says. "And trees."

This explains why there are very few large native pine trees. Medium and small evergreens are scattered among scrub oaks, leaving the forest looking jagged. The landscape would be completely dismal if it weren't for the manzanita trees. Their smooth bark is red, their branches unruly, and their leaves bright green and shiny. They're like a flash of beauty in a ravaged ecosystem.

"This view is a bit depressing, Sam," I say.

"It's the product of unconscious humans," Sam explains. "The world is filled with scenes like this."

"The world doesn't have to be this way," I say, feeling sentimental.

"It *is* this way, Detroit," Sam replies sharply. "Who cares whether it *has* to be or not."

"Why are you so critical? And pessimistic?" I take his hand in mine as we walk, happy to be alone with him.

"I'm not pessimistic," he declares. "I'm realistic. Humans are idiots."

Maybe you're the idiot.

I don't argue with Sam. I don't care if he thinks humans, in general, are idiots. As long as he doesn't think *I* am an idiot. Besides, I also think clear-cutting forests is idiotic behavior.

"I know you believe ending desires is the way to end suffering. But do you believe there's a Higher Intelligence that humans are aspiring towards or evolving into?"

He smiles. "You mean an Intelligence that might cure them of their stupidity?"

"Yeah." I laugh.

"Yes, actually, there is a Higher Intelligence. It's called the Absolute," Sam says with his usual certainty. "It has nothing to do with humans though, and is not what most humans are aspiring towards. In fact, the Absolute couldn't care less about humans or any other part of this relative world."

We walk in silence as I chew on Sam's statement.

"Is the Absolute the same as God?"

"Not even close," Sam answers. "God is just another form of idiotic."

I learned while studying the Kabbalah that the Transcendent and the Immanent are two faces of the One God. Sam is implying this One God is entirely Immanent and contains two faces. Its two faces are composed of opposites, like life and death, matter and energy, good and evil. All of which Sam is categorizing as idiotic.

But the Transcendent, that which Sam is calling the Absolute, he claims is altogether different. It's beyond opposites and appears to be the object of Sam's seeking. I wonder if the Transcendent is where we end up when all desires are gone. I wonder if the Transcendent is the Abyss Sam also talks about.

Intriguing.

This could clear up a lot of my confusion. It might explain my troubled relationship with God. Maybe the Absolute is what I'm actually searching for.

We come to a clearing in the forest and stop to rest near a group of boulders. I climb onto the biggest one, lie down, and let the sun warm my body. The smell of pine is strong and enlivening. A squirrel rustles in the brush.

I wonder how the Absolute came into being?

I let my mind wander into the nuanced texture of this question.

I've been at Sam's for less than one full day, but already I know I want his life. Despite the challenges of meditating and doing awkward yoga poses, I appreciate the simplicity, the quiet, the time to deeply consider things. I want more time in my life for study and contemplation, for understanding my psyche, and deconstructing my past.

I suspect this is what I've needed all along. Time with myself.

"I'm glad I'm here, Sam," I say, feeling grateful for his generosity. "Thanks for inviting me."

"Just don't waste the opportunity," he says, dismissing my gratitude.

"I won't," I assure him. "I promise."

After a while we hike back to the house, talking about the history of yoga coming to the west. Sam tells me about Swami Vivekenanda's visit to the Parliament of Religions in the late 1800s, and Paramahansa Yogananda's arrival in the 1920s. Yogananda established the Self-Realization Fellowship and wrote about his life in *Autobiography of a Yogi*. The book is on my reading list.

As Sam and I approach the house, he informs me his cousin Barb will be joining us during the last week of my stay.

"Your cousin?" I'm intrigued, and annoyed another visitor will be intruding on my time with Sam.

"My second cousin once removed," Sam clarifies. "She lives in New York. I told her about you. She wants to meet you. You'd be good for her."

What does that mean?

"How old is she?" I ask.

"Thirty-four. Single mom with a four-year-old kid."

"Cool," I reply, eager to meet a relative of Sam's.

A few mornings later, after our second meditation period, I find Robert standing in front of the bookcase in the living room. Floor-to-ceiling shelves hold books on every religion or philosophy I could ever imagine. Sam has read them all.

"What are you looking for?" I ask.

"This!" he says, grabbing a thick purple paperback off the lowest shelf. "It's by Ram Dass."

"Who's Ram Dass?" I ask.

"He was a Harvard professor who experimented with psychedelics back in the sixties. He had profound experiences with LSD and spoke publicly about them. After he got fired from Harvard he went to India and met his guru. After a while, his guru told him to come back to the States and share what he learned. *Be Here Now* was his first book."

"Interesting," I say. "I'd love to check it out."

"Check what out?" Sam asks as he walks into the room.

"Ram Dass," I say, beaming.

"Great idea," he says, unimpressed. "We can check out whatever you want, in the car. Get your shoes on. We're going out for breakfast."

We're driving an hour north on Highway 5 to a restaurant, Heaven on Earth, where Sam says they make cinnamon rolls the size of my head. I'm staring out the window, enjoying the landscape of forest and ranches, when I ask Sam about psychedelics.

"What do you think LSD did to Ram Dass?"

"Opened him to other dimensions and perceptions."

"Which ones?" I want more information.

"The most significant One. The One that proved to him that none of the other ones are real. Or that they're only relatively real. On psychoactive drugs the mind becomes more fluid and permeable. Ram Dass was able to see what he couldn't see in his normal mental state."

"Have you ever done LSD?" I ask Sam.

"Nope," Sam answers. "I don't need to. I meditate."

I remember my first experience with psilocybin mushrooms. It was the spring term of my sophomore year at the University of Michigan when I spent seven weeks in New Hampshire with twenty other students. We were attending an offsite literature course run by a group of professors who, when I think about it now, were probably familiar with Ram Dass, maybe even knew him personally.

The program provided an opportunity for my eighteen-year-old self to explore some deep philosophical questions. In reading Thoreau I learned what he and so many other mystics and poets found in nature and through concentrated introspection.

One day halfway the through the term, before hiking into the mountains, four of us drank psychoactive mushroom tea. By the time we hit the trail my body felt like a helium balloon. I began singing love songs out loud to the sky, sensing my connection to everything. Later in the day, I painted with watercolors, mesmerized by the fusion of pigment with water and paper.

The experience inspired me to wonder in new ways. I began to crave knowledge of other landscapes, internal and external. That fall I dropped out of college and moved to California.

"So what exactly did Ram Dass' guru want him to teach people?" I ask as we pull into the parking lot.

"Any realization of truth acquired via psychedelics isn't sustainable when you come down from the high of such mind-altering substances," Robert reports. "Meditation and spiritual practice are needed to stabilize any meaningful realization."

I wonder about Ram Dass' guru. I wonder what it would be like to have a guru.

We arrive at the restaurant, a rustic log cabin built with lumber from the surrounding forest. In the entry sits a table filled with homemade jams and local honey. These are surrounded by pamphlets with pictures of Jesus.

We take a booth by the window and order two cinnamon rolls and three cups of black tea.

"Freeze!" Sam says as the waitress walks away with our order.

"Freeze" is Sam's version of Gurdjieff's "STOP" exercise, one of his better known methods of jarring his students awake. I'm in the middle of swallowing a sip of water and setting my glass on the table. Robert is next to me about to toss his backpack across the booth to Sam. Robert's arm is suspended over the table holding the bag. On Sam's command, Robert and I have become statues. I hold the water in my mouth and don't let my hand lower the glass even one micrometer. I breathe.

I pretend I'm on LSD. Just for fun.

I imagine that my thoughts are particles. I observe them moving away from me like tiny receding bubbles. I blow on them and watch them turn to fairy dust. Then I bring my attention to my aching arm. The pain rising in my shoulder feels like molten lava.

I remind myself to breathe.

What is pain?

I consider this question.

Who's considering?

Now my shoulder is pounding.

Whose shoulder?

"Thaw," Sam says.

As if pushing the play button on a VCR, Robert hurls his backpack at Sam and I lower my glass onto the table.

"Shit, Sam," I almost spit my water in his face. "Why do you call Freeze when we're in such compromised positions?"

"Every position is a compromised one," Sam says and smiles.

The waitress delivers warm cinnamon rolls with icing that glistens like wet snow in the sunshine. Sam and Robert each cut off a section of their roll, put them on an extra plate, then hand it to me. We eat in silence.

I pry apart the layers of sticky cinnamon dough as my thoughts turn to this afternoon, when I will begin my recapitulation process. I'm ready. I've recorded on paper every sexual encounter I can remember. My first memory is from kindergarten when Michael Schwartz kissed me on the playground during recess. I have no sexual memories before then. I know people who remember having orgasms before they turned five. But I don't. Heck, I didn't even figure out how to masturbate until I was nineteen, two years *after* I started having intercourse.

When we finish eating, we sit drinking tea for another hour as Robert and Sam talk about Swami Chinmayananda, a Hindu spiritual leader and teacher. Robert heard Swami lecture in the Bay Area last month. I sit quietly, listening to them discuss the tenets of Advaita Vedanta, a non-dual system of thought found within Hindu philosophy and religion. Apparently, Advaita Vedanta is a sub school of Vedanta and underscores the notion that the true self is pure consciousness.

I slowly sip my tea, contemplating the notion of self, and pure consciousness.

"Is the Absolute made of pure consciousness?" I ask Sam.

"Consciousness, capital C, *is*," he answers, "but it has no relationship to consciousness small c. Except, of course, when we use our small-c consciousness to be conscious of this truth."

What the hell is he talking about?

"Is the Absolute the same as the Abyss?" I ask, wanting to get the terminology straight.

"Yes."

I collapse into myself to think, while Sam and Robert continue talking about Swami. I hear their voices as if through a tunnel. I'm busy putting a bunch of puzzle pieces together in my mind. Seeing if they fit together.

My brain hurts.

On the ride home I doze off in the back seat.

7

It's late afternoon when I enter the meditation room with my recapitulation list. I close my eyes and begin the process. I imagine the first scene on my list, the afternoon Michael Schwartz kissed me. I remember what the school playground looked like and how it smelled of damp wood chips. I recall how my body felt light, and I can practically hear the sounds of young children giggling. I turn my head to the right as I inhale, imagining any part of myself I might have lost or given away during that experience. I hold my breath as I turn my head from left to right two more times. Then I exhale, releasing any beliefs or acquired habits from the experience that I no longer want.

My mind launches an attack, creating logical reasons why the process of reconstructing and re-living an experience to filter out its negative impact is stupid.

What could you have lost or given away? This is pure nonsense.

I decide to let my mind have its point of view and proceed with the practice, regardless of its efficacy.

Breathe in.

Breathe out.

Remember.

Return.

Release.

Pause.

My next memory is when I'm in fourth grade at a party in the basement of my best friend Rachel's house. Her parents are away and my parents don't know this. They never would have let me come if they'd known. There are eight of us here, four girls and four boys. The lights are off. *The Best of Bread* is on the turntable, the track "Baby I'm a-Want You" is playing.

I inhale the joy, take it back. Exhale my fear, give it away.

I'm with Mark Kramer sitting on a purple beanbag chair. He puts his arm around me.

Inhale excitation. Exhale anxiety.

He moves in to kiss me on the lips. I let him.

Inhale. Exhale.

His mouth is open so I open mine. My lips bump into his metal braces. Our tongues swirl like lost kites entangled in a windy sky.

Inhale pleasure. Exhale shame.

His hand is now on my breast. I flip my loose hair out of the way in a gesture that thrusts my torso forward.

Inhale explorer. Exhale slut.

Mark's hand doesn't move from my flat chest. It rests there like a suction cup devouring my nipple. I smell him. His sweat. A hint of cologne? I open my eyes to peek. His are closed and his breathing is getting quicker and louder. My arm is around his neck and I'm loving it, the whole thing. Wanting more. Not knowing what more would be. Wondering if he likes me. If he'll ask me to "go steady" when we're done. Wondering what the other kids are doing.

Inhale youth, innocence, curiosity.

Exhale self-consciousness, caring what other people think, comparing myself to others.

Inhale staying-in-my-body. My body. This body. This life.

Exhale trying-to-please. To do it right. To be sexy.

Inhale sexy. Inhale sexy. Inhale sexy.

Exhale dirty. Exhale stinky. Exhale ugly. Exhale not-enough. Exhale too-much.

The memory ends. I continue the breathing and head-turning while waves of emotion wash through me. I realize these are emotions not connected to any particular memory. They come on the tails of the feelings already released. Leftovers.

It's like we're clearing junk out of a scary dark attic.

I spend two hours every afternoon for the next ten days activating, feeling, and releasing my past. Recapitulating helps me bear witness to the stories of my life and then turn away from them. I am compelled to reside more fully in the present moment.

After my final memory is recapitulated, I sit silently in "regular" meditation for a while to seal the entire process. I rip up my sexual memory list and bury it under a tree in the yard. Feeling satisfied, I walk into the kitchen as Sam is preparing dinner.

"I feel great, Sam," I report. "I've uncovered a sense of self beyond my personal story."

Something's crystalizing in me.

"Don't get too caught up in this new you," Sam's tone is cautionary. He's standing at the counter chopping broccoli with a large knife.

"Why not?"

"As we've discussed," he turns to me, "there is a self inside you who wants the ultimate truth more than anything else. This is the one who brought you here to Oregon in the first place. I sense that the recapitulation has cleared out some false beliefs and allowed the truth-loving part of you to feel more in control. This is probably what you're noticing. It's a relief to deconstruct the thought patterns pulling you into the past or pushing you into some fantasy of a future. But it's not the end of the road."

I sit down at the dining room table. Sam dumps the vegetables into a pot, adds water, and places the pot on the stove.

"Put it this way," Sam continues. "This self you've unearthed must also be deconstructed, recapitulated, and ultimately destroyed. For now, she's helping remove the other ones. But even she must jump into the Abyss, too. In fact, she's the only one, in the end, who'll actually be excited to jump."

I like this self. Maybe mine won't want to jump.

"You'll see," Sam declares. "In the meantime, go ahead, feel good about yourself. Knock yourself out. Just don't get too comfy as *her*, is all I'm saying."

I leave Sam standing by the stove in the kitchen. I don't want to listen to what he's saying. He's pissing me off. I'm going outside to be with the anger welling up inside me.

I step onto the deck. Sam built this deck as a way of channeling *his* anger after the break-up with his last girlfriend. Apparently she couldn't tolerate his eccentric lifestyle. He spent months cutting raw redwood planks and pounding nails, all without a plan. The deck meanders like an abstract sculpture in front of his house, the wood now black because Sam chose not to put a finish on it. Raw and exposed wood suits Sam. There are no railings anywhere, and on the northern edge of the deck is a set of steps leading to nowhere.

A hanging swing is suspended on one of the outposts.

I plop my deflated self into the rope seat and turn to face the setting sun.

Don't worry. Sam might not be right about everything.

I just busted my ass recapitulating for ten days and am feeling lighter and more hopeful than I have in a very long time. I was expecting Sam to be happy for me. I was hoping he would celebrate my accomplishment.

That's not his job, remember?

I guess so. But it doesn't mean I have to like it.

Who's not liking it?

8

I agree to have sex with Robert over the next three afternoons, feeling curi-ous about what I might learn. I'm approaching our encounters as oppor-tunities to further discover my authentic sexuality. Even though I'm not all that attracted to Robert, he *is* somebody I can trust. So I'm treating our exploration as an exercise, not dissimilar from the exercises I've experi-enced at the Sex, Love, and Intimacy workshops.

It's a hot afternoon with temperatures spiking into the hundreds. I'm heading to the guest cottage where Robert is staying. The scent of drought-resistant star thistle permeates the parched hillside where I'm walking. The pollen feels heavy in my nostrils, like it wants to invade my entire body.

I knock before I enter. The entry room is where Robert meditates and reads. The adjacent room, where he sleeps, has a large mattress in the center of it. There's a floor lamp in one corner and a stack of milk crates filled with clothes and personal items against the wall. A fan is circulating air through the room. The curtains are closed to keep out the heat.

Robert is lying on the bed. He's wearing gray shorts and a bright white t-shirt. He pats the bed next to him indicating I should join him.

I slide off my flip flops and lie down on my side, propping my head on my elbow.

"So what do you have in mind for today?" I ask.

Last night, we finalized our specific intentions for these sessions. Our plan is to each choose one aspect of sex we wish to investigate. Today is Robert's day. He gets to design the exploration. Tomorrow will be my turn. How we spend the third day is yet to be decided.

"I want you to massage my whole body, ending with my penis," Robert says. "When you get there, go slowly, keep me hard, but don't let me ejaculate. I'll guide you."

Sam, Robert, and I have had a few conversations about Tantric sex, a catch-all term in the Western world for sacred sexuality. One theory promotes the belief that when men don't ejaculate they're more focused and have more energy for spiritual practice. Robert has been practicing restraint of ejaculation.

I'm stroking his penis and admiring it. It's not too big and not too small. I enjoy the feel of it in my hands. I'm watching Robert ride waves of sensation as they ripple through his body and he twitches or moans. Instead of letting the energy escape through ejaculation, Robert focuses on keeping the energy moving within. He uses his breath and visualization to direct it. Robert raises his hand when he's close to orgasm so I know to back off a bit. I witness him use his breathing to stay in that sweet spot, and I help him sustain it. It's quite beautiful.

And fun.

The next afternoon we're exploring the spot on the ceiling of my vagina known as the G-spot. I've asked Robert to massage it without touching my clitoris. There's another area deeper inside my vagina I yearn to explore, but I'm not ready to invite anyone in that deep.

Robert is rubbing rose scented massage oil on my inner thighs. Then he enters me with his middle finger. He's rubbing my G-spot side to side, then in circles. It's painful and stimulating at the same time. I instruct him to slow down. After ten minutes I begin to cry.

"You okay?" Robert asks.

I don't know what's happening.

"I'm okay and not okay," I manage to say.

"Do you want me to stop?" he asks, adjusting his position on the mattress.

"No," I answer. "Keep going."

Let's see what happens.

Robert continues steadily stroking me. I'm calmly observing the sensations in my body and then breathing into them, the same way I do when I'm experiencing pins and needles in my legs during meditation. I take long deep inhales to receive Robert's strokes and, just when I think I can't take any more, I relax and keep going. I ask Robert to pause while I place an extra pillow under my head. Now I'm partially upright. When Robert starts again, almost immediately a throbbing sensation starts pulsing through my groin. Concentric waves of warmth reverberate throughout my pelvis. I put up my hand telling Robert to stop. I close my eyes and let the waves reach the edges of my skin. Then I roll over and sob into the pillow. I have no idea what the tears are about. They just come.

Robert, Sam, and I are gathered on the porch after dinner. I'm feeling tender from my experience this afternoon. I sit alone on the ground leaning against a post. Sam and Robert are sitting on the couch. It's still quite warm and we're all naked.

Sam asks me how the afternoon went.

I'm mad at Sam for not being the person who rubbed my G-spot.

"What do you want to know?" I ask, feeling antagonistic.

"I want to know what happened." His voice is kind.

It's none of your business.

"Robert rubbed my G-spot," I report. "I had an implosive orgasm and I cried a lot."

As if sensing my distress, Sam joins me on the floor and my defenses weaken. He grabs a pillow off the couch and sets it next to me. I lie down and put my head on it. Sam spoons me. I begin to sweat.

"Listen, Detroit," he says into my ear. "You've done a lot of work since you got here. You recapitulated your entire sex life, for Christ's sake. Deeper layers of sexual intensity are now available to you. But so are deeper layers of pain. Don't push too hard."

I'm here to find the truth. How can I push too hard for that?

"I feel really emotional," I admit.

Sam puts his hand on my chest, pulling me closer.

"Can you feel my hand between your breasts?" he says.

"Uh-huh." I begin to cry.

"Bring your attention here," Sam guides me.

We're breathing together and my agitation settles. My chest relaxes, and then my whole body.

"Remember, your emotions are just emotions," Sam reminds me. "They only tell you the truth of how you feel, not the truth of what is. Just feel them, then let 'em go."

I close my eyes, feeling myself soften. My body is different from when I arrived three weeks ago. For one, my vagina feels clearer. Lighter. Sparkly.

I want to make love to Sam right now.

Don't even go there.

The next morning I feel rested and renewed. After my sexual and emotional release yesterday, I don't feel like experimenting with Robert today. We agree to take a hike instead. While walking, we talk about love, trying to discern how love is different from other emotions such as happiness or excitement.

Arriving at the giant boulders along the trail, Robert and I lie down to rest. I take off my dress so I can be naked on the hot rock. Undulating waves of warmth start pulsing through my pelvis again. I breathe with their rhythm until I'm imagining the current extending into the boulder I'm lying on. Soon I feel the warmth pulsing through the forest all around me.

Robert and I remain silent together for more than an hour.

The following day Robert returns to California. Sam and I have a couple of days to ourselves before my final week, when his cousin Barb will join us. So we get in his little Toyota and drive three hours to the Oregon coast. We rent a room in a mom-and-pop motel for two nights. We swim in the pool and eat at local restaurants. We hike in the redwoods and walk barefoot along the shoreline. If it weren't for sleeping in separate beds, we could be any normal couple.

But we aren't.

Barb arrives the day after we get back from the coast. Barb is short and chubby with long dark hair. She wears Birkenstocks, a flowery muu-muu, and no make-up. There's a gap between her two front teeth that gives her smile a certain brilliance. When we meet, Barb hugs me as I imagine a loving Italian mother would. Deliciously comforting and a bit smothering.

My final days at Sam's revolve around Barb. It turns out I'm okay with this. I'm actually happy to have the focus be on someone else, and to have some time to myself. Sam advises Barb on how to deal with her ex-husband, counsels her on her health, and teaches her to meditate. I journal, sit, and take long walks alone in the woods.

In the evenings, the three of us gather on the porch.

"I'm considering moving to Ann Arbor," Barb says to me on our last night.

"Really?" I reply, surprised.

"Yeah. Sam's helped me realize I need to get out of New York," she explains. Then, without any hesitation, she asks if I'd be up for having a roommate.

Barb's request surprises me and reminds me how I felt the first day I met Robert when he asked me to have sex. I barely knew him either.

"What about your daughter?" I ask.

"She'll come too."

I look at Sam. He smiles an I-couldn't-help-myself smile.

I imagine what a big step moving out of New York will be for Barb. She's in major transition after ending her difficult marriage and is now an unemployed divorced single mother. I consider what living in Ann Arbor will be like for me. Though I can imagine having a roommate, I'm not so sure I want to live with a young child. I'll be starting a new job and don't want my home life to distract me from the focus on my spiritual quest. Still, living with Barb could be beneficial for a number of reasons. We're both interested in the same quest and living together would cut my expenses. Plus, she knows Sam. I'd be able to talk with her about the complexity of my relationship with him. Nobody else would understand.

"I'll think about it," I answer, feeling open to the possibility.

I haven't had a roommate since the yeshiva.

It might be good for you.

wild

1

I was seventeen in 1980 when I moved to Ann Arbor the first time. I was a freshman at the University of Michigan, eager to explore life beyond the sheltered suburb I was ready to leave behind. Ann Arbor has changed a lot since then. I've changed a lot, too.

I'm driving through town looking at places for rent. I've decided I want to live with Barb and her daughter Elana. I'm headed to look at a two-bedroom apartment on the south end. It sounds perfect. The complex is filled with young kids and is close to my new job.

I turn onto East Anne Street where I shared a house with two other girls during my sophomore year. *Déjà vu* washes through me. I stop in front of the house, staring at the living room window. The exterior is a different color but the window frames are the same. I flash back to the night when a stranger entered the house and raped my roommate Jeanine at knifepoint. Though I recapitulated this event at Sam's, the memory overtakes me now.

A muted terror races through my body. I begin to sweat.

It could've been you.

Our third roommate Eileen and I slept through the attack. It wasn't until after Jeanine called the police that she woke us up. She was in shock pretending she was fine. Eileen and I were in shock, too. But we didn't pretend we were fine. After the police left and we escorted Jeanine safely to a clinic, Eileen and I banded together like traumatized soldiers. Besides abstaining from dating men for a while, we became active in the *Take Back the Night* movement on campus, marching to stop violence against women.

I lay my head on the steering wheel to cry.

They never caught the guy.

I wonder where Jeanine is now.

Early in the morning, two days before I start my new job, Barb pulls up to the apartment in a maroon Mazda jammed with suitcases and bags of clothes and toys. Elana is squeezed in between two green duffel bags in the backseat. That same afternoon a moving van arrives. Barb has shipped her furniture from New York because she can't bear to part with it.

Once unpacked, it doesn't take long for Barb and me to establish a rhythm living together. She takes part-time work as a secretary and focuses mostly on helping Elana adjust to the move. Many mornings Barb and I meditate together before Elana wakes up, and in the evenings we make time to sip tea and talk. On weekends Barb and I take a yoga class together.

Though I wish it weren't so, I find myself mostly tolerating Elana. The noise she makes disturbs my peace, and I feel burdened by her demands for attention. I try to be kind, but after spending my workday with chatty teenagers, my patience is thin.

I want a quiet home life.

It's almost Halloween. The weather is turning cool and the leaves are changing colors. I'm up early on a Saturday, driving to Diana's, excited about this next course of study. Today's teaching is in preparation for the winter solstice. We're learning a ritual designed to connect our personal growth with the rhythm of the seasons. There are fifteen men and women at Diana's when I arrive. Angela and I sit together near the fireplace. Diana's four-month-old son Nathan sleeps in a basket in the corner of the room.

"This ceremony happens four times a year," Diana begins. "On every solstice and equinox we stop to acknowledge the movement of time and the changing seasons of our lives. The solstices and equinoxes are four pivot points within each year-long cycle of the earth around the sun. The Native people experienced these turnings as sacred moments of opportunity for self-reflection. We begin the ritual by taking an honest inventory of our lives."

Everybody has brought a notebook or a journal. In a few minutes we'll begin writing, meditating on our lives, identifying areas where we're content and areas where we feel stuck or want to grow.

"Once you've taken stock," Diana instructs, "you'll spend time praying and listening for guidance. Between now and the solstice, you'll meditate and contemplate, paying attention to coincidences and dreams. Watch for signs. You're asking this question: "What will align my life more fully with my unique purpose and destiny?"

I sense the potential for this ritual to be a powerful examination of my actions and intentions. Diana suggests I view it as a homecoming to my Self. An opportunity to correct my course. When the solstice arrives, I'll gather the insights I've received. Then, through ceremony, I'll set clear, accountable goals for myself.

This practice could help me with self-discipline.

You've got to be joking. "Pay attention to signs and dreams." What fantasy world are you living in?

I've got to stay connected to the sense of self I experienced while in Oregon with Sam.

The only thing you experienced in Oregon with Sam was his fanatical lifestyle.

I focus on the assignment. In my journal I organize my findings into five separate categories: physical, emotional, mental, spiritual, and sexual.

I'm writing a stream of consciousness about my emotional life, assessing how I'm doing in this arena. Mostly, I'm feeling confused. I'm not sure how to be in relationship with my emotions. I still struggle with a persistent melancholy, which I find easier to accept during meditation practice than while at work each day. In meditation I'm able to observe my sadness, then rest into the silence behind *all* my emotions. But when I'm teaching, I find it hard to bring forth the vital enthusiasm I yearn to share with my students.

Diana's been teaching us that emotions are merely pockets of energy in motion.

"Harness the energy to create something beautiful," she advises.

I have no idea what she means. My depression isn't creative at all. Sam says it's best to simply let my emotions be and cautions me not to *do* anything with them. The less attention I give emotions the better.

I sense Diana and Sam might be pointing to the same truth from different perspectives, but I'm not certain. I wonder if I should try harder to get creative with my sadness or if I should somehow move it through. Neither of these tactics feels available to me right now. I can't harness my sorrow or let it go.

I note all this in my journal, then write about my maddening relationship with thoughts.

On the eve of the winter solstice I sleep with my journal tucked under my pillow. Deep into the night I have a dream.

I'm in a classroom learning about human anatomy. There are large colorful charts of each system of the human body displayed on the walls. The instructor looks like me. She's speaking about the heart and blood flow in a language I don't recognize. She's naked. I stand up from my seat to move closer to her, imagining it might help me understand what she's saying. I am gasping for air. The instructor doesn't see me struggling to breathe and continues teaching. Suddenly the charts come alive and fall off the walls. They circle me. A skeleton sidles over and forcefully punches me in the chest. His bony hand travels right through me. I wake up.

I grab the flashlight from my nightstand and write the dream in my journal, wondering what it means. Unable to fall back asleep I read the entries from earlier this month. I linger on this one:

> I feel troubled by a consistent fatigue and intermittent sore throat. I realize I've had these symptoms since high school. I don't feel "sick" to the degree that would seem to justify going to see a doctor. But I definitely feel unwell a lot of the time.

I close my eyes as the realization comes to me. My symptoms have to do with taking penicillin every day for ten years after having rheumatic fever as a kid. At the time, my parents were convinced by the pediatrician that a regular dose of antibiotics in my little body would prevent me from getting sick again. Maybe the medicine did serve some purpose. More likely it suppressed my natural immune system and weighed me down in some way I don't yet comprehend. For years I've been overriding tiredness with caffeine and sugar, assuming exhaustion must be part of growing older. After all, I'm nearly thirty.

The dream is showing me something about my health.

I wonder why the skeleton punched me.

I set my journal down and manage to sleep a bit more, then rise to hold my solstice ritual. Barb and Elana are in New York for the weekend, so I have the apartment all to myself. First I go outside for a short walk in the neighborhood. I gather a bunch of frozen leaves and dead branches. I build a large altar on the floor in the living room. I identify the four directions with my compass and put a pillow in each direction. On each pillow I place a branch or a leaf. I take my seat in the north. I light a candle, wrap myself in a blanket, and close my eyes while turning my attention inward. I speak a prayer aloud to "all those beings who might be here with me, watching over me, blessing me." I ask them for support and inspiration.

My body settles as my awareness expands.

I chant my favorite Cherokee song. "*Yala waneyna heynayno…*"

The Cherokee song morphs into a Hebrew prayer. "*Kol haolam kulo…*"

Then my prayer turns into a spoken petition.

"Oh Sacred Ones, I ask for your guidance. I'm still not sure if I believe you exist or if any of this ritual stuff works but, please, bear with me while I make a sincere attempt."

"Hear my prayers."

"Help me move forward in my life with clarity and purpose."

"I will now speak my intentions for this coming three-month cycle. I ask that you show me where I might be off course."

In the north, the place of air and the mind, I plan to continue studying with Diana, review the Castenada books, and read all of Lynn Andrews' works.

In the south, the place of water and emotion, I will stalk my sadness, and attend the next level Sex, Love, and Intimacy workshop in order to cultivate a healthy relationship with love.

In the west, the place of earth and the physical, I will explore ways of finding out what's at the root of my body's fatigue.

In the east, the place of fire and the spiritual, I will sit for twenty minutes each morning, take three yoga class each week, enjoy a Sabbath once a month, and do a vision quest in the Spring.

In the center, the place of pure energy and the sexual realm, I will continue to explore my sexuality by engaging with various partners and each of the masks.

"And now, Sacred Ones, if there's any information you feel I should have, show me," I whisper.

I get very still.

I listen.

I wait.

I hear a voice telling me to consider attending massage school. Or maybe it's a thought of my own. I can't tell the difference.

What if there is no difference?

While recovering from my second abortion, I had a moped accident. The accident led me to experiencing my first therapeutic massage. When the therapist placed her hand on my sacrum, I burst into tears, unleashing a rush of grief. In addition to stimulating an emotional release, the massage also helped heal my low back pain. Since then, I've received massages when I'm able to fit one into my budget. Until now, however, I've never considered becoming a therapist myself.

Last night's dream has new meaning. I was, after all, in a school of some sort, studying the human body.

Am I making this shit up?

Diana emphasized the importance of suspending our rational beliefs. She encouraged us to intentionally bring faith into these ceremonies in order for them to have power.

Faith in what? What can you trust?

Diana emphasizes that life is fundamentally a mystery. "We overlook the awesomeness of life," she says, reminding us not to be distracted by what we think we know. "Engage always with the mystery. Learn to trust it. When you come to ceremony, open your perception to something greater than you already believe you are. Remember, nothing is set in stone, and time is not linear. It winds through our lives, appearing to take us in a straight line. But infinite options are available to us at every moment of our lives. Change *is* possible."

I wonder about free will.

I write down my commitments, including looking into studying massage. I place the list in an envelope and put it in my nightstand. The envelope will remain sealed until the spring equinox, when I'll revisit my commitments and see how well I did with follow-through.

A week after my ceremony, I spend winter break in Florida. My brother David has recently relocated and bought a restaurant in Fort Lauderdale. My mom and dad are renting a condo on the beach nearby. Jacob, Adam, and I spend a week with our parents, getting tan and eating. My sister Ellen is in the Bahamas with her friends.

Jacob and I are walking on the beach. It's early in the morning and the surf is calm. Jacob is leaving for Israel in a week. He'll be attending a year-long program studying psychology and philosophy while living on a kibbutz. He's hoping to kickstart a life for himself apart from baking bagels. Though we don't see each other often, I like knowing Jacob's never far away. Realizing he will soon be *very* far away brings me pause. What if I need him?

"I'm going to miss you," I tell him.

"Come visit," Jacob says as he stops to pick up a perfect sea shell partially buried in the wet sand.

"Maybe I will," I reply, knowing I won't.

We walk in silence, comfortable to not have to speak.

"You seem happy," Jacob says to me and hands me the shell.

"I mostly am," I say, not wanting to burden him with the whole truth right before he leaves on his adventure. I clutch the shell and imagine placing it on my nightstand for safekeeping.

2

Three months pass quickly. I'm so busy I barely notice the gradual explosion of yellow on the landscape. I'm taking an evening class in anatomy and physiology. The class is part of a Therapeutic Massage certification course. We're studying the digestive system so I'm experimenting with diet and exercise. I've eliminated dairy and run a mile each day before work. While jogging this morning, seeing the forsythia against the gray backdrop of a long Michigan winter, I finally acknowledge the arrival of spring.

On the equinox Angela and I are driving three hours into the middle of Michigan where we will experience our first vision quest, a Native American rite of passage. I will use the quest as preparation for my equinox ceremony and ritual. We arrive just before noon.

This beautiful land belongs to Diana's assistant, Carla, whose family has owned these 1,200 acres for more than a century. After greeting Diana at base camp, our task is to wander the area until we find our individual questing sites.

I choose a site under an oak tree next to a dry creek. I spread out a Mexican blanket, then set a gallon jug of water against the trunk and head back to the main camp.

We are nine women total, five of whom I already know from Diana's previous classes and two I've only recently met. We set up our tents around base camp and then finish building the sweat lodge, a temporary domed structure made of willow branches. It stands next to the fire pit. Our job is to cover the frame with layers of wool blankets and plastic tarps until it is airtight and womblike.

Tonight we will sleep in our tents here at base camp. Diana says it's necessary. "One night at base camp will help you transition into your solo time. You'll let go of the city and settle into the forest," she tells us. "In the morning, we will sweat. This will be the final group ritual before you walk alone into the wilderness."

Our questing sites are within earshot of the main camp but isolated from one another. I'll spend two nights and three days sitting on my blanket praying, making myself available for insight and possibly a vision.

I've brought my medicine bag filled with the sacred objects I've gathered this past year. Each object represents a quality I'm cultivating in myself. A quartz crystal carved into the shape of a pyramid for worldly strength and courage. A hawk feather, representing clarity of mind. A small ceramic cup to be filled with water, to encourage emotional equanimity. And a candle to represent fire, the alchemist's most precious symbol of transformation.

I put the bag at the door of my tent so I will remember to take it with me tomorrow. Everything else is piled in the far corner, ready for my return in three days.

I crawl into my sleeping bag.

What if you don't have a vision?

Then I won't have a vision. My intention is to be open. That's all I can do.

You could probably do more.

Diana blows the conch, calling us to sweat. Giant stones have been heating up in a fire-pit since dawn. Soon the hot rocks will be carried by shovel and placed into the pit at the center of the sweat lodge. When we're all gathered inside Diana will pour water over them, initiating our sweat.

I leave my tent, wrapped in a towel, and walk in silence to the lodge.

Carla is drumming while Diana smudges each of us with sage and gives us her blessing. The nine of us enter the lodge, first dropping our towels in a basket just outside the entrance. I'm glad to be sitting by the door. I've participated in a number of sweat lodge ceremonies with Diana and sometimes I feel claustrophobic. Should panic arise today, I may want to get out fast. I like knowing the exit is close.

Diana enters last, closing the flap. It's pitch black. I blink, then get very still, resting into the cool earth. I put my attention on my breath. We begin to chant in rounds, our voices sounding a call to the ancestors. I wrap myself in the intensity of the darkness, the heat, the bodies tucked in close, breathing together. The smell of sweat mingles with the scent of the damp ground. I feel cocooned by the lodge. Expectant. When the chanting trails off, we each pray silently.

"Oh Sacred Ones, please hear my prayer. I'm here to deepen my knowing of what is true. I ask for your help."

I want a clear sign.

I want any sign.

Something burns.

It sweats out my pores.

In single file we leave the lodge. Then we jump into a cold pond. The freezing water shocks me awake. When I'm dry, I walk back to my tent and dress for my quest.

I've been sitting on my blanket under the tree for more than twen-ty-four hours. I know how long because the sun has already set once and is now directly overhead. It must be close to noon and I'm hungry. I spent the night alternating between meditating, praying, and lying under the stars in that half-awake-half-asleep zone. I've had no insights or visions.

I begin to struggle with my desire for food. I've never fasted for longer than a day. I hate that I'm struggling already. A sense of inadequacy floods me.

Why are you even bothering with a vision quest? You're not Native American. You're a white girl. A Jewish American Princess.

I sit up straight to shake off my inner critic. And my hunger. I take long deep breaths to stabilize my increasing anxiety. I imagine capturing any lingering doubts with my inhale and casting them out on the exhale.

I do this for a few rounds. Then my blood sugar crashes. I begin to shake. I drink some water. It doesn't help. I lie down and rock myself.

Misery seeps in.

I'm desperate for food.

Diana prepared me for this. She spoke about how to "allow room for feelings of hunger" and then notice how I use food as a crutch. I've heard all of this from Sam, too, but in this moment I'm struggling to stay present and allow.

How can I get clear about "truth" when my body's freaking out?

I'm rapidly losing energy trying to stabilize my frightened body. I need the energy to get me through this quest.

Accept that your body is freaking out and just relax.

I sit up and take another drink, holding the water in my mouth for a while before I swallow. I close my eyes to visualize my body absorbing energy directly from the wetness.

Doesn't it make more sense to just go grab some food from your tent and then return to continue the quest?

I wonder.

No. Don't do it. Don't give in.

I get up and walk around my site, hoping increased blood flow will help. When I feel a little better, I decide to move beyond the boundary of my blanket. It's not forbidden to take a walk while on a quest. But it is discouraged.

Diana impressed upon us, "Best to incubate in one place."

Best to follow your intuition.

I stagger towards the ridge nearby.

The sun's going down. A lone pine tree stands to my left and I inch towards it, now crawling on all fours. I call forth my will to override my body's desire to collapse. I embrace the tree, rubbing the bark with my fingers.

I sit with my back to the tree and let the trunk hold me upright. Fluid pulses up and down my spine. I imagine the sap in the tree's veins pumping in sync with the rhythm of my spinal fluid.

I inhale the tree's exhale. She inhales mine.

We are one.

He falls from the sky, landing directly in front of me on the shoreline of the earth. He is turquoise and teal, iridescent and transparent. He is a turtle without a shell. He is throbbing. His wings fold in on himself and transform into feet. Now he's carrying a hard shell, brown like the earth, gritty like sand. He's giant, dense, and steady.

Suddenly he is a she. Her eyes like a cat's. She waddles towards me, her shell creaking as she approaches.

"Stay the course," she says with her eyes. "You're doing great."

"I'm scared," I say, mesmerized by the realness of the vision.

"I know. It's okay to be afraid. Just keep going."

"In which direction should I go?"

"In the one you're headed."

"But which way is that?" I ask with urgency. "I need more information. Where do *you* see me headed?"

She smiles. Walks right into my chest.

My ribs stretch to receive her.

A sharp pain pierces my upper back, right between my shoulder blades. The bark has grown nails and is now clawing me.

I hear drumming in the distance, pulling me back into reality.

It's Diana.

She's here with you, holding you, just as the ancestors are holding you. Dreaming you along.

I must be crazy. This can't *really* be happening.

A raven caws in the distance.

I sit motionless as the sun sets. I stare at the fiery orb and wonder why the sun moves so quickly once it gets close to the horizon. I want to slow it down, extend my view of this blazing sky. Rapid swirls of red, gold, and orange explode between the heavens above and the darkness below.

The day hovers on the threshold of night.

This is the in-between.

This is where I am.

As the darkness descends I trudge back to my site. Once I reach my blanket I start shaking again. I lie down and look up at the canopy of leaves. Stars begin to peek through. The waning moon won't rise for hours and the night feels thick.

You should go back to your tent. Eat something. Sleep.

I should stick it out until tomorrow liké everybody else.

You should follow your own path.

I close my eyes and search for the spaces between the voices of my various selves.

I listen for guidance. Whether to stay or go.

First I push aside all the voices telling me to go, not trusting their intentions, sniffing out the inner saboteur among them.

Then I shut out all the voices telling me to stay, not trusting them either, sensing a martyr in the pack.

I breathe deeply to ground myself.

"I don't know if I can make it through the night," I say to the silence. "I need to know what to do."

I'm suddenly weighted down by an invisible force. It's hard to move my limbs. I sense the turtle aiming to root deeper into my body. I surrender.

I feel a nudge on my tailbone in the direction of the drumming.

The turtle's pushing you back to your tent.

I wait for another nudge before I agree to go.

The prod comes.

Along with a feeling of doubt.

Shit. Why is there always another opinion?

I cut a deal with my inner critic, promising to continue my quest in the tent once I've eaten something. Before I'm tempted to change my mind, I quickly roll my blanket, grab the water jug, and follow the sound of Diana's drum back to my tent.

3

Early in the morning, the other eight women return from their sites. I crawl out of my tent at base camp, hoping nobody will notice. We sit in a circle around a smoldering fire where we will keep the coals warm until every woman has shared her vision quest experience. This is an integral part of the ritual. We offer our visions to one another as a way of solidifying them. It's also a way to bless one another.

"Suddenly the wind picks up and the next thing I know a jaguar is staring at me," Marilyn reports. A nurse with two teenagers and a husband who cheats on her, Marilyn came on this vision quest seeking courage.

"When the jaguar leaves, a glow remains where it stood. I crawl to touch it. When I do, the glow enters me through my fingertips and I feel suddenly strong. I walk back to the center of my blanket and stand until the sun rises, singing a Cherokee spirit song."

A jaguar? Really?

I wonder if Marilyn's making this up to impress us.

What if it was all in her head?

Stephanie shares next. She spent her quest resting on her blanket.

"For me," she says, "there were no dreams or visions. Only a deep yearning, practically an ache, for something to enter me and fill me up. I prayed a lot. Nothing tangible showed up. But I do feel an energy hovering, as if some sort of blessing is imminent."

Did she even struggle with hunger at all? Am I the only one who wimped out?

It's my turn to share. I pause to make eye contact with each woman in the circle. I remember how their faces looked when we first arrived. Their beauty was hidden behind a dullness they wore like bad makeup. Now their faces are radiant.

I'm hesitant to speak. My vision feels too personal.

Just tell them.

What if they dismiss me?

Who cares what they think?

My voice starts off shaky, but sharing the vision aloud gives my experience more substance and calls forth a rush of self-confidence. I'm surprised by the details that come through in the telling.

While describing the turtle morphing into a she, I hear the turtle whispering to me.

Giving voice to your story is an act of power.

I stop speaking and listen carefully to her.

She is now giving me a name.

"My medicine name is Turtle Dreamer," I say aloud.

The turtle is resting quietly inside my chest.

My new name feels like an amulet attached to my heart, directly linked to my turtle guide within.

Diana asks about my decision to leave my site early, return to my tent, and break my fast.

See, I told you. You should've stuck it out.

I'm reminded of the time when the rabbi at yeshiva questioned my decision to break a rule on the Sabbath. I told the rabbi my disobedience was the right choice in order for me to remain connected to the Sabbath. I tell Diana the same thing.

"I chose to leave my site in order to remain connected to the quest, not to abandon it."

You followed your own path.

Diana nods in approval, but I suspect she's thinking I should've stayed.

Loser!

The feeling that I "did it wrong" lingers.

I vow to do another vision quest someday.

Carla has prepared a celebratory feast for us. She sets it out on a picnic table. As the coals turn to ash, all nine stories finish weaving themselves into a tapestry of shared experience. I linger in the warmth and beauty of our connection. Before we make the long drive home, we dine on fresh salad, cheese, and homemade blackberry pie. We've closed the circle, dropped the ceremonial etiquette, and begun to socialize.

This is when I get to know more about Stephanie.

She's in her early fifties, still youthful and pretty with flowing auburn hair and hazel eyes. She bulges a bit at her midsection and shows signs of aging in the loose skin on her neck.

I fill a plate of food and sit down next to Angela just as Stephanie is sharing her decision to sell her business.

"What's your business?" Angela asks.

"I own an escort service," Stephanie answers as casually as if saying, "I own a beauty salon."

"Really?" I chime in.

I'm rattled, but I'm not sure why.

"You're not the kind of person I picture owning an escort service," I say, feeling like an idiot.

When have you ever pictured anybody who runs an escort service?

"I'm sorry," I quickly add. "I'm just, well, I'm intrigued."

Angela's eyes get big.

Stephanie says nothing, as if she's waiting for me to continue.

"How does it work?" I give voice to my curiosity.

"It's pretty straight forward," she answers. "I have employees who provide a service and customers who pay for it."

She gives me a look that suggests a question. Something like, "What is it *exactly* that you want to know?"

Angela is also looking at me quizzically. She's about to speak when I cut her off and ask Stephanie the age range of the girls she employs.

"Most are in their early twenties," Stephanie says.

"Would somebody like me be too old?" I ask.

Angela kicks me under the table.

I can't believe you just asked that.

"Would somebody like you *want* to work for me?" Stephanie smiles.

"I think she might," I say, feeling bold.

"Whaaat?" Angela cries with a mouthful of food.

Stephanie laughs, then stands up to leave. "I've got to pack up and get on the road. Let's talk about this later." She reaches into her purse, takes out a pen, and scribbles her number on a napkin.

"Call me," she says, handing me the napkin and walking away.

"Are you crazy?" Angela is practically screaming.

"No, I'm not crazy." I retort. "I'm *open*. I'm paying close attention to where Turtle Dreamer is leading me."

I smile proudly.

"It's so obvious and perfect," I say, holding up the napkin. "My first post-vision-quest task is to call Stephanie."

Last month I attended the third of seven levels in the Sex, Love, and Intimacy series of workshops. As I've progressed through the levels, I've learned to sharpen the distinctions between sex, love, and intimacy while choosing to consciously join them where it's appropriate.

These workshops, along with the Native American teachings, are helping me discover my authentic sexuality. I'm finally feeling comfortable in my body and enjoying my sex life. Working as an escort is a fantastic learning opportunity. I view it as my own personal workshop.

Why doesn't Angela see this?

Angela looks at me sideways. "Working for Stephanie is where you think your vision is leading you?"

"Yes," I assert. "Meeting Stephanie through Diana and sharing this vision quest experience together means I can trust her. She just offered me the opportunity to explore a hidden dimension of myself and my sexuality. I couldn't have manufactured anything more ideal!"

Angela stares at me like she doesn't know how to respond, then stands up with her empty plate. "Let me digest this a bit. We can talk more about it on the drive home. I'm going to go pack now. We should leave soon."

"Okay," I say, "but try to be open-minded, would you? This could be really amazing."

As I walk past the sweat lodge on the way to my tent, I squeeze the napkin in my hand. The last phone number that was scrawled onto a piece of paper and handed to me was Sam's.

Good reason to exercise caution.

I crawl into my tent and pull my journal out of my day pack. I find the section on the sexual masks. I review my notes about the Professional mask. "Offering sexual services in the form of a professional agreement is civilized, allowing two responsible individuals to enjoy sexual pleasure on its own terms. Without shame."

I close my eyes and imagine having sex with a man purely for *his* pleasure. No strings attached. My whole being is energized.

On the drive home, Angela grills me. "Why would you want to sell your body? What if something bad happens? Why can't you just role play the Professional mask?"

I feel Angela's fear but I don't let it get to me. I deflect answering her logistical questions until after I talk to Stephanie. Then I challenge Angela's beliefs about prostitution.

"Christianity crushed healthy sexual expression by making sex sinful outside of marriage," I tell her. "It also made sex sinful for priests and nuns, those people supposedly devoted to God and His creation. It's not hard to see how this has screwed *all* of us up sexually."

"I agree," Angela says as she sets the car's cruise control. "But you aren't bound by those laws. You *can* have sex freely. You *do* have sex freely. Why would you want to prostitute yourself?"

"When a man who isn't interested in marriage wants to have sex, he needs to find a woman, or a man if he's gay, who's willing," I explain. "When a woman who isn't interested in marriage wants to have sex, she must also find a partner who's willing. Look around. It's pretty easy for a woman to find a man with no strings attached. Right?"

Angela nods from her personal experience. She's had numerous one-night stands with guys she's picked up in bars.

I continue. "For men, it's much harder. If they approach a woman in a bar purely for sex they could get charged with harassment, or worse. Men are almost always forced to pay for sex in one form or another. They pay in the form of dates, marriages, children, gifts, and who knows what else. What if men could just pay for the sex straight up?"

Angela was raised a Christian. I realize that my liberal middle class Jewish upbringing might make me more open to this way of thinking.

Open? More like naive.

I continue my argument. "What if we could remove all religious overlays of judgment and shame? What if simply sharing sexual pleasure wasn't viewed as sinful? What if selling sex didn't revolve around drugs or involve ownership or suppression of women? What if it was a clean arrangement between two responsible adults solely focused on the power and beauty of the sexual act. When all a man really wants is sex, it would be much better if he could just be honest about it. Don't you agree?"

"I never thought of it that way," Angela admits.

I can almost feel her reorganizing her beliefs.

"So, why *wouldn't* I want to be of service to my brothers in this way, if I have the chance to? Besides, I'm curious about what it would actually feel like to be a prostitute," I continue. "Aren't you?"

"No!" Angela cries.

"Well, I am," I state boldly. "I honestly didn't realize how curious, until now. And this might be my only chance to try this mask on, for real."

"Okay," Angela says. "I get it. Whores *do* serve a purpose. But it sounds like you believe you can be a prostitute in a *sacred* way." Angela's voice is softer now, genuinely curious and caring.

"I *know* there's something sacred about sex," I say. "I'm still figuring out what that is. For now I'm approaching every sexual encounter with the intention of showing up in a sacred way. Whether I'm working as an escort or dating the guy I eventually marry, what difference does it make?"

I look out the window at acres of farmland, imagining my future as a sacred prostitute.

"But what if you have to be with a creepy guy? Or get a sexually transmitted disease?" Angela asks.

Or get beaten.

"That'll be part of the experience then," I tell her, unruffled. "Just like everything else in life, there are risks."

"I think you might be acting impulsively, is all," Angela asserts.

I'm too tired to respond or explore with Angela why my excitement makes her so uncomfortable. I turn away. We drive in silence. I recline my seat and close my eyes.

What if this ends up being the stupidest thing you ever do?

It won't be.

What if your father finds out?

I consider this question.

What if he's one of your customers?

I gasp out loud.

"What's wrong?" Angela turns to me startled, keeping a firm grip on the steering wheel.

"Oh," I sit up. "I was just choking on the thought of my father ever finding out." I laugh.

"What do you think he'd do?" Angela asks.

"I'm not sure," I admit. "Not much he could do. But he certainly wouldn't be happy."

I slightly cringe at the thought, because I never want my father to hurt on account of me. The possibility of him finding out brings me pause. I can't imagine what he would do if he knew.

Don't worry about how this will impact others.

I lean back in my seat again and remain quiet. I don't want to defend what I know I'm going to do. Impulsive or not.

I feel the turtle rustle in my heart.

When I said good-bye to Diana, she told me this: "Turtle wisdom teaches us to walk in peace and to stick to our path with determination."

I wrap my arms around my chest and thank the turtle for being with me.

About an hour later Angela pulls off the road for gas and I take over driving. As I'm buckling my seat belt and arranging the mirrors, Angela taps me playfully on the shoulder.

"What?" I say, not really wanting to get back into our discussion.

"What will you wear?" she asks, smiling.

We giggle.

"I don't know," I reply. "Wanna go shopping?"

4

I call Stephanie two days later. She invites me to attend her annual business luncheon. On Saturday afternoon I drive to the Hilton where I join fourteen other women in a conference room. We eat from a buffet and socialize around tables covered in fine linen. There's nothing obvious that would identify us as escorts. We could just as easily be at a fundraiser for the National Organization for Women.

I sit down next to Anne, a sweet brunette with perfectly made-up brown eyes. She's twenty-four and finishing a degree in advertising. Then I meet Dawn, a lanky blond with perky breasts. She's twenty years old and a single mom, working day shifts for Stephanie so she can attend night school. We chat about our lives, our families, and our futures.

I'm pouring myself a cup of coffee when I meet Sharon. Sharon looks older than the other girls. When I ask, she tells me she's in her late thirties. Sensing my next question and my hesitancy to ask it, she adds, "Men sometimes want an older woman."

At twenty-nine, I wonder who'll want me?

I'm at the dessert buffet when Tracy, Stephanie's manager, introduces herself. She's my age and has been working with Stephanie for seven years.

The two of us sit at a table eating tiramisu. Once I start working, I'll be reporting directly to Tracy.

Stephanie joins us and briefs me on the specific details of the job.

I get to choose when I'm on call. I must be home by the phone during that four-hour shift. When there's a client, Tracy will call and give me the information: his name, meeting place, and time. I meet the client either at his home, his office, or a hotel room. When I arrive, the first thing I do is check the client's ID. Then I take payment: $250 in cash. After that I call Tracy and let her know I've arrived, tell her the name of the client, and confirm that payment has been made. I spend an hour with the client. I call Tracy before leaving and then again when I get home. The following day I purchase a $50 money order and mail it to Stephanie.

"You'll get the hang of it after a few times," Stephanie assures me.

I imagine you will.

"Any questions?" Tracy asks.

"How many clients will I see per night?" I ask.

"Only one," Stephanie answers. "I want you to be at your best for each client."

"How many evenings a week will I work?" I ask, trying to imagine how I will arrange my schedule.

"As many as you want. I just can't guarantee you business every night. It depends on who else is on call and how busy we are."

Tracy rummages in her purse and pulls out a hand-held phone.

"Stephanie just bought this for me." She shows it to me, obviously delighted. It's black and a good deal larger than her hand. "At some point all the girls will get 'em, and then we won't have to be home sitting by the phone during the shifts we're working."

"Wow. That's very cool," I say.

I'm surprised such a thing is now available. I remember in the late seventies when I was in high school my dad had one of the first mobile phones in his car. It was the size of a toaster.

Tracy drops the phone back into her bag. "Any other questions?"

"What do I wear?" I ask, visualizing shopping with Angela.

"You'll need to invest in some nice clothes," Stephanie explains. "My girls dress like professional business women. The look you're going for is sexy and put together. Dress so that men will find you desirable but not presume you're an escort simply by looking at you."

"Dress as if you were going on a date with an attractive, sophisticated New York businessman," Tracy offers.

I've never been on a date like that.

"And wear the sexiest lingerie you own," she finishes.

I don't own any lingerie.

I thank Stephanie for the opportunity to work for her. My skin tingles with anticipation.

"Call me when you're ready to start," Tracy says. "Regular clients always look forward to meeting a new girl."

"Oh, and by the way, you need a name," Stephanie says.

I blink.

"Allison" falls out of my mouth.

"Allison it is," Tracy winks.

5

The snug black dress falls to just above my knees and hides my new ruby red lace garter belt and bra. I choose sheer black hose with a seam up the back because sliding into them turns me on. I wear a red Anne Klein silk jacket, tailored and bright. Looking in the mirror, I see a well put-together woman. I actually *do* look professional. In a way I never have before.

Energy pulses through my body like a current of warm honey.

I'm excited.

And afraid.

I walk into the living room where Barb is seated on the couch reading a book.

"How do I look?" I twirl for her.

"Wow!" she exclaims. "You sure do clean up well."

I smile and lean over to give her a hug before I dash out the door.

I drive to my client's home on the other side of town. He's a retired banker and recent widower. He answers the door in khaki pants and a loose dress shirt. His thinning dark hair is cut short and he wears glasses. I feel at ease, imagining he could be a friend of the family.

In the foyer, he takes my coat, hands me cash, and shows me his ID. I call Tracy from the kitchen phone, telling her I am with Stanley and have received payment. Then I join Stanley in the living room where we sit and talk. The television is muted, and we both laugh at a silly commercial. Stanley tells me how his life has been difficult since his wife died. He tells me about his three children and five grandchildren. He spends as much time with them as he can, manages his investments, plays golf. He's not interested in dating, but acknowledges his loneliness, his desire for touch, and his sexual needs.

I like him.

Stanley escorts me to the guest bedroom where we'll have sex. We won't use the bed he shared with his wife. Something about it doesn't feel right, he says.

We both undress. I move slowly so that Stanley sees me in my sexy lingerie. Then we get comfortable under the sheets.

We lie together for a while, holding one another. Then we move gently into being sexual.

I place a condom on his erection and we have intercourse. Nice and slow.

Do we make love?

That's a good question.

What do we call this?

I feel love for Stanley, I guess. After all, he's a lovable human being.

But you're not "in love" with him.

How did we come up with that distinction? What's the difference between "love" and "in love"? I'm here for Stanley. With him. Touching him. Holding him. There's room for his grief and his pleasure. I let his need for sex be without shame. It's easy to do.

It feels natural. Kind.

Note to self: Escorting is about connecting and caring.

Stanley and I shake hands when I leave, like we've just completed a business deal. Which we have. It feels a little weird, awkward, like I should hug him, call him later.

And it feels fine.

Tidy.

Uncomplicated.

6

When I arrive home, Barb is waiting expectantly in the same spot on the couch. She's in her pajamas now, eating a giant bowl of popcorn.

"How was it?" she asks, muting the TV.

"Fun," I say as I drop my purse and grab the phone to call Tracy.

When I hang up the phone, I change into sweats and join Barb on the couch.

"Who was he? What was it like?"

"You know I can't tell you who he is. But he was a nice guy. Kind of ordinary, actually."

"Were you attracted to him?"

"Not his looks. But it didn't matter. I liked *him*."

"But what was it like kissing him? Was it weird?"

"We didn't do much kissing. And none of it felt weird."

I pause to consider if I'm feeling anything I might be hesitant to admit. There *was* one Oh-my-God-I-can't-believe-I'm-doing-this moment, but it only lasted a second.

"How do you feel now? Now that's it's over. Your first time as a hooker." Barb is practically giddy and I wonder if she might be living this experience vicariously through me.

"I feel relieved that it was so simple. I'm actually surprised by how easy it was. How natural. And how happy I feel to have been of service to my client, giving him some loving touch and pleasure."

"I have so many mixed feelings about sex," Barb says as she grabs the throw and drapes it over the two of us.

"Tell me about it," I smile.

Barb and I talk until past midnight. She tells me all about her marriage and the guy before her husband, the love of her life she let get away. I tell her about my two abortions, Jeremy and Judaism, the masks, and the sexuality workshops. As I talk, I'm aware that *studying* about my sexuality and *living* it are two completely different experiences. This seems obvious, but I take a moment and appreciate my courage to try new things. Listening to Barb makes it clear to me that stepping into this experiment with Stephanie is not something very many women would do.

Moonlighting as an escort fills out my schedule. Five days a week I teach school until early afternoon. One weekend a month I attend massage school. The rest of the time I'm either studying or giving practice massages. One or two evenings I'm on call for Stephanie.

I set aside a drawer for my new undergarments. I've never worn anything like them before and I'm intrigued by how sexy they make me feel. Sometimes I just wear them around the house.

My clients are diverse. A forty-year-old white businessman from Pittsburgh. A Chinese professor of Economics. A young buff black construction worker. Each encounter is its own adventure. Since this is a job and I pride myself on being an excellent worker, I'm extremely professional and fully engaged. I view escorting in exactly the same way I regard my position teaching school and my work as a massage therapist. I feel the same when giving a high school student my attention, laying my hands on a massage client, and giving the retired banker pleasure. Though my actions are different in each case, the quality of service feels consistent. My engagement is based in kindness and love.

Is this sacred?

I miss Sam but I'm so busy I barely notice. He's planning a visit during the summer. Until then we talk regularly on the phone. He thinks my escorting is great. We talk a lot about relationships, sex, and spirituality. When he asks me if I'm still meditating, I tell him I don't have much free time. Sam cautions me to not let my practices slip away.

"Your disciplines are what keep you tethered to yourself and your goal," Sam says, referring to meditating, fasting, studying, and silence. I tell Sam not to worry. I have my inner turtle to tether me.

Tonight I'm headed to an office downtown. A lawyer has requested my services. The building is mostly dark. A burly security guard greets me and escorts me into the elevator. I wonder if he knows why I am here. I consider how many other women he's let up to this particular office after hours. I say I'm a client needing to sign some papers. He just smiles.

Mr. Smith lets me into his office. It's palatial. Turn-of-the-century desk, fine leather chairs, mahogany bookshelves. Classy. Elegant. Sexy. He's probably in his forties. He has dark curly hair and is wearing a navy blue suit.

We move through the usual steps: ID check, money exchange, and phone call to Tracy.

Then Mr. Smith throws me down on the desk and takes my clothes off. I usually like to have some dialogue first, ask what the client wants, and negotiate any boundaries or considerations, but this guy is not interested in talking. He knows what he wants. He takes me. And I let him.

I learn the art of surrender with Mr. Smith. He is forceful but not overpowering. He responds to my body's timing, not with might, but with sensitivity. I trust my body to know when to push back and when to yield.

I'm fascinated by my body's excitation and orgasmic response.

Note to self: Escorting forces me to face my perceived limits.

After Mr. Smith has climaxed, he's ready to talk. He lights a cigar and pours himself a scotch while I dress. I slip into my garters and put on my heels, then sink topless into his leather chair and smile. He hands me a glass of soda water.

He tells me about his day with a difficult client and a challenge with a conservative judge. He asks me about myself. I give him shades of me, just enough to let him feel like he's having a conversation with a real person and not a complete fraud, but not enough to really know me. I tell him I work with kids, that I like to do yoga and read philosophy books. My father is a lawyer, I say. We laugh about this.

"What would your dad think if he knew what you're doing?" he asks.

"He'd probably be annoyed that I'm working for somebody else and not running my own operation," I say.

Mr. Smith laughs.

He escorts me back to the elevator.

We say good-bye.

I wonder if he likes me.

7

I meet Dave at the grocery store on a weekday afternoon on my way home from school. He's tall and olive skinned with wavy black hair. He wears a brown leather jacket and snug jeans. I watch him buy tortilla chips, salsa, and a six-pack of Dos Equis. I'm turned on by the way he moves.

I smile at him at the checkout. He smiles back. A chill runs over my skin and I want to touch him.

He can tell.

He knows I know he can tell.

I follow him out of the store.

"Want a ride?" He asks while putting his groceries into a hard-case attached to his motorcycle. It's big, his bike. I say yes and climb on, leaving my car parked till later. He hands me his extra helmet and tells me his name is Dave. I hold him tight as we hit an open country road. I whisper in his ear that I like the ride. He drives faster, then takes me to his house. To his bed. And he becomes my regular guy for sex. I don't tell him about moonlighting. Or meditating.

One day Dave and I take a long ride on his bike and end up at a cabin in the woods that belongs to his aunt and uncle. There, we spend two full days of wild abandon. We eat, have sex, drink alcohol, smoke marijuana, and even snort a few lines of cocaine. We wrestle and cuddle. We play loud music and dance. We watch stupid TV shows and laugh. I lose myself in all of it. I don't "observe" what I'm doing. I do it.

I let myself lose control with Dave, viewing our time together as an opportunity to explore the Unbridled mask: "Able to be horny, lusty, promiscuous, voyeuristic, or exhibitionist."

All the while, I imagine Sam criticizing me, telling me I'm not following the voice inside me who wants to wake up. I should be home meditating and studying, not hanging out with Dave. Or at the very least I should be mindful when I am with him. But everybody needs a vacation now and then.

There is no such thing as a vacation.

The more Dave drinks, the more I taste danger in his kisses. I don't consciously intend to invite his darkness, but somewhere inside I must want it.

This is crazy. What are you doing with this guy?

I do another line of coke and smoke a cigarette to numb my inner critic. I tell myself I have everything under control. Dave is all about me unleashing my wildness. With Dave I don't have to be of service to him. Sex can be for me.

Waking up can wait.

Angela and I have lunch the following week. She's asks me if I'm okay. She says I look a bit drawn; I seem depressed and tired.

I tell her I'm fine, just busy. I tell her massage school and escorting are both going well. Plus, I'm doing some great mask experimentation with Dave. I tell her I'm exploring my edges around domination with him. When she asks whether Dave is safe for that, I assure her he is. Again, I convince myself that I'm handling it.

I tell Angela not to worry.

But soon, *I* begin to worry. Dave has no interest in anything remotely spiritual. Being with him is starting to feel like a waste of time. To go deeper into the masks I need a partner who is doing it *with* me. Dave is not that partner. I tell myself it's time to break up with Dave and get back on track.

Start meditating again.

But I don't.

I take more baths. Try to wash off my attraction to Dave and to danger. Or is it self-sabotage I crave? In a clear moment I decide to end it with Dave, but when I call to tell him, I collapse into my desire for him. He comes to get me, lifts me onto his bike, takes me to his bed and into his darkness. I don't stop him.

Sam phones on a night when I'm on call. I answer, thinking it's Tracy.

"What's going on with you? Why haven't you called?" he asks. "Barb says you're hardly ever around."

"I've been busy," I say, closing the door to my bedroom.

"Busy with what? Detroit, what's going on? Tell me."

I hesitate. I sit down on the floor next to my bed. I have my sexy lingerie on under my robe.

"Detroit?"

Sam's concern nudges something in me.

"Detroit!" he yells. "It's me! Talk to me!"

I break down and tell Sam all about my behavior with Dave.

I'm so ashamed of myself.

When I'm done Sam asks me a simple question.

"What do you want, Detroit?"

"I WANT IT ALL," I scream, suddenly furious. "I want the intensity of the sex with Dave and the darkness of being kept. I want the peace of being with myself, sovereign and content. I want the warmth of a loving committed man. I want the freedom to come and go as I please. I want meaningful work and I want to not have to work at all. I want to help people. I want to kill people. I WANT TO KILL MYSELF!"

Sam is silent. I hear him breathing. I stand up and hold the receiver out in front of my face.

"SATISFIED?!" I shout. It feels so good to yell. I throw the phone at the wall.

I fall onto my bed exhausted, smelling alcohol in my sweat.

Sam stays on the line even though the receiver is now on the floor.

I hear him calling me. His voice is far away. I don't want him to see me this way. I don't want his self-righteousness. I don't want his judgment. I don't want him to tell me to quit drinking, dump Dave, and start meditating again.

And I want him to rescue me.

I roll to the end of the bed, grab the receiver off the floor, and hang up on Sam.

I take a hot bath.

8

The next morning I call Dave. I'm feeling desperate to see him.

"Come get me after work today, okay?" I say.

He's there waiting for me when I get home. When I park my car I see that his bike is loaded with supplies. He and Barb are chatting in the living room when I enter the apartment. Dave winks at me from the couch and my body shivers.

"We're going to the cabin," he tells me. "Get your stuff."

I change my clothes and pack an overnight bag. It's Friday. I can be away for one night.

Barb hugs me goodbye.

Saturday morning Dave and I are in the shower and he has me pinned against the tile wall. We've been partying all night. He presses into me with the full weight of his gorgeous six-foot-three toned body. He enters me. His throbbing is like a lid on a pot of boiling water. He smells like a wild animal. The shower is too hot. I can't move to adjust the knobs.

"Dave. You're hurting me. Back off a bit," I tell him.

"Fuck you, bitch."

"Excuse me?"

He's never talked to me like this before.

"Fuck you. You're my woman and you'll do what I tell you. I won't let you leave me. I need you." He's yelling at me.

"Dave. What are you talking about?" I try to be calm.

"Shut up!" He pushes into me harder.

I look into his eyes, but he's not there. He's a madman, inaccessible and completely unreasonable. I'm alone with him in the woods in a remote cabin with no phone. I'm naked and he's fucking me. Hard.

I shut up, close my eyes tight, and let him pound. I feel bruises coming on my shoulders where he's squeezing me with a force originating somewhere deep inside him.

If you can just bear this until he's done.

I leave my body.

I flash back.

I'm on the Jersey shore. It's the summer of my sophomore year of college. I'm wandering the boardwalk and meet a guy named Peter. Peter runs a booth where he sells mugs and photo t-shirts. He lives in the back of the booth. We flirt for a while. He invites me to stay the night. I say yes. He closes up shop, shutting the booth with a silver gate that functions like a garage door. He bolts it from the inside with a padlock. I assume there's another door somewhere, but I'm wrong. He leads me into the back. I follow.

He sleeps in a small room with a big bed next to a stack of cardboard boxes holding clothes and sundries. There's a tiny bathroom with the only window in the entire place. We're lying in bed after having sex when he asks me if I've ever had sex with a woman. I tell him yes. I don't think anything of it. He freaks out, says he wishes he'd have asked me before we did it. Some form of religious-fundamentalist-demon overtakes him. I'm now being called the devil. With no way out, I try and talk him down, tell him sex with a woman was no big deal. Just a one-time thing, I lie. I swear to him it was innocent. I was young. I didn't even like it, I lie. Will never do it again, I lie. I ask him to unlock the gate. He says no. I change the subject, ask him about his business, ask him if he wants a back rub.

I wait for him to fall asleep, then carefully slide out of bed, desperate to not wake him. I search for the keys to the padlock. I can't find them. Peter stirs. I hold my breath. It's three in the morning. I go into the bathroom and shut the door to consider my options. I stare at the window above my head. It's the kind with glass slats that open when you rotate a handle. I bend the metal that holds each piece of glass in place. There are six of them. I quietly slide them out and stack them on the bathroom floor. I push the screen out and hear it crash on the ground. I hold my breath again.

Please don't wake up.

I zip my purse shut and toss it out. I climb onto the back of the toilet. Then, feet first, I wiggle my butt through until I'm holding on to the window sill hanging three feet from the concrete below. I let go. I tumble, then stand and shake myself off. I face an eleven-mile walk back to my apartment. I don't consider how close I was to being in the kind of trouble no girl ever wants to be in. It was just a bad judgment call, I say to myself. And look how resourceful I can be. I escaped! I feel a sense of pride and exhilaration as I stick my thumb out for a ride.

Now I'm standing alone in a shower trembling. Dave is gone. The sun is rising. I let the warm water wash over me. It feels thick, like a humid summer rain. I dissolve into a puddle on top of the drain. I am crying.

What are you doing?

I have no answer.

I turn off the shower and dry myself, checking for blood. I put on a bathrobe and walk quietly into the bedroom. Dave is passed out on the bed naked and wet. I'm relieved. I stare at his face. It's so gentle now. So handsome. I leave him there and go to the kitchen to make a cup of coffee and consider my options.

This cabin is too far from town to walk. Plus, if I leave, he'll surely follow me.

You need him to think you still love him.

We're scheduled to head back this afternoon. I can wait. I can do this.

I make myself some toast.

Dave strolls out dressed and cheerful. He grabs me from behind and kisses my neck. I cringe and turn rigid. I hope he doesn't notice.

"Sorry I crashed, baby. You just wear me out," he smiles.

He has no idea what just happened in there.

"It's okay," I lie, as I turn to face him.

"Hey," I force a smile. "What do you say we head back a little earlier than planned? I'm feeling like getting back in time for dinner. I haven't seen much of Barb and Elana lately. It would be sweet to have dinner with them."

"No way," he turns towards the pot of coffee. "There's still half a gram of coke left. I think we should head home *later* than planned. Let's stay till tomorrow. We have enough food. Barb can wait."

"No, really," I try to hide my desperation. "I shouldn't be away the entire weekend."

"Bullshit," Dave says as he walks into the other room. "It's beautiful here. We're staying."

I surrender because it's my best option. I need to stay calm. Not make him angry. I'll get home eventually.

You hope.

An hour later I make myself a gin and tonic. I take the razor blade and cut four fluffy lines of cocaine. I turn on the music really loud. I do two lines, one in each nostril. I dance. Dave asks me to do a striptease. I do. My body sizzles.

You're sexy. Desirable. He wants you.

I ask him to take me. He does. When he enters me, I feel his largeness reaching towards the place deep inside, the spot I can't quite locate but know is there, the area I crave for someone to access and break open.

He doesn't quite reach it.

9

When Dave finally drops me off Sunday just before dusk, I want to run from him. But I slide off his motorcycle slowly, kissing his cheek as I grab my bag. I'm not sure how he'll respond when I leave him for good so I proceed gradually. I tell him school is demanding, I'm spending the coming weekend with my parents, and I'll be in touch. He grabs me and kisses me with an open mouth. My resolve sinks.

Shit.

"Okay, baby. You're the best." He grabs my breast.

I love it when he calls me baby.

"Thanks." I take his hand off of me and turn towards the door.

I go inside to unpack my suitcase and my experience. My head is killing me.

There's a note on the kitchen counter from Barb. She and Elana are at the clubhouse watching a movie.

I get in the bath and discover a bruise on my thigh I hadn't noticed. I close my eyes and submerge myself into the wetness. Baths are still my sanctuary. Covered with water, I imagine I'm cleansing myself from the inside out. I take a washcloth and scour Dave off of me.

You're out of control.

Three days later I'm giving a fellow student a massage in order to complete my practicum hours. I glide massage oil on his broad back. Rubbing his shoulder blades, I settle into the subtle movements beneath my hands. Touching grounds me and reminds me how much I love this work. I haven't spoken with Dave in these three days. When thoughts of him surface, I push them away and find something to get busy with.

Angela and I meet for lunch later in the week. I'm feeling relatively stable, so I don't mention what happened at the cabin. I don't want her to worry.

I've got it under control.

I haven't spoken with Sam since I hung up on him.

Tonight my resolve to stay away from Dave is beginning to slip, so I call Tracy and tell her I'm available to work. I want to replace Dave's imprint on my body with somebody else's body. Anybody's. It might help lessen my obsession with Dave.

Tracy calls with an assignment. A private home an hour's drive away.

"A regular guy, but a bit quirky," she says.

"Oh great," I balk, not sure if I can handle quirky right now. I was hoping for handsome.

"Don't worry, you can handle him," she assures me.

I put on my working clothes and take two aspirin.

I pull into the driveway as the garage door opens. An overweight middle-aged man stands at a door leading into the house and motions for me to enter. The garage walls are stacked with floor-to-ceiling boxes. Each one is labeled. I drive my car in as he closes the garage door behind me. I flash back to the shop door closing at the Jersey shore. I panic. I breathe. I get out of the car.

I offer a forced cheerful greeting.

"Come on in," Joe says without smiling.

I follow Joe into his living room. I take off my coat and check his ID. He hands me worn bills. Mostly twenties. I'm wishing I was with the kind, attractive, wealthy client I saw last week. The one who I secretly fantasize will rescue me from my life, marry me, and create a family with me. My fantasy guy always pays with crisp hundred dollar bills, plus tip.

Note to self: When escorting, never fall for a client.

Joe asks me to undress to my lingerie and stand in front of him with my back to him. We are in his living room. His house is as cluttered as his garage. Stacks of newspapers, books, and magazines litter every tabletop. His couch is faded and worn. The room reeks of dust. I smile and do as he asks.

Joe bends me over and begins to pleasure me. I climax once. And then again. And again. And again. Though I'm perched doggy style on his La-Z-Boy, he has yet to bring his penis near me. His hands send me climaxing over and over again. I can barely catch my breath. I'm actually hoping he will stop. It's too much.

But this is Joe's time. His pleasure. And his pleasure is clearly to please me. Or something like that. I call forth the sacred prostitute inside of me and ask her what I should do.

Her message is clear: "Receive without resistance."

After forty-five minutes Joe throws me on the musty couch and enters me. He thrusts without looking at me. He's squeezing my breasts under my bra, which he has never taken off. He grunts. His belly bounces with him. His receding hairline begins to pucker with beads of sweat. The television is on in the kitchen. The evening news is the background music we fuck to.

Joe's pleasure releases into the condom. He grabs the edges before he pulls out. He walks into the bathroom, leaving me there lying in disbelief. I've never had this many orgasms in one sexual encounter. I'm dizzy.

I get dressed.

Note to self: Never underestimate the number of orgasms you're capable of having.

Joe returns from the bathroom and motions for me to leave. I exit the same way I entered.

He finally speaks. "I have you use the garage because I don't like my neighbors to wonder. A different car parking in the driveway every other night could draw attention."

Every other night?

"That's why I have you girls drive all the way in," Joe smiles. "Thank you, Allison. I hope to see you again. Please keep your lights off until you get to the end of the street."

I get in the car and turn the key. I'm placing the gearshift into reverse as the garage door opens behind me. I slide out as easily as I slid in. In the darkness, I drive to the end of his street. Then I turn on my lights, picking up speed.

10

The school year is nearly over and I'm strategizing how to leave my career in education in order to enter the field of healing arts full time. I'll receive my massage certification in two weeks. I prefer the quiet of doing bodywork over teaching a chaotic room full of kids. When I'm massaging a body, I'm meditating with my hands. Plus, I can freely speak with my massage clients about a wide range of topics regarding health and wellbeing. Though the alternative school is much more open than the Hebrew day school where I previously taught, I still feel a split inside myself. I'm not able to speak freely with my teenage students about sexuality or the ways I'm exploring and experiencing sex. And I'm only allowed to talk about spirituality from a third-person perspective. I struggle with my own hypocrisy. I desperately want my insides to match my outsides. I want to be completely transparent.

I've managed to stay away from Dave for two whole weeks. Today I woke up aching for him and am struggling with my resolve. When I get home from school, Sam's sitting on the couch talking with Barb. My body shrinks. I knew he was coming, but I lost track of time.

Sam smiles at me.

I wish he'd leave.

"Hi," I say walking towards my bedroom.

I want to cover up my lingering tobacco breath, my pulsing vagina, my shame.

Who cares what Sam thinks?

"Hey, you ready to talk to me yet?" Sam says.

If I were, I'd have called.

"What do you mean?" I say nonchalantly as I put down my things.

"You know what I mean, Detroit."

"Listen, Sam, I'm fine. Really. Sorting stuff out. I have a lot going on. I know we've had this visit planned for a while, but in this moment, the timing is not ideal. Why don't you just hang out with Barb on this trip?"

I feel Sam's stare piercing my back as I walk into my bedroom.

"Well, I'm here for five days," he shouts. "So if you change your mind, let me know. You can spend time with me or not. Up to you."

"Thanks," I say and close my door. I draw a bath and fill it with the lavender-scented bubbles Dave bought for me. I pretend Sam's not in my house and put on music to drown out the sound of him cooking dinner with Barb.

When I'm finished bathing, I walk by the dining room where Barb and Sam are now sitting and drinking tea.

"I'm going out," I say with my back to them. I grab my purse and walk out the front door before either of them respond.

I drive to Dave's and ask him to fuck me. Then we watch TV and drink scotch. I cuddle with him on the couch, nestling into his body as tight as I can, hoping maybe I'll disappear.

I walk quietly into the apartment after midnight. Sam's asleep on the couch. I tiptoe into my bedroom and fall into a deep, fitful sleep.

The next morning I go to the kitchen to make coffee. Sam's been up for hours meditating and is now eating oatmeal.

"Coffee, huh?" he says in a judgmental tone.

"Yeah," I counter with reciprocal disgust. "Want some?"

"No thanks."

Sam's smaller than I remember, especially compared to Dave. But his energy is big, bigger than I remember. It fills the room. I'm both drawn and repulsed.

"Detroit," his voice is inviting. Soft.

I make the mistake of looking into his eyes.

I tear up.

Sam doesn't move. He stays present, watching me. It's like he's waiting for me to ask him to hold me, but I don't.

"Sit down," he says.

I sit on a chair at the kitchen table.

"What do you need?" he asks.

Not this question again.

"I don't know, Sam," I say.

You're pathetic.

"Why don't you tell me the truth about what's been going on?" he says.

"Because I don't want to," I cry.

"Why not? Why are you so hard on yourself? Why are you hiding from me? If you're struggling, just talk to me. We all struggle. Why are you so afraid of exposing yourself?"

I don't know.

"Because I'm a loser, that's why. And because a part of me doesn't want to stop being a loser," I admit.

"Well then, you might as well kill yourself now."

"Huh?"

I kinda like his suggestion.

"'If you think you're going to be able to remove your desires and change your habitual patterns so easily, then you might as well throw in the towel now. But if you're in for the long haul, you'll remind yourself that every warrior falls down along the way. Then she picks herself up. Over and over and over again."

"I don't know if I have what it takes," I confess in a wash of self-pity.

"Bullshit, Detroit. Of course you have what it takes. The only question is whether you're going to use what you have and commit fully to the journey."

"It's not that simple," I yell at him.

"Yes it is," Sam's steady voice cuts through my defenses. "It may not be *easy*, but it sure as hell is simple."

"Shit, Sam," I say, wiping the tears from my face. "I don't even know where to begin."

"Just tell me everything."

And so I do. Sam's the first person I tell about what happened at the cabin with Dave. Sam listens. He doesn't turn away. I surprisingly don't feel his judgment, only compassion. When I'm done, Sam stands.

"Come with me," he says.

Sam takes my hand and leads me to the bedroom.

He takes off my clothes, then his.

He guides me to the bed and tells me to lie on my side.

He gets into bed with me, snuggling real close, spooning me.

Sam holds me as I cry. His chest attaches like velcro to my bruised shoulder blades. We remain spooning, alternating from side to side, breathing as one breath, until the morning.

11

A week after Sam leaves, I'm at my parents' house for Friday evening Sabbath dinner. It's just the three of us. We're beginning the dessert course when I tell them my news.

"I've decided to make a big change," I say. "I'm going to leave Michigan and go live with Sam for a while."

I slice my dad a piece of seven-layer cake.

"What?" my mother chirps. "When?"

"At the end of July," I answer.

"Why? What're you going to do there?" my father asks as he sips his cup of instant coffee.

"I'm going because, after visiting Sam last summer, I knew I wanted to get back there at some point. I just didn't know when."

My mother is silently eating fruit from a small bowl.

"And what exactly did you do out there with Sam last summer?" My dad begins his interrogation.

"I've told you, Dad. We meditated, did yoga, and studied different religions and philosophies."

My dad sets his coffee cup down and looks at me squarely.

"What about work?" he asks.

"I'm not certain about work just yet," I lie, not wanting to tell them Sam will be supporting me. I don't want them to judge me, to think I'm not capable of making it on my own, to see me as submissive or weak. "I'll see how things go once I get there. I plan to take my Oregon Massage Board exams and get licensed to do bodywork out there."

"You mean to tell me you got your master's degree in education, spent three years teaching, and now you're going to walk away from education altogether? What's wrong with you? Why did you even bother with all that schooling? I don't understand why you can't stay with one thing and see it through." He's exasperated.

Yeah. What's wrong with you?

My mom cuts my dad a second slice of cake and offers me one. I decline.

"I don't understand why I can't stay with one thing for very long either, Dad," I say coolly. I don't want to fight with him. "Believe me, if I knew the answer to your question I'd probably be a different person. Maybe a happier one."

"You don't need to *know* the answer," my dad clarifies. "You just need to *do* the answer. I mean, just follow through with *something*. Anything. You don't have to figure out the meaning of life first. That's your problem."

"I don't know if that's true, Dad. I hear what you're saying and, honestly, I've considered your view. But the fact is, there's something I need to know about myself *before* I can commit to anything for an indefinite amount of time. Sam's offering me the time and space to be with myself. It's been seven years since I left California, and I'm still struggling. Emotionally and spiritually. Sam's is the only place that makes sense to me right now. He's giving me an opportunity to simplify my life, slow down, and turn inward. I know that may not be what you would do, or what you would want me to do, but it's what I want. I feel like *this* is what I need to follow through with, not some teaching job."

"You might be happier if you just got on track with a normal life. Get married. Have kids."

If only I were normal.

My mother is now standing at the kitchen sink wearing bright yellow rubber gloves. She's washing the dinner plates under a stream of hot steamy water, then putting them in the dishwasher for good measure. She's heard everything I've said to my dad. She says nothing. All I hear is the squeaky sound of her gloves rubbing on the wine glasses.

When I inform Dave I'm leaving town for an indefinite length of time and not to contact me, I tell him at my place, not his, with Barb there, during the day, so I feel safe. He reluctantly acquiesces, saying he understands and wishes me the best. Secretly I'm afraid he will stalk me, so I lie about where I'm going. I tell Dave my leaving is not about him. I'm going to be doing some personal growth work.

I hope he doesn't try to find you.

Next, I resign from teaching, telling the director I'm going into spiritual retreat for a year. Although I feel badly about leaving after only one year of working for her, I'm clear I need to go. The director says she understands and promises me a job if things change.

Then I resign from my job as an escort. My three months in the role of sacred prostitute have taught me so much. I hate to let my position go, but I console myself with a promise that my discovery of my sexuality will continue through other means. I send Stephanie a gift, thank her for the opportunity she's given me, and express my gratitude for all I've learned.

Barb and Elana move into a one-bedroom apartment in the same complex. We have a garage sale where I sell or give away practically everything I own. I ship a box with art supplies, books, and clothes to Sam's.

The rest of my possessions all fit in my car. When my students throw me a going away party, I give each of them a personal item from my collection of clothes, jewelry, and art. To one of my favorite students I give the enamel box I brought from New York.

Stripping myself of my material possessions feels liberating.

I intend to arrive in Oregon empty.

I meet with Diana the day before I leave. We sit together under the giant oak tree in her backyard. Diana brings out her medicine pipe and blows sacred smoke into the space around me. This is how Diana blesses me.

"May you walk in beauty, Turtle Dreamer," she says aloud. "May you be held by the ancestors and align with your destiny. May the Great Spirit keep you safe. And may you be of service to all beings with your deep heart and wisdom. Aho."

"Aho," I say as I close my eyes to let Diana's blessing penetrate.

Diana takes the ashes from the pipe and carefully folds them into a small piece of tinfoil.

"It's not the most elegant way to package the ashes," Diana smiles, "but this way none will fall out. Place this in your medicine pouch and keep it always, so that my energy can go with you to protect you."

"Do you think this a good step for me, Diana, moving to Oregon to live with Sam?" Though I have not worked one-on-one with Diana very much, she's been a teacher to me for almost four years.

"I trust you're following your inner guidance," Diana says. "This is the most important guidance to follow. More important than mine or anybody else's."

"I know," I reply. "I just value your input. And I'm going to miss you."

"I'll miss you, too," Diana says, then suddenly stops moving.

Something has pulled her attention. I can tell she's listening to her Spirit Guides.

"Where will you be living?" Diana turns back to face me.

"With Sam, in a small house, in a small rural town in southern Oregon," I answer. "Why?"

"I'm not sure," she says, looking a bit more concerned than I would prefer. "My guides are expressing a tone of caution."

"Caution?" I say, feeling worried.

"Yes." Diana continues. "They're not saying anything specific. Just a general concern for your wellbeing."

"Should I be nervous?" I ask.

"Of course not," Diana shakes her rattle around my body, scaring away any dark forces. "Just pay attention to signs. And take good care of yourself. Call on me if you need to."

I hand Diana my gift for her. It's a Guatemalan shirt, hand woven by native women. It has colorful flowers around the neckline. It's beautiful. Like Diana.

Diana and I hug for a long time.

As I drive away, I decide the dark forces Diana's guides were seeing must be Dave's lingering energy hovering around me.

What else could it be?

I make a mental note to purchase a rattle of my own.

still

1

I set my compass west and don't look back. Sitting in the car all day is brutal. My poor body aches. I was hoping massage school would influence my own physical wellbeing. In some ways it did. I learned a lot and changed some behaviors. But most likely my toxic relationship with Dave cancelled out any positive impact therapeutic touch, diet, or exercise may have had on my health.

I'm not sure what my body needs now.

I'll sort it out when I get to Sam's.

As I cross over the Missouri River in Council Bluffs, Iowa, my mind begins to get dreamy. I realize I've been driving for ten hours straight.

To stay alert I imagine myself sitting cross-legged in a field of white daisies, perfectly still, pondering the value of solitude. I picture myself wearing a thin cotton dress and a beaded turquoise necklace with a turtle medallion. The turtle's head rises and falls with the movement of my chest.

I'm imagining wind flowing through my long hair when I'm pulled from my reverie by the view through my windshield. Thick gray clouds are rolling in from the north. The clouds shoot bolts of intermittent lightning in my direction as the wind blows petals off the surrounding flowers.

I turn my wipers on high, drive on to Lincoln, Nebraska, and stop for the night.

I take a wrong turn in Colorado and head south on Highway 76. I decide to take advantage of the detour and visit Bryce and Zion National Parks in Utah. On the third night of my drive I camp in Zion. Fierce steel-colored peaks frame the campground. It's beyond gorgeous, but my campsite sucks. There are noisy people everywhere. My tolerance is low for obnoxious humans and their unconscious idiotic behavior.

They remind me of Dave.

They remind me of you.

I take my camping gear to the periphery of the grounds where there are no official camp sites. I pitch my tent in a spot tucked out of sight and close to the creek. I hike the canyon overlook trail and return to my site at dusk. I'm invigorated and exhausted.

I undress inside my tiny one-person tent and crawl naked into my down mummy bag.

I'm in a deep sleep when I'm awakened by a scary choking sensation. I bolt upright in a panic. I frantically unzip my sleeping bag and throw it off of me. This doesn't help. I still can't breathe. I'm suffocating. I rip open the tent door and stumble into the dark night, gasping.

Now I'm naked in the middle of nowhere, alone and hysterical under a brilliant canopy of stars. Ancient rock formations surround me. Like wrinkled elders, they bear witness to my madness. I shake myself in a desperate attempt to slither out of what feels like a full-body straight jacket. I'm afraid I'll die if I don't escape.

Get a grip. Just breathe.

I can't! It's too tight.

What's too tight? You're outside your sleeping bag, your tent, and your clothes!

My skin!

OH MY GOD. THIS BODY!

I'm trapped inside myself!

I begin to sob. My breath comes in staccato-like bursts. I drop to the ground and claw at the earth, digging because I'm not sure what else to do. I want out. The only out I can see is death. But I'm not ready for that. Yet. All I can do in this moment is keep reminding myself to breathe. To relax. There is no other out.

You can't unzip your skin, honey.

I pace up and down along the creek taking deeper and deeper breaths. I hold my breasts in my hands because they're heavy and I hate them.

Love this body. It's your home.

I don't love it! I feel trapped inside of it!

Where else would you rather be?

Anywhere but here.

Are you sure?

I can't answer, so I walk until my bare feet are caked with dirt and the panic subsides. But I can't go back inside the tent. I drag my sleeping bag out into the night and lay it on the naked earth. I get in, leaving it unzipped. I lie on my back, rest my hands on my belly, and look up at the sky.

"If the universe is infinite, then there are no walls closing in on me, right?" I say this out loud.

The sound of my voice helps me orient myself in time and space.

"What's happening to me, then?" I ask the silence.

I wait for an answer.

The only response I get is the creek's steady trickle and a light breeze on my forehead. I feel the panic hovering right above me. If I'm not careful it will enter and overtake me again. I slowly count my breaths to help me remain calm while I wait for either a welcome insight or sleep, whichever comes first.

I'm still awake and unsettled when the dawn paints the sky soft blue. I quickly get dressed and pack up before anybody catches me camping where I don't belong. I throw my stuff in the car feeling grateful for daylight.

I have a mission.

Find coffee.

2

Two days later I arrive at Sam's in tatters. For the first month I resign myself to coping with the remnants of tobacco and alcohol in my system. Cravings tug at me. Sam's presence is barely enough to keep me from acts of self-sabotaging behavior. Some days I feel so ambushed by my incessant desires, I can't imagine life without them. I can't imagine it's even possible to decrease them. On really tough days I question my decision to leave my job, my family, and my promising professional future in Michigan.

Who in their right mind wants to get rid of their desires? So what if you drink or smoke? You're human, after all.

Sam has wholeheartedly welcomed me into his home and is mercifully accepting of my persistent grumpiness. He prepares simple nourishing meals and draws a bath for me almost every night. When I apologize for my mood, he simply reminds me of a warrior's attributes: control, discipline, forbearance, timing, and will. He tells me to stop feeling sorry for myself and grow up. He models maturity through his formidable presence and unwavering self-discipline. He then begins to train me as a warrior. We begin gently by taking slow silent walks together in the woods, sitting for short periods of time, and studying together.

But mostly I sleep.

By the second month, thoughts of Dave have receded and cravings for alcohol and tobacco have mostly subsided. I feel like a different person. I'm ready to begin the more rigorous schedule of activities Sam and I have planned. I feel like a kid starting the new school year, anticipating the smell of fresh textbooks, crisp and unmarked, filled with stuff I don't yet know. I'm excited and determined to excel.

"We'll start with a cleansing," Sam says to me the night before we commence. "We haven't discussed this part, but you don't need to know anything except to be ready at sunrise."

The next morning, Sam comes to my room carrying a stainless steel basin of warm water and a red washcloth. A white towel is draped over his shoulder. I'm naked in bed. He instructs me to lie back, bend my knees and spread my legs. He places pillows under them so I can fully relax without angering my hips.

Sam carefully washes my private place with the warm wet cloth, covering my opening and letting the steam penetrate my tissues. He sits at the edge of the bed, concentrating on his task. He dips the washcloth twice more, each time pressing a bit firmer on my crotch with the palm of his hand.

Each wipe pulls something from me, like a leech sucking poison.

As he finishes, I tilt my head back and thrust my chest towards the ceiling. I feel something snap.

It's you who's shattering.

I weep. Then whisper a prayer.

"Oh Sacred Ones. Please. Release me from my past. I want to start over."

There is no such thing.

I'm worried this might be true. And yet, as Sam dries me with the soft towel, I feel a certain innocence returning. I close my eyes and sense the echo of my nine-year-old self sitting on the toilet. I reach towards her as I consider the possibility that I'm striving to get to a place that is already here, buried under my confusion.

Though I don't fully understand what's happening, I surrender. I give up trying to keep my shit together, pretending I'm in control, thinking I know what I'm doing. I let my body collapse into the bed and sob uncontrollably about nothing and everything.

Sam sits quietly at my feet.

For the next thirty-nine days Sam comes to me in this way. With tenderness he washes me, and with urgency I silently pray. Though I still don't know for certain who or what I'm praying to, I make the effort. Something or someone must be listening by now. After all, I made it here.

One thing I do know for certain. The morning ritual has solidified my intention to allow Sam and his years of experience to be my guide. I commit myself to fully being here for a while. I vow to not stress about the future, to let go of the past, and to dive deeply inward.

Sam agrees to share with me everything he knows, while simultaneously demanding I discover the truth for myself. I have the feeling that, by allowing Sam to help me, I'm somehow helping him.

On the final day of the cleansing, Sam arrives dressed in black and enters my room empty handed. He walks over to the closet and takes out my white cotton dress, the same one I wore the first time I met him at the airport in Detroit. Sam lays the dress on the bed.

"Put this on and meet me in the meditation room in ten minutes," he says.

In the meditation room, a basin filled with warm soapy water is sitting on the floor in front of a simple wooden chair. When I enter, Sam directs me to sit on the chair and place my feet into the basin.

Sam kneels on the floor holding the red washcloth and begins to wash my feet.

I close my eyes and focus on the sensations coursing through my body. Wetness. Warmth. Touch.

Sam works slowly, his lean body crouched over, attending to my feet like a shoeshine boy.

When Sam finishes drying my feet he sits quietly for some time, then abruptly says, "You're not who you think you are."

"Huh?" I'm jarred by the sound of his voice.

"I said, you're not who you think you are."

Sam reaches for the bottle of oil next to him.

"I know, Sam," my voice practically a whisper. "That's why I've come here to live with you. To discover who I *really* am."

"I'm referring to something else. I'm referring to the you who's seeking, not the one you'll uncover."

I look down at the top of Sam's head as he begins to anoint my feet with oil. He starts with my right one, massaging with a confident touch.

"What are you talking about?" I ask.

"You're my wife," he says.

"Very funny," I say, dismissing him.

"I'm serious, Detroit. I had a dream about this a few months ago, but I didn't say anything until I was sure what it meant."

He pauses and looks up at me, his eyes fierce with sincerity.

"I've just been waiting for the right time to tell you," he adds.

"Sam, what are you talking about? How can I be your wife? You're a celibate monk."

I'm bothered that he's distracting me from feeling what's happening with my feet. As if reading my mind, Sam pauses the conversation and allows me to relax again. But not for long.

"Wife doesn't necessarily mean we have sex, Detroit. It means you're my partner on this spiritual journey."

"And what does *that* mean?" I ask.

"I'm not a hundred percent sure what it looks like, because this has never happened to me before, but what it *means* is you're my primary partner," Sam says, resting my well-oiled right foot on the towel and picking up my left.

"Are you asking me to marry you?" I say quasi-seriously. I know Sam well enough to know he's not joking. I also know he has absolutely no interest in getting married in any conventional sense. I feel a distinct discomfort in the back of my throat. And I'm flattered.

"No, birdbrain," Sam says, using his term of endearment for me, "I'm telling you we're *already* married."

Is this really happening?

"What? No ring?" I use humor to hide my distress.

This is ludicrous.

I feel energy moving up my leg and into my pelvis. It feels like warm white Elmer's glue. A bit sticky but nice. Nobody has ever touched me like Sam touches me. Not just physically. Sam is refreshingly present, radically honest, and completely devoted to my personal evolution. Like a dry sponge finally making contact with something wet, I'm soaking myself with Sam.

Maybe this is love.

"Listen, Sam, you know I love you." I want to slide off the chair and join him on the floor. But he's not finished yet, so I stay seated. "Still, I'm not sure if what you're doing with your life is what I want to do forever with mine. I can't marry you, or anybody, for that matter, until I have a clearer sense of who I am and what I want to do with my life. Your friendship is helping me discover what is true. That's why I'm here, Sam. Nothing else matters. I want you to help me get clear. Please reassure me that this is what our relationship is about. Please don't muddle things."

My stomach hurts.

I don't want to be his wife.

I close my eyes to center myself. I can't deny there's something compelling going on between us. Sam and I *are* tied together. I just don't know in what way or what our bond means. And I don't want to admit how much I'm captivated by him. Not now. And certainly not to him. I need him to help me sort things out. I need him to give me time and space to be with myself. That's all.

I don't want to be a monk and give up my wildness forever.

"I'm not muddling things, Detroit. I'm naming them. But you're still too invested in your romantic fantasy of marrying a handsome successful jerk who's hot to make babies with you. You're still brainwashed by happily-every-after and all that crap. That's what's confusing you. Not me. Not us. What you and I have is way more real and genuinely intimate than anything you've ever experienced."

This is true.

Sam stands and takes my hands.

"Stand up," he says. "Don't say anything more right now. Go outside and sit alone on the deck. I'll meet you in the yoga room in an hour."

I walk slowly through the dark house and out onto the farthest edge of the deck where a rope swing hangs suspended from a high arch. I settle into the seat with crossed legs and look up. The moon is resting on the horizon, about to set.

"If I were not here to see the moon, would it exist?" I wonder out loud.

I morph into my nine-year-old self staring at the stars through the bathroom window.

My questions are still the same. My wonder is still the same.

If you weren't here to seek the answers to these questions, would you have ever met Sam?

3

Sam and I eventually settle into a steady daily rhythm. We sit for fifty minutes upon rising early in the morning and again in the late afternoon. We practice yoga poses called *asanas* and yogic breathing exercises called *pranayama* for two hours every day. We study from a variety of spiritual source texts in the evenings. Most afternoons we take long walks.

Our practice periods are scheduled around healthy meals and quiet solitude. I remember my visit last summer and how strongly I craved this life. Now that I'm living it, I feel a deep sense of relief.

One day on a walk in the woods, Sam tells me about Sonia, a woman he met through Robert. A few weeks before I arrived in Oregon, Sam and Sonia spent two days together on the coast meditating and discussing spirituality.

As I listen to Sam describing his visit with Sonia, I begin to feel uncomfortable. I push my discomfort aside. I nod my head as Sam tells me how intelligent and funny Sonia is. I pretend I'm unruffled by her existence, as an enlightened spiritual woman should be. Until he tells me they took a bath together.

"You took a bath with her?" I say as calmly as I can.

How could he? He knows baths are holy to you.

"Yeah," Sam says. "Why? What's wrong?"

"It bothers me," I admit, wishing I would've said nothing.

"It was just a bath," Sam says.

If you're gonna be his wife, you're entitled to be bothered by this.

"There's no such thing as *just* when it comes to baths with other women," I raise my voice slightly, embarrassed by the me who's showing up.

You're so unevolved.

"Woah, Detroit. You're jealous," Sam stops and stands directly in front of me. "Talk to me."

We step off the path to a clearing and sit down on a bed of pine needles.

"At some point you'll realize how ridiculous it is to waste your time being jealous," Sam says.

"You say that as if I have control over my feelings, as if I'm *choosing* to feel jealous." Now I'm pissed.

"Jealousy is not a feeling, Detroit. It's a state of mind," Sam's tone changes and I know better than to dismiss him. Though I want to punch him for taking a bath with Sonia, I take a deep breath and listen to what he has to say.

"You're choosing to be jealous. What you're probably *feeling* is insecure or scared," he says.

Right now I feel exposed.

"Your mind is attaching your discomfort onto a story you've made up about our relationship," Sam continues. "Onto a story about me, actually. As if I'm responsible for causing your feelings. And for fixing them."

My brain turns fuzzy.

"I don't understand what you're saying, Sam." I feel defeated.

"I'm capable of loving more than one person at a time, Detroit." His voice is soft. "As are you. As is everybody. Regardless of how I feel about Sonia, you're still special to me. My feelings for each of you don't cancel out the other."

Logically, I understand this. But some part of me revolts. I'm in a panic.

You must receive Sam's undivided love in order to be safe.

"But it doesn't feel that way, Sam! It feels like your attraction to Sonia affects your feelings for me." I'm arguing now.

"Who cares how you *feel?* Remember, Detroit, your emotions are only telling you the truth about how you *feel*, not the truth about what is *so*. Stop and take in what I just said." He pauses. "What *is* true is that a bath with Sonia has in no way lessened my love for you or changed the intimacy you and I share."

I know Sam's right, but I hate him at this moment. Most of me is not in alignment with the undeniable truth of Sam's words. I prefer being comfortable in my delusion rather than uncomfortable in facing the truth.

Is that so?

I stand up and walk away from Sam. I step back onto the trail.

"I don't know if I can do this relationship thing with you. Or even if I want to!" I shout at him and turn to walk home, letting my rage work its way out of me as I pound the earth with my feet.

It feels good to be angry.

Arriving at the house, I go directly into the meditation room. My cushion and I have a complicated relationship lately. In addition to consistent chaotic mental rambling, I've been struggling with pins and needles in my legs again. But I need my practice right now, so I let my body sink into a more comfortable position by leaning against the wall as I prepare to face myself. I wonder if I'm even capable of observing my jealousy. I'm curious about whether what Sam says about me *choosing* to be jealous is true or not. I search for the feeling he claims is hidden underneath my jealousy.

I'm sweating.

I put my attention on my breath.

My chest feels like somebody's pressing on it. With my back flush against the wall, I feel pinned. I breathe deeper, making room for the pressure so it doesn't snap me in two. I know better than to push it away. I need to meet this force.

Then we'll destroy it.

I begin a conversation with myself.

What's with the jealousy?

I'm not sure. The story goes something like, I need to be the one and only in somebody's eyes. In a man's eyes.

What if what Sam said is true? That the love he has for you doesn't decrease when he loves another?

I don't care if loving another person *increases* his love for me a gazillion-fold. I don't like him having his attention focused on another woman. I don't like him loving her. There's not enough room for another woman here. Period. I need to be the only one.

What does it mean if you're the only one?

It means I'm special.

What does special mean?

I suddenly hear my father's voice. "Lis, baby," he says as he swoops me into his arms. I'm two years old. He kisses my forehead.

Special matters.

I want to be special.

I need it.

I DESERVE IT.

Are you sure?

Yes, I'm sure!

Do you want to feel special more than you want to realize the truth of who you are?

Fuck you. Unfair question. Feeling special and finding out the truth are two separate matters. I'm allowed to have both of them.

My breathing becomes shallow as my chest rips apart. Wanting-to-feel-special and wanting-the-truth pull at me in a tug of war. I can't choose one over the other. It'll kill me if I do. I need both. I deserve both.

You can't have both. You must choose.

Is this true?

You must be one-pointed in your search for truth or you'll run in circles your entire life and never find the inner contentment you crave.

But the need to feel special is critical. Being special completes me in some way. I don't want to sacrifice it for the truth.

Feeling special comes and goes. Just like all feelings. Specialness, in anybody's eyes, is unsustainable. You'll be chasing after it forever, like an addict.

I'm suddenly disoriented. My mind carelessly scatters, trying to distract me from focusing. It takes all of my inner strength to corral my attention back and return to my breathing.

I want to shift my body, but I don't. I sit still and burn in the heat of my discomfort until I set myself on fire. Rage is burning me up from the inside out. I have a visceral urge to kill somebody.

The ache in my chest tightens.

Every time you expose and then expel a lie, you move closer to the truth.

How do I remove my desire to feel special?

You just do. Every time you want to feel special, turn away from it. Turn towards truth.

I can't do this.

The heat in my chest stirs again. I see myself running out of this room, this house, Sam, my life. I imagine running until I fall over, until I die.

It would be so much easier.

Death is not an option, wimp.

I take short, quick breaths to calm my urge to escape. Then I begin to sway. I take deeper, successively longer inhalations until a growling sound erupts from my throat.

I lie down and rock myself as the desperate moaning overtakes me. I pound the floor with my fists, snot dripping onto the shag carpet. I rage until my chest stops hurting.

I consciously roll onto my back and become still. My breathing calms and the room is quiet. The silence is like still water.

I reach for my cushion, place it under my head like a pillow, and fall asleep.

"Okay," I say as I walk into the kitchen hours later. Sam is at the stove cooking pasta, his favorite food. Bright green asparagus is already steamed in another pot and a red sauce simmers on the far burner.

"Okay what?" he says without flinching.

"Okay, you can take baths with other women." I sit down at the table. "But I don't want to talk any more about it right now."

"Okay, birdbrain, whatever you say."

4

Most days I thrive, because I like the ways Sam challenges me. I *want* to become self-disciplined, cultivate a regular meditation practice, perfect my yoga poses. But, other days, drill-sergeant-Sam pisses me off.

Today I'm ready to leave.

I woke up with a strong urge to go shopping. I don't want to sit still this morning. I want to buy a new dress. When I tell Sam about my impulse, he rolls with it. But not exactly in the way I was hoping for. We drive to the mall and spend the afternoon walking for hours in and out of stores, "shopping" with no intention to buy.

I haven't been out in public in a long time. I notice people staring at us and begin to wonder what they're thinking. Sam's unkempt hair is long and loose, and his beard's starting to grow in straggly. I have no bra or makeup on and feel self-conscious of the way my breasts hang and how pale I must look.

Sam pays no attention to other people. He's concentrating on teaching me how to track my desire to consume, and then how it feels to restrain myself from acting on the craving.

"Your longing for material possessions is pulling you away from the truth of who you are," Sam says. "Instead of unconsciously buying something to satisfy your urge, see if you can calmly bear witness to the desire itself."

"Buying something would make the desire disappear quicker, Sam," I suggest.

"Very funny."

"It doesn't even have to be something expensive," I say as we walk past the GAP.

Desire is visceral, I realize. I can easily build a case for not buying another pair of shoes, since I already have all the shoes I *need*, but reason doesn't remove my want.

"It's not rational, Sam!" I'm feeling slightly alarmed now. "The desire is coming from my body. Or some alien force within me beyond my control."

"Good awareness," Sam says as we walk into the women's section at Macy's.

"Nothing's going to make this desire go away besides satisfying it!" I'm coveting the dress on the mannequin.

"Not true," Sam says and abruptly stops walking. I almost fall on top of him. He turns and brings his face close to mine. "You must give it more time."

"But I'm uncomfortable!" I shout, taking a step back. "I don't want to give it more time. Restraining desires is a stupid practice. It feels too hard."

"Who cares how you feel?" Sam is heartless.

I do, asshole!

"Be with your agitation, Detroit, just like you do with hunger when you're fasting."

"Yeah, but eventually I eat, Sam."

"And eventually you'll buy something, Detroit. But not from an impulse or a craving for a fix. You're training yourself to take action from a grounded clear place inside. Don't buy new shoes because of how shopping makes you feel, birdbrain. Buy shoes because you need them to walk."

"But I haven't shopped in months, Sam! You promised me that my desire would *disappear* if I restrained it." I'm whining now.

"Eventually it will," Sam assures me. "Depending on the strength of the desire, sometimes it takes many years of restraining until it finally gives up and falls away."

I turn away from Sam, not wanting to hear any more of his preaching.

All I want is a new dress, for chrissakes.

I stop at a row of skirts and fondle them. I take one off the rack and hold it up to my body to see if it would fit. Now I don't even want it.

Sam's taken all the fun out of shopping.

"I'm ready to go home," I tell him, feeling defeated.

The next night Sam challenges me again and I find myself questioning his motives. It feels like he gets off on pushing me just for the sake of the challenge. The problem is, I can't tell whether my questioning his intentions comes from sensing something might not be right with Sam's approach or from my resistance to doing what he's asking me to do.

You need to listen deeply if you're ever going to know the difference.

Sam suggests I commit to restraining another desire of mine: picking pimples.

"Are you kidding me?" I laugh and fondle the scab from the one I popped yesterday.

This might just push me over the edge.

"No, actually, I'm not," he answers. "Picking pimples is another example of how you behave impulsively, habitually."

I want to say, "Fuck you. You're joking. Pimples?" But instead I consider how satisfied I actually felt upon returning home from the mall empty-handed. Clearly I'm getting *something* from most of Sam's challenges. So I agree to a one-month experiment of not picking my pimples. I even agree to fast for thirty-six hours if I do pick because consequences help me follow through on my word, and fasting is my nemesis.

As I walk through the forest the next morning, I feel agitation coursing through my body. Soon, I'm marching instead of strolling, my hands coiled in tight fists. I'm not certain what's causing my upset, but I'm especially concerned because this is precisely the sort of stress that stimulates me to pick at something. Pimples. Cuticles. Scabs.

I stop and lean against a pine tree. I bend over, place my hands on my thighs, and scream "FUCK!" really loud, over and over.

When I finish, the silence is pronounced. I close my eyes.

It's not about pimples, I realize. My agitation has been building for a while. The mall trip helped bring it to the surface. My angst is about my relationship with Sam.

I'm in love with him and repulsed by him.

Sam's sitting in his brown wingback chair reading a book called *Spiritual Materialism* when I return from my walk. He looks up at me and I feel a hot wave of contempt.

Just talk to him. He'll understand.

I sit down on the floor at Sam's feet because there are no other chairs in the room. He sets his book in his lap.

"I've decided what *your* nickname is," I say.

"Oh?" he looks down at me.

"CHA."

"CHA?" he smiles with curiosity.

"Yes," I say, relieved to be telling him. "It's an acronym for Cold, Harsh, and Aloof."

I suddenly feel like a mean, horrible person. But I don't care. I need him to know what I think.

You need him to stop being a jerk.

"Yeah. That fits. Thanks for the compliment," he says, sounding genuinely gratified.

"Compliment? REALLY? Don't you see? This is what drives me crazy about you. You actually don't *mind* being an asshole, even though it doesn't reflect the truth of who you are. You're incredibly generous in so many ways. When it comes to helping people spiritually, you pull out all the stops. But most other times you're grumpy and insensitive. Sometimes downright nasty."

The Sam I know and love is not the same Sam the world sees. Sam doesn't realize how he comes off to strangers.

"You're cold, Sam," I continue. "And you're aloof. Half the time when you go out in public, you don't even speak to people. When you do talk, you barely look at the person you're talking to. And you're curt, often rude. Your wild look *alone* is enough to make people uncomfortable, but your *behavior* makes you seem like a nutcase. I hate it."

I'm remembering our walk through Macy's when I witnessed two salespeople whispering while pointing at us. Then I remember the time Sam barked at a gas station attendant for filling our tank too slowly. During a recent phone call with his mother, he yelled at her for not speaking up for herself.

All the ways Sam expresses his impatience and contempt for the human race pester me now.

He's radically insensitive.

"Ah, so that's it." Sam smiles coolly, folding his hands in his lap. "This is actually about you, not about me, how *you* feel about *me* being CHA. How *you* look."

He's onto you.

"Don't turn this into being about me." I'm almost shouting now. "Let's stay with you for a minute. For a change!"

"Okay," he backs down. "Let's stay with me. I'm cold, harsh, and aloof. True. What about it?" He leans back in his chair.

"It's mean, that's what."

"Says who?"

"Says me!"

I'm about to cry. I stand and begin to pace right in front of him.

Why are you wasting your time trying to change him?

I press on. "It's not just that I don't like your behavior. I think it's actually a problem. Like a flaw in your character that you might want to consider working on!"

Silence.

"Detroit," he finally says, then pauses.

I know this tone.

"It's not my goal to be nice," he says. Quite nicely, of course. "Most people are idiots. I'm not interested in idiots. And I'm certainly not interested in social niceties. They're a waste of my time and energy."

"But it's *not* who you are," I yell. "I know you! I live with you. Your kindness runs deep. Why not show the whole world your generosity? Regardless of whether people are idiots or not!"

"Because the world is screwed up, Detroit. I spent a lot of time hoping other people were interested in what I'm devoting my life to. But they're not. I have nothing in common with the majority of humans. So why bother with them?"

"How can that be, Sam? There are probably hundreds of thousands of people who meditate! Everybody can't be that screwed up!"

"Most meditators aren't concerned with the objective I'm focused on, Detroit. They're fascinated by useless promises, like stress reduction, or experiencing altered states, or enhancing their libido. Stuff I couldn't care less about."

"How do you know *your* purpose for meditating is the *right* one? That Emptiness or the Abyss or whatever you call it is the correct and ultimate goal?" My pulse is racing and my cheeks are burning. "How do you know you're not just making it up? Hoping for it to be true? Running from something? Running from life? What if *this* is all there is? This life that you call an illusion? What if all us screwed up humans are in it together? Including you and me. With no way out. And 'ending suffering' means something totally different from what you believe? What if you being CHA in no way serves your fucking enlightenment?"

I feel like I just hurled a piece of phlegm in his face.

"Because I know," Sam says.

His words suck the air right out of the room.

Sam's certainty is immovable.

I want it.

I stop pacing and stand in front of him, my hands on my hips.

"So then, for you, being CHA really isn't a problem at all?" I need to make sure I understand his position.

He raises his eyebrows then slightly nods his head.

"If the goal is to die into Emptiness, then it doesn't matter how you behave while you're alive?" I reframe the question, just to be clear.

"Correct. You're getting the idea," he smiles.

I feel the lawyer in me building a case, anxious to trap him.

"Well, if it *really* doesn't matter, why not just be nice then?"

Ha! Gotcha!

"Because I'm not a nice guy," Sam says coldly.

His deadpan unapologetic declaration ends our conversation.

I stomp out of the room.

I can't sleep. I don't like what Sam's admitting about himself, nor what he's saying about humanity. I don't want a CHA husband. I want it to matter how Sam treats people.

I take the focus off of Sam for a moment to consider how I treat people. I wonder what it would feel like to consciously behave insensitively to others.

Maybe CHA is a better way to be in the world.

I contemplate the possibility that a life unencumbered by social niceties might make it easier for me to stay focused on what really matters.

Sam just might be onto something.

But I don't like his perspective on humanity as a whole. He makes humans sound so pathetic and everything seem so hopeless.

Look around. He may be right.

If he is right, then I wouldn't have to worry about anybody but myself.

This could simplify things.

Later that evening I get out of bed and stand naked in front of the picture window, my skin prickling in the cool air. The thought of not having to be nice to people, not needing to act any particular way other than the way I decide to behave in the moment, is exhilarating. With no expectations influencing my actions, I might actually become authentic.

I grab a blanket, wrap myself in it, and sit down on the bed. I spin scenarios in my mind where I bluntly speak my truth to strangers and watch them react. It's a bit unsettling, not knowing how my coldness will impact others. But more, the freedom to be radically honest is invigorating.

I imagine how it'll feel when somebody asks me how I'm doing and I answer "shitty" instead of "fine, thank you."

To not care could have its advantages.

I crawl back into bed. The sheets smell amazing, like cedar and sky, still fresh from drying outside on the clothesline this afternoon. I doze, intoxicated by the scent.

I'm hiking up a mountain trail at dawn. The path is dusted with golden powder. I'm barefoot and I've been walking a long time. I realize I'm dreaming.

I reach a plateau where an old man is sitting on a giant rock. I quietly approach him.

He's naked except for a loincloth.

His legs are crossed as if sitting in an oversized chair at home in his living room.

He smiles at me. His eyes are dreamy brown.

"Hi," I say without actually speaking.

"Hello," he says back.

"Who are you?" I ask silently.

He smiles.

I sense that I've got something for him hidden somewhere on me. I remember packing it before I started on this hike, but now I can't recall where I stashed it. I pat down my pockets.

"Who are you?" he asks.

I still can't speak.

You don't have an answer because you don't know who you are.

The man leans over and touches my shoulder.

My body shudders.

He whispers into my ear, "Who are you?"

His gentle voice echoes into the basin of my pelvis.

I let the sound waves ripple through me.

Then I'm suddenly awake in my bed again.

The setting moon creates an opalescent glow throughout my bedroom. I roll over and bury my head in the pillow. I want to sleep more. I want to find my way back to that mountain, that man, and the secret hidden somewhere in my body.

When I enter the meditation room, Sam is already there. I wrap my blanket around myself and cross my legs. Closing my eyes, I see him again, the man in my dreams. He smiles at me. As the image fades, my thoughts quiet down and I relax into a profound stillness.

Later in the morning I'm doing a headstand in yoga practice when I experience an unusual tingling sensation in my vagina. I've been putting off deciding what to do regarding my desire for sex. I haven't had any sex since I left Michigan nine months ago. Since Sam isn't available as a partner, I can either practice restraining my desire and become celibate with him or I can find a lover somewhere in Oregon. Neither choice is appealing. But this morning's tingling reminds me that a decision must be made.

During *pranayama* I breathe the tingling up and down the front of my body until it settles. Then I decide to return to the meditation room to sit again. I tell Sam to eat breakfast without me.

In the meditation room I lie in *savasana* instead of sitting upright. I put my hand on my vagina and ask her what she needs. Without any added stimulation, I climax, sending a rush of energy into my chest. I fill my lungs with air and hold my breath. When I exhale, energy flows into my arms.

Sam is reading at the dining table when I walk into the kitchen. A pot of warm oatmeal is on the stove. I fill a bowl and sit down to eat.

"I've decided what to do about sex," I say to Sam.

He looks up at me.

"I'm going to have sex with myself as a disciplined practice. I'll investigate the sexual energy in my body, paying attention to how pleasure, both with and without climaxing, affects my spiritual practice. I'll schedule an hour session every morning after yoga and *pranayama*."

"Why not become celibate and let your desire for sex rest?" Sam asks.

"If sexual energy is simply energy, as we've discussed, then theoretically I can channel it in any way I wish. I want to teach myself how to channel it. Instead of restraining my desire to have sex, I'll run this experiment for a while."

"You just described the same practice I'm doing through being celibate," Sam says.

I've never fully understood Sam's celibacy.

"Do you channel the energy?" I ask.

"Of course. That's the whole point," Sam explains. "Whether I'm having sex with another person, with myself, or with nobody, the intention is the same. I'm always channeling the sexual energy into my spiritual practice and the realization of my goal. The difference with being sexually active and being celibate is one has stimulation involved, the other doesn't. I contain the energy in order to channel it. You'll stimulate the energy. Either way works."

"Excellent," I declare. "Then that solves my sex dilemma. I don't have to take on celibacy, which feels like too much for me to handle right now, and I won't have to go find a partner, which feels too complex to integrate into our scene. I'm happy to be on my own in this arena!"

I remember the time I explored the healer sexual mask at a retreat with Diana. I aroused Angela and then, brushing her torso with my hands, swept her orgasm up to her injured shoulder. Afterwards, Angela said she had more mobility in that joint than she'd had in months. Given the way the energy easily traveled into my arms this morning, I'm curious to see if sexual arousal and orgasm will shift my body's unrelenting fatigue.

"Sounds good." Sam goes back to reading his book.

I eat my oatmeal slowly, feeling a slight quiver in my G-spot.

"Hey, Sam."

Sam glances up at me with a will-you-stop-bothering-me look on his face.

"I had a lucid dream last night," I tell him. "It felt significant. I met a dark-skinned man in a loincloth on a mountain. He kept asking me who I was. I saw him again in my sit this morning. What do you think it means?"

"How did you answer him?" Sam asks.

"I couldn't answer him because my voice was trapped. It was kinda frustrating, actually."

Sam stands up and walks to the bookshelf. He grabs a book from the Hindu section and brings it to me.

On the cover is a picture of the man I saw in my dream.

"Oh my God. That's him!" I squeal.

"Read the book," Sam says and drops it on the kitchen table.

I spend the entire afternoon on the deck reading about Ramana Maharshi, a famous Indian yogi and guru. The essential point in Ramana's teaching is the existence of one indivisible reality or truth. The term for this reality is the Self. Ramana's primary instruction to his devotees is to practice silence. When not being silent, Ramana suggests the practice of self-inquiry. Ramana makes this promise to his students: "By repeatedly asking one's self the question 'Who am I?' the fundamental reality will eventually appear."

I consider all of the ways I could answer the question, "Who am I?"

"Nearly all mankind is more or less unhappy because nearly all do not know the true Self. Real happiness abides in self-knowledge alone. All else is fleeting." I read this sentence over and over.

I put the book down and lie back on the deck and let Ramana's words sink in. I hear a familiar bird song coming from the forest.

"Who are *you*?" I whisper to the unseen bird.

I relax my body and let my breath slow way down. I visualize the mountain from my dream. I imagine myself walking up the trail until I see Ramana, still sitting on the same rock.

I smile.

"Who am I?" I ask him.

"Find out," he answers.

5

Months go by. Sam's encouragement to not care about anybody else helps me stay disciplined and focused on myself. When Kate, an old college friend, calls to ask if she can visit, I say I don't want to be friends anymore. I put it nicely, saying it's nothing personal. "I'm taking time to concentrate on myself and I don't wanna have to explain what I'm doing or be interrupted." Kate's upset, and I do feel badly. But more significantly, I feel great freedom in being bold and honest. I can't afford to be distracted by people who aren't aligned with what I'm doing. Kate's in law school, excited to marry soon and have babies. I'm on a completely different path.

My family is a bit harder to separate from emotionally. I'd really like for them to understand what I'm doing and to even partake in self-inquiry. But they don't seem to be interested. After returning from Israel, Jacob purchased his own bagel shop outside of Detroit. He says he'll visit Sam and me at some point, but I don't imagine he'll ever make time. My sister Ellen is now in grad school on the East Coast and Adam is in law school. My older brother David is still in Florida running his restaurant. My father calls every couple of months. He asks me annoying superficial questions. When he calls, I sometimes say "hi" to my mom.

Ramana says this: "Your own self-realization is the greatest service you can render the world." Since Sam and I are completely devoted to self-realization, I'm hoping that somewhere inside themselves, my family and friends accept my distance as a form of loving-kindness. To help release any guilt as I detach from them, I decide to recapitulate my entire life. I figure it'll take me about a year.

I'm a few months into the recapitulation process and lost in a time warp, hardly speaking to Sam between sessions. Yesterday I recapitulated an experience I had when I was seven years old. I still feel shaken by it. I was in the hospital with rheumatic fever. I was admitted during the daytime and had no chance to say goodbye to David, Jacob, or Ellen because they were at school. Adam wasn't born yet. I was placed into a long large hospital room with eleven other girls between the ages of five and twelve. There were six beds on each side of the room, each bed with its own metal nightstand and wrap-around curtains. Evelyn was one of the girls I met during my month-long stay. She was tiny and dark skinned, with tight braids woven close to her scalp. She was in the bed directly across from me and we sometimes made funny faces at one another from across the room. Late one night she had an asthma attack. Doctors and nurses rushed into the ward, trying to be quiet. They closed the curtains around Evelyn so I couldn't see what was happening. I liked Evelyn. Just that afternoon she and I had worked on a jigsaw puzzle together.

When I awoke the next morning Evelyn was gone. I never saw her again.

Can you imagine the impact that had on you?

I recapitulated the scenario two more times in order to release the experience's hold on me.

I remind myself that humans are incredibly resilient.

And terribly fragile.

I'm heading outside for a walk when Sam calls to me from his wood shop. He's working on a series of murals depicting the alchemical process of transforming lead to gold. Sam says alchemy reflects the process of transforming the small ego self into the full realization of truth. Sam contemplates the alchemical process as he cuts and glues exotic woods.

"Your dad called today," he says as I open the sliding glass door and poke my head in.

"What did you tell him?"

"I told him you were busy and that I'd let you know he called."

"Were you nice to him?" I ask.

"I was me," he says. "And I'm pretty sure he still doesn't like me very much."

My chest tightens.

The last time my dad called, he seemed worried about me. He wanted to know when I was coming home for a visit. It's been more than two years since I left Michigan. I told him I have no plans to visit. When I hung up, I was hoping he wouldn't call again for a while. I wish he'd just leave me alone.

"Ugh," I say to Sam. "What should I do?"

"Since you don't want to go visit him, I think you should invite your dad to travel here to visit you. If he's so concerned about your wellbeing, let him come see for himself what you're up to, where you live. Assure him that you're not being held against your will. That you want to be here. That you're happy with your life. Then maybe he'll leave you alone."

"I don't know if I can do it." I say.

"Why not?" Sam asks.

"Because I'd have to fake certainty or happiness for him, and faking is the last thing I want to do."

"Then don't fake it, Detroit," he presses into me. "Show him the truth. And then let the chips fall. You don't owe him anything. And you don't have to prove anything to him. My guess is, unless he sees you some time soon, he's not going to leave you alone."

I shut the glass door and turn my back on Sam.

"Hi Dad," I say, when I get around to calling later the next day.

"How are you?" he asks.

Ugh. There it is, right off the bat, that stupid question.

Just answer him. He's your father, for God's sake.

My honest answer would go like this: "Well, Dad, I'm actually busy deconstructing myself in order to find out who I am underneath all the stories I've been told about myself and about life. Recapitulation is intense. In fact, I just recapitulated the time mom wanted a divorce and how you convinced, probably manipulated, her to change her mind. I waffle between feeling in love with and being repulsed by Sam. I'm actually his wife, by the way, but don't be upset, nobody was invited to the wedding. Not even me."

What I actually say is, "Fine, Dad, how are you?" I immediately hate myself for lying. I should've set up a consequence before I called him. I should've agreed to fast for a week if I didn't tell my dad the truth.

"I'm fine," he answers.

My father's a liar, too.

Who do you think you learned it from?

"So, why did you call?" I probe.

"To see how you are," his tone turns defensive. "Like always."

"Well, Dad. The deeper truth is I'm going through some intense stuff and I don't feel like talking about it right now."

One step towards honesty without telling him to fuck off. Good job.

"How would you feel if I came to visit?" he says.

Sam was right.

"When?" I ask.

"Whenever you want." He's being generous, careful to not push me farther away.

"I have to think about it, Dad," I say.

How can you say no? He's your dad. The poor guy is probably freaking out, thinking you've joined a cult or something.

"Well, let me know, baby."

"OK, Dad. I will. I need to check with Sam."

I hang up and go to Sam in his shop.

Sam puts down his sander and takes off his goggles.

"Well?" he asks.

"I feel like a bitch," I report.

Being CHA sucks sometimes.

"I told him I would talk to you about him visiting," I add.

"You have a clear choice, Detroit," Sam says flatly. "Either you suffer by continuing to pretend to be the daughter you're not, or you tell him the whole truth, endure the torment of being perceived as a bitch, and break free of your attachment to your father."

"I hate both choices," I complain.

I hate Sam.

6

The recapitulation process continues to envelop me. Days fold into one another, barely separated by the subtle wrinkle that forms with the sun's arrival and departure. Only the seasonal weather tells me life continues to move in a forward direction.

The boundary of our property is like a wall separating me from the outer world and, with no television or newspapers on the inside, my life feels completely cut off from the mainstream. I'm not surprised when Sam has to remind me my father's arriving tomorrow. It's been six weeks since I spoke to him.

I drive to the airport alone.

My dad steps off the plane onto the tarmac looking old and hunched over with a full head of white hair. I watch him through the window, then walk to the gate to greet him.

"Hi Dad," I say.

He hugs me a bit too tightly, like he's just rescued me from stepping off a cliff. He's probably just happy to see me, but I feel repulsed by his gesture.

I still need space.

"Let's get you to your hotel," I say, pulling away from him. "You must be exhausted."

"Sounds good," he answers.

As I'm about to leave my dad at the hotel, I hesitate.

Look at him. He's more like a little boy than a grown man. Don't leave him here alone.

Once upon a time, he was the one looking after me, a young man who would make it to every piano recital, coach me on how to wrestle my brothers, and teach me how to drive a stick shift. Now he seems frail and unsure of his place in the world.

Unsure of his daughter's place in the world.

I want him to feel comfortable.

He's not your responsibility.

My heart aches. He's my daddy, after all. No matter what.

I don't know how I'll survive this visit.

The next afternoon we drive to a magnificent glen of redwoods at the Oregon Coast a few hours away. My dad loves nature and I'm hoping this will be the perfect setting for us to get real with one another. This morning we had breakfast with Sam. It was awkward, but polite. Sam was on his best behavior and even smiled a couple of times. My father fidgeted a lot, drank his coffee, and asked Sam about business.

As we're driving, I start the conversation, "Dad, can I ask you a question?"

"Sure," he answers.

"Are you happy with your life?"

He shrugs his shoulders as if tossing something off.

"I don't know, baby. I just do my best."

I wait for more.

"Are you happy in your marriage? Your work? Your relationship with God?"

He does that twitch with his shoulders again.

"Life's not all about my happiness," he says, sounding philosophical.

This is potentially a good sign.

"I just want you kids to be healthy and happy," he says.

"But what if my happiness means I do something other than what you want for me?" I ask.

"Well, isn't that already the case?" He looks directly at me.

I feel myself becoming defensive. "Dad, I'm not doing what I'm doing in order to annoy you. You know this, don't you?"

He nods unconvincingly.

"I'm here in Oregon because it's where I *want* to be," I tell him. "What's frustrating for me is that I believe you can understand what I'm doing here and that you could even participate with me in my spiritual journey if you wanted to. But you don't seem to want to."

"Lis, baby. It's not that I don't want to be a part of your life. I honestly don't understand what you're doing. Or how I fit in. If you really want me to understand, you need to meet me at my level. Talk to me in a language I can comprehend."

What a complete cop out.

The sunlight catches his wavy hair and reveals some darker strands hidden underneath.

"I don't believe you," I say. "You're an intelligent man. And a religious one. If anyone in the family can sympathize with my quest, it's you. I think you just don't want to. Having a real relationship with me, as a fellow human being, not as your daughter, might force you to face yourself in uncomfortable ways. Maybe you're scared. I'm not sure. But, Dad, please don't say you can't. Just be honest and admit you won't."

All your dad really wants is for you to be who he wants you to be, so he can be comfortable.

"This is not just a phase, Dad," I add. "I would love it if somebody in the family was even remotely interested in genuinely inquiring about my life."

My father says nothing.

We're quiet for the rest of the drive.

As we park at the trailhead, I make a decision. I'll have no part of helping him stay in denial of what he's capable of. It goes against everything I stand for. If my dad isn't going to step into realizing his full potential, then we just may have to go our separate ways for good.

We get out of the car and begin our hike.

We walk in silence, dwarfed by the majesty of the ancient trees.

I wait for my dad to initiate further conversation. But he doesn't. So, I keep quiet and enjoy the redwoods. I witness how much my dad enjoys them, too.

When I return my father to the airport the following day, we hug good-bye tentatively at the gate. I have no idea if or when I'll see him again.

"I love you, baby," he says as he kisses my forehead.

"I know, Dad," I respond.

I don't say "I love you too, Dad," because I'm not sure if I do.

I don't know what love is anymore.

7

Sam greets me at the top of the driveway when I return from the airport. I let myself cry during the entire ride home, and now I feel lighter.

"Let's take a walk," he says as I toss the car keys onto the porch.

When we reach the trail, Sam says, "I think it's the perfect time for a *sesshin*."

A *sesshin* is a meditation retreat where we sit ten to twelve hours a day for 8-12 days in a row. The first time I sat a *sesshin* with Sam, I thought my head was going to explode on the first day. I couldn't imagine how I was going to make it through nine more. But I persevered, concentrating on one breath at a time. By the third day something shifted and I was able to relax. The last seven days were incredibly powerful. I was able to steadily observe myself and my environment. As the witness, I began to sense a profound stillness all around me.

Sam and I sit a *sesshin* every few months.

"Why now?" I ask Sam.

"Because if you don't want to collapse under the emotional stress of your father's visit, you'd better turn up the heat and burn out your attachment to him. Sitting a *sesshin* is the perfect way."

Sam and I walk in silence.

"Okay," I agree. "But only if I can continue to recapitulate in the afternoons."

"Of course," Sam says, taking my hand in his. "Now tell me what happened when you dropped your dad off at the airport."

The next morning Sam and I enter the meditation room at 4:00 am. I don't know if it's because I'm so tired or because I've now been sitting for years, but I easily nestle into the space between being asleep and awake, my body perched upright on my cushion.

Silence closes in on me like a dense fog.

I turn my consciousness towards the silence.

The alarm rings.

The sound of the bell guides my awareness towards the origin of the sound, and finally back into my body.

Sam and I step into the living room for a walking meditation, which we do between sits. Hands clasped at the sternum, eyes cast down at the floor, I walk two feet behind Sam. We move in super slow motion and in ten minutes I take only three steps. Then we bow and return to the meditation room and our cushions.

Eight sits a day for ten days in a row, *sesshin*s are like shamanic journeys. Vision quests. Self-imposed solitary confinement.

Breathing.

Observing breaths.

Thinking.

Watching thoughts.

Boredom.

Wondering if I'm crazy.

Watching again.

Breathing.

Observing.

Now thinking again. About food. Sex. Tomorrow. The rest of my life.

Shut up!

Back to watching.

Sharp pain below my right shoulder blade.

Don't you dare move!

Breathing.

Being breathed.

In.

Out.

Thinking about God.

Searching for the silence.

Watching.

Pins and needles.

Heebie jeebies.

Waiting for the alarm to ring.

Over and over again.

By day four, going in and out of meditation has a hypnotic effect on my mind. Though I continue to be tempted by the theater of thought, I'm able to wrap myself more tightly in the silence. Soon my mind chatter recedes. The silence takes center stage for the remaining six days.

Sam and I ended the *sesshin* this morning and are driving to town for groceries. As we make the turn where we get a view of the entire valley,

I gasp. Before us is the most perfect rainbow I've ever seen, each individual color thick and bold.

"It's so beautiful, Sam." I'm in awe.

"Be careful, Detroit." Sam's tone is harsh.

I brace myself against his voice. I miss the silence already.

"Huh?" I say.

"This is the perfect test to see if you get sucked back in."

"Sucked back in to what?"

"To life," Sam doesn't hesitate to answer. "After ten days of turning inward, it makes sense that looking out would be exciting. Compared to the internal view, the outer world is now extra tantalizing. But don't forget it's all a mirage, Detroit. The rainbow is light playing tricks on you. It's not real. If you let yourself be tempted, you'll be drawn into life like an addict grasping for an unsustainable high."

Where once Sam's perspective made no sense; now it does. Now that I've personally experienced the silence, I understand his point of view.

"It's not real," I echo, wondering if maybe the rainbow and the silence can *both* be real.

"What *is* real?" I ask Sam, more as a rhetorical question.

"Emptiness is real," Sam answers. "Silence is real. The Void is real. Stillness is real."

I nod in agreement and stare out the window.

The rainbow seems as real to me as the silence does. Just different.

As the rainbow begins to disappear, a familiar melancholy starts to creep in, like smoke seeping under a closed door. I take another peek at the rainbow before it's completely gone. I let my awe take a seat right next to my melancholy. I decide to let them co-exist and see what happens.

At the market, I hold up a piece of fruit and stare at it. I know it's a pear, but I also know it's not. It's a miracle that some human decided to *call* a pear. Maybe the pear is Emptiness. I place the miracle into my basket and stare at the people rushing all around me, loading their carts with miracles, too.

8

It's the winter of our fifth year living together and I'm beginning to push up against Sam with an urgency I haven't experienced until now. I consider that I may be hormonal, or have a case of cabin fever. All I know is I'm feeling trapped. Sam says this is a good sign. He tells me to sit with my aversion, be still in my boredom, just like I do with every other emotion. Just like I've done for years.

With the exception of Robert's and Sonia's brief visits every couple of months and Barb's yearly week-long retreat with us, Sam is the only person I've spent time with for more than half a decade. Maybe I'm sick of him and craving intimacy with somebody else. I have no remaining girlfriends. I talk with Barb on the phone every once in a while, but even Angela and I stopped communicating years ago. It happened gradually. We just stopped calling each other.

"I have an idea," Sam says in response to my obvious edginess. "Let's take you and your agitated mood to the desert and send you both on a vision quest."

Instantly an image of Diana surfaces in my mind sending a surge of warmth into my chest. I smile, feeling my love and appreciation for my teacher. I miss her. Diana and I stayed in touch for about a year after I moved to Oregon and, though we haven't talked since, I've continued doing solstice and equinox retreats and ceremonies. I sense that, more than any other practice, this quarterly ritual is what's keeping me tethered to myself. I recall Diana's guidance to keep things simple and stay connected to nature. Then I recall the premonition of darkness she had on the day she blessed me with her pipe.

Maybe what you're going through is the darkness Diana saw.

I decide to find out.

"A vision quest sounds perfect," I say to Sam.

Sam and I drive three days to get to the Anza-Borrego Desert where we set up base camp in a funky motel built in the fifties. Our sage-colored room blends into the hues dominating the landscape outside. Cacti and other wild flora sit in stillness along the broad expanse of the quiet desert. Sam and I prepare for my two-night solo journey by clarifying our individual intentions. My intent is to summon guidance and insight regarding my recent feelings of confinement. Sam's objective is to support my mission.

We drive a few miles south of town, park along a sparsely traveled road, and hike in to the open desert to find my questing spot. I'm enchanted with the Joshua trees, waving to me like wild green allies. The temperature is supposed to be in the eighties during the day, dipping into the fifties at night. I've brought a thick blanket to lie on and a lighter one to wrap myself in, a sweatshirt, and a wide-brimmed hat. I'm carrying a gallon jug of water in my hand and my medicine pouch around my neck.

I'll be fasting, but I brought a bag of almonds just in case.

We hike for just over an hour when I find my spot. I know it's right because my mind goes suddenly blank and my skin trembles ever so slightly.

I'm learning to trust my knowing.

Sam and I agree on a meeting place nearby and mark it with a large stone. I'll come here in the mornings and place a small rock next to the large stone so Sam knows I'm not dead. Sam will come by around noon each day, check for my small stone, and bring more water.

I say goodbye to Sam and lay out my blanket.

I sit cross-legged facing west.

Being alone in the desert feels completely different from questing in a forest. There's nothing here to obstruct my view and the silence extends to infinity, rippling through sagebrush as it goes.

I pray out loud, "Sacred Ones, I offer gratitude for your presence, your guidance, and your support. I ask that you be with me during this quest and lead me forward on my path. I ask for clarity."

I open my medicine pouch and place a stone in each of the four directions to anchor this spot. I walk four circles around my blanket to set a boundary: all beings unwilling to assist me must remain on the outside of this border; all allies are invited to enter.

I sit back down on my blanket and wait.

I merge into the silent expanse.

As the sun sets and the desert air turns cool, I put on my sweatshirt.

I sit calmly for many hours deep into the night.

The moon is just a sliver in the sky.

It's amazing how much I can see in the dark.

The wind picks up and begins to whistle over the top of my ears.

I feel guided to lie back.

Now I'm looking directly into the sky.

Oh my God! It's spectacular!

I stare at the stars without blinking until they morph into psyche-delic splendor, twinkling like giant multicolored fireflies.

The universe is pure magic!

So are you.

I wait. I watch. I listen.

Then, as if choreographed especially for me, shooting stars begin to streak across the sky. Four in a row. Big ones. Long trails of light. So close I can almost reach out and grab them.

I feel my heart skip a beat. I want to get up and move in some way.

Instead, I stay still, letting the delight pulse through me like an orgasm. I grab onto the pleasure's tail and guide it through my entire nervous system.

"You're alone," a voice says into my left ear. "Essentially alone."

"Keep going," it says, now into my right. "You're on track."

Feeling split, I close my eyes to orient myself.

I don't dare move.

"Who are you?" I ask.

I wait for the voice to answer.

A coyote howls in the distance. I'm not sure how far away it is, so I sit up. A shiver cascades up my back and my nipples turn hard.

I expect another coyote to howl back, but there's only one, alone in the night.

I listen intently with my whole body.

The coyote howls again. I know it's a she. I don't know how I know. I just do.

She howls once more. It's not a beseeching cry. It's celebratory. A love song to her self. A tribute to her independence and thriving alone in the wild.

She croons another verse.

Am I the only one listening?

I turn my head to the left and bump into a pair of eyes. I gasp and restrain the impulse to scream and run.

The eyes are green and blue, flashing before me like two tiny hummingbirds. They hover for a minute, vibrating fast while remaining perfectly still, peering into me. I take a deep breath. We commune, and then they're gone.

The sound of the wind softens as the silence takes over. I dive into the silence and disappear.

The dawning light revives me.

I emerge from sleep to wakefulness via tender movements cascading in sweet succession through every joint in my body.

I sit up and stack my vertebrae.

My mind is calm and alert, refreshed like the air after a thunderstorm. I bring my attention into my belly to be with what I experienced last night.

My skin feels tight.

I choose to view this containment as an embrace rather than a straitjacket.

I'm alone in this body and it's okay.

The sun rises behind me, a giant flaming orb, as I walk to the meeting spot. I move carefully, scanning the ground for a small rock. I pick one up and hold it for a while before I place it on the big rock for Sam to see.

I return to my blanket and sit facing south, the direction of the water element. In tribute, I drink. I feel the water sliding down my throat and filling my belly. I welcome it dripping into the caldron of me. I close my eyes and imagine watering my whole being.

I wonder what pops out of a seed first, the roots or the stem?

Something cracks in my pelvis with this thought. A bolt of energy, hot and rigid, thrusts out my vagina down into the earth. I'm immobilized by it, so I hold onto it with my attention as if it were an arrow just shot from a bow, and follow it.

I remain still until the sun is directly overhead.

You don't have your hat on.

Little critters start tickling my scalp, massaging it, fluffing my hair. I resist flinching and shooing them away. Instead I move into the sensation.

It's creepy, but it also feels really good.

My ears begin to buzz as though bees are swarming in them.

The thought occurs to me that bees might actually be walking on my head right now. I grab the thought before it has a chance to take me away from this moment. I stop the thought dead in its tracks. It's a miracle the way I capture it, kind of like catching a fly with chopsticks. I find this quite astonishing. I smile but stay focused on the catch.

What follows is a complete dismissal of thought itself. Usually, thoughts illuminate the darkness of my psyche like burning street lamps. I see clearly now how thoughts themselves are actually obstructive, incapable of revealing what's hidden in the darkness.

Being still allows me to experience this truth.

I wait patiently for the darkness to reveal its wisdom. It moves in closer, ready to devour me. I let the darkness completely swallow me as if being submerged into a giant vat of cosmic black tar.

The rod of energy now descends from my skull all the way down to the earth's molten core, where the heat mirrors the sensation on my scalp. I extend my awareness from the bees on my head to the echo in my belly and down into the fire at the center of the earth.

I stretch my awareness.

Careful. Don't let it snap.

Now I'm floating, like a giant human balloon, like the ones in the Macy's Thanksgiving Day parade.

Big and fat and full and high. And funny. So fucking funny.

I start laughing hysterically. Giggles roll through me like aftershocks from a tectonic earthquake. This goes on for a while, until I explode, like a neutron star morphing into a sun. There's light everywhere.

I am the light.

I inhabit all space and the space has no boundary. Actually, it's not even space. It's the darkness.

Paradoxically, I'm also still me, sitting alone on a blanket in a desert on planet earth getting a wicked sunburn.

This is the miracle.

I am two.

I am alone and I am everything.

I am me.

I am nobody.

I am.

Sam meets me at the pile of stones the next morning and we walk out of the desert together. He reaches out to take my hand, but I pull away. I shake my head in a gentle no.

Not now, Sam.

Not yet.

Sam and I spend two more days hiking the maze of desert wadis, swimming in the hotel pool, and meditating in our tiny casita. Sam asks about my vision but I choose to not share it. I'm not sure if I don't want to share because I don't yet comprehend it for myself or because I'm nervous Sam will try to shape my experience to fit into his view of things. I just know I need to keep my vision to myself.

When we return to Oregon, on impulse I call Jacob. Even though it's been a long time since we've talked, I trust he'll respond to me as if we'd spoken yesterday.

"How's it going in bagel land?" I ask.

"I'm so happy to hear your voice," Jacob says. "You okay out there? How's Sam?"

"We're good," I tell him. "So much has happened. I wish I could share everything with you."

"Some day, holy sister," he promises. "Some day."

But I wonder if it will ever happen.

Jacob's voice always tugs at my heart. This time it also pulls me into another vortex of memories. I watch them unravel in my mind's eye and wait patiently for them to finish.

"Listen, I have bagels in the oven about to burn," Jacob's voice begins to trail off. "If it's nothing important you want to talk about, I really gotta go."

"No, nothing important," I respond, wishing there was something more I could say.

"I'm glad you called," Jacob says. "Maybe I'll get out there this summer. Bring Sam some bagels."

I smile at the thought.

"I love you," I say.

I know what love is, when it comes to Jacob and me.

"Love you, too," Jacob says and hangs up.

I stand by the phone, unable to move.

I miss Jacob.

I miss my whole family.

No you don't.

I miss what we were.

Those days are gone.

I let my tangled emotions unwind and watch them completely dissolve into nothing.

9

This message comes during my equinox ceremony two weeks after the vision quest: "Move deeper into stillness."

Geez. How much deeper can you go? For the love of God! You're basically an ascetic monk. You spend half your waking hours sitting still!

Since Sam and I returned from Anza-Borego I've continued to feel antagonistic towards him. The vision quest solidified something in me, but it did not resolve my tension with Sam. If anything, it's been heightened. Almost everything Sam does irritates me.

Your angst has nothing to do with Sam.

It has everything to do with Sam.

When I ask Sam what he thinks is happening, he says this phase of internal agitation is to be expected and could remain with me for a very long time.

"Until you successfully remove all the selves inside you who aren't committed to complete dissolution into Emptiness, they'll exist as irritants," Sam explains. "Sometimes, the farther along, the noisier they get."

"How come you're not grumpy like I am?" I ask. "What are you doing that I'm not doing?"

"Nothing," Sam assures me. "The process just manifests differently for each person depending on their personality."

I don't know if I can live with this degree of irritability for the rest of my life. I could live another fifty years!

"I guess I need to isolate this particular defiant self," I say. "She feels like a slippery one. But if I can clearly identify her and her agenda, I'll know what must be done to get rid of her. Then I can feel more settled with however long it takes for the rest of them to disappear." I'm starting to feel encouraged. "And then maybe I can stop blaming you!" I add.

"Great," Sam says. I can see his mind already working, ready to help me come up with a tactic. "How do you want to want to go after her? A *sesshin*? A long fast? Another vision quest? You name it. We'll do it."

"All of the above," I say, as the perfect strategy hits me. "But I need to do this one alone."

Today the preparation for my ideal solo retreat begins. Sam and I are adding a bathroom onto the guest cottage. On January first, I'll move in. I'll spend three months isolated in silence.

I'll be completely alone with myself.

You mean your selves.

Over the years my life with Sam has been seasoned with the smell of cut wood, the sound of electric saws, and the sight of Sam as he works bare-chested, his tool belt snug on his hips. Sam's grandfather was a carpenter and it's as if the skill has been passed on to Sam through blood. I love it when I get to help him on a project.

Sam hands me the silver knob at the bottom of the chalk box and sends me to the far end of the piece of sheetrock balancing on the sawhorse before us.

"Put it down on the mark I drew over there and hold it tight," Sam says as he moves to another mark directly across from mine. A chalked blue string now stretches between us, lying snugly on the board.

"Snap it," he orders.

I lift the string a few inches off the board and let it go as if plucking a stringed instrument. It makes a popping noise, and leaves a perfectly straight blue line, Sam's guide for the cut.

As I hold the board and Sam cuts it with his hand saw, I imagine carpentry as a metaphor for my life. The analogy goes something like this: Many moons ago I arrived at Sam's, a twenty-nine-year-old, two-story house, fairly well-built, but with significant structural damage and an outdated electrical system. Since then, I've torn down ceilings, rewired circuits, updated the plumbing, and repainted a few dreary walls. But now the foundation is in trouble. It could be rotten. If it is, do I tear down the house and start over or shore it up?

"Remodels are always a bigger pain in the butt than new construction," Sam says as he sinks the final nail on the ceiling directly above our heads.

"I know," I answer, wiping the dust off my cheek.

But it's too late to build myself from scratch.

10

It's been almost forty days since I entered the cottage for my twelve weeks alone. Thus far the solitude has been easy and comforting. Being a recluse suits me. Alone and with nowhere to go I'm ready to face myself with the courage of a warrior.

I've committed to a certain number of hours of sitting daily, but allow them to happen organically, in tune with my natural rhythm. When I feel like eating, I eat from the one simple meal Sam leaves on the porch each morning. I walk once or twice a day in the forest and luxuriate in long uninterrupted periods of reading, journaling, and staring out the window.

Being silent for this long is becoming a bit surreal. The only sounds I hear indoors are the ones I make myself through daily living: stirring a cup of tea, brushing my teeth, turning the pages of a book. These noises no longer register as identifiable sounds. Instead they reach my ears as random tones and timbres. Outdoors the wind registers as if the earth herself is breathing. My steps on the trail relay like an auditory heartbeat.

Internally I feel swaddled by the silence, but not always in a good way. Sometimes I feel vacuum-packed. All my voices are trapped in here with me and there's not enough air. Though my physical voice remains dormant, the noise in my head can be deafening.

I'm not sure what I was expecting when I committed to not speaking for so long. I guess I'd imagined the outer silence would stabilize the inner silence, making it obvious which voices I need to remove next.

Just the opposite is happening.

Each voice is distinct and has its own agenda. When there's an exchange between two or more inclinations, it can sometimes be harmonic and exhilarating, like great jazz. But when the voices pit their positions against one another, the sound is like horrible rock music bouncing off the inside of my skull.

If I could just take the perspective of silence and stabilize there, maybe the voices wouldn't bother me so much. Maybe they might even obey me.

Today is day three of a five-day water fast and heavy metal is blasting throughout my head. I'm getting pummeled.

Fasting for so long! What were you thinking?

It seemed like the right choice to push myself farther than I ever have. But now I regret it. My blood sugar is low. My body is demanding sustenance. I flash back to my first vision quest and how I gave in to my hunger. I strengthen my resolve.

I will not give in this time.

My attention is all over the place, racing from the ache in my belly to the dizziness in my head, darting between the voices shouting "Eat!" and the ones yelling "Don't eat!" Distracted by the ones ranting about nothing relevant at all.

You're hopeless.

The witness is strong in me. She usually manages to stay relatively whole amidst the chaos of my thoughts and feelings. She helps me discern which voices to follow, strategizes which ones to ignore.

Today she's worthless.

It doesn't seem to have any relevance that I've successfully eliminated some of the voices through years of unwavering detachment, recapitulating my entire life, and meditating for a gazillion hours; there are still enough voices in my head to leave me wondering if I've accomplished anything of significance in all my hours of dedicated practice.

Tears rise from deep in my throat where the disappointment has settled.

The voices are so chaotic I start pounding on my head to shut them up.

I'm aware I might shatter.

Who's aware?

"I DON'T KNOW!" I shout inside my head. "I thought the witness was the aware one in here. I thought I could rely on her."

Where is she now?

"FUCK YOU. I DON'T KNOW!" This time I scream out loud. The sound of my own voice throws me against the wall with its ferocity. There's a winter storm beginning outside and, as if responding to my cry, the wind sends a branch crashing onto the roof. I crumble into a ball, swept into the sound of the pelting rain.

As the storm gets louder, the silence gets louder too. Moves in as if coming to embrace me, like the darkness did on my vision quest.

Are the silence and the darkness one and the same?

The silence squeezes me, then expands and hovers, as if lingering to tell me something. But I can't hear the message over all the noise.

If only I could unzip myself and cast all the voices out. Let the silence take over.

Eating might help.

Fuck you. I'm not giving in this time!

Or should I?

I crawl over to the table and rip out a page from my journal. I write Sam a note.

"I'm losing it. I need help. I need to talk," I scrawl.

I put on my boots and walk over to the main house and slide it under the front door. I let the rain soak me on the three-minute walk back.

Then I wait.

I hate to shatter the cocoon of my confinement, but I don't know what else to do.

I imagine the words I'll say to Sam, but I dread speaking them.

I rehearse the speech in my mind. I can imagine Sam's response. Because he's a zealot for self-discipline and austerity, he'll encourage me to push through. Though I love this about Sam, I hate it in this moment. He'll want me to stay with the fast until the end. He'll say I have nothing to lose and everything to gain.

Maybe I'm wrong. Maybe he'll let me off easy this time. When Sam sees me suffering like this, maybe compassion will trump his fanaticism.

Doubtful.

Within the hour, he's walking to my cottage and tapping on the door.

"What's up?" His voice scrapes like sandpaper and I regret inviting him over.

I begin in a whisper, barely able to make sound. It hurts as much to drag the words out of myself as it does to let his words in.

"I want to break my fast early," I manage.

Try to keep this short. Make your point. Get his input. Ask him to leave.

"Why?" he says.

I give him my story. He listens carefully, then closes his eyes to consider.

"I don't think you should end it," he answers.

Please don't say this.

"I can't do it, Sam. I'm losing it. I hate this." I burst into tears. "Please, say it's better for me to eat." I'm begging.

Wait! You're begging him to free you of a commitment you made to yourself? Are you paying attention?

"Detroit!" He rattles me present with my name. "*Why* are you fasting?"

This is the pertinent question.

I go over the reasons in my head. Austere practices break down our egos, our voices, whatever we want to call them. Once destabilized and subsequently removed, what remains can surface.

I'm here to find what remains, as if my life depended upon it.

Because it does.

"To find out who I really am," I answer soberly.

"Then stay with the fast," Sam says flatly.

I stand and pace the small room while Sam watches me.

"What if it's not what I need to do? What if pushing myself so hard physically right now is what's actually keeping me from realizing the deepest truth of who I am instead of taking me there? Who's pushing, Sam? Who's being pushed? Who can I trust inside of here?" I plead.

"Find out." His voice slams into my argument.

I stop walking and stare at him. I search for a region of my psyche where I can pretend I'm not alone. For a moment I imagine we're in this together, Sam and me. I pretend he has my back, that he'll change his mind and bring me some food.

Sam grabs my arm and pulls me towards him. He hugs me tight and says, "Detroit, you can't give up now. This fire is too hot. Focus your will and root your identity once and for all in your center. Finish the fast even if you feel like shit. You're not going to die. I promise. Stop being harassed by your voices and stabilize as the one who's committed to ultimate freedom."

"Is that the witness?" I reach for understanding. "Or am I searching for someone else inside of here?"

"Find out for yourself."

I feel so confused.

"Who's in charge in there?" He gently taps my head as he pulls away.

Nobody, asshole. Obviously, nobody.

I know Sam's right. So right.

And I know he's wrong. Terribly wrong.

There has to be another way.

"I don't know if I can do this," I say.

"Of course you can," Sam declares, his certainty stabilizing my wobble. "Use everything you've got. Stay awake, Detroit. This is an important moment."

He turns his back to me and leaves.

11

It's after midnight and I'm in deep distress. This must be insanity. The storm outside is in full force and a torrential rain batters the cottage roof. I'm huddled in a fetal position, wailing. I'm furious at myself. At all of my selves. I'm mad at God. At Sam. At my parents. At life.

I stand up, struggling to balance my head on my shoulders.

You're such a loser. Can't you see you're wasting your life? You should be out there living, not in here going crazy.

What do you know? Out there life sucks.

You say that cuz you're scared of it.

I'm not scared. I'm smart! I'm doing something with my life that's way more important than having a career, a marriage, or kids!

You think you're so special.

Fuck you. If I could just get *you* to go away, I'd be fine. I actually love my life here with Sam. It's uncomplicated. Simple. It's not my life that's the problem. It's *you* that's the problem! And all the rest of you *yous*!

Bullshit. You don't love it here. You're just trying to convince yourself that you do because you don't know where else to go. Look at you. Tell the truth. You're still depressed and, at this point, probably psychotic. Why don't you just admit it? Get some help.

You're the one who's sick. Not me.

YOU ARE ME, YOU IDIOT!

I pace the tiny room like the raccoon on my balcony years ago. I remember how scared he looked, screeching for someone to help get him out of the daylight and back into the dark. Here I am now, screaming for help to get out of the dark and into the light.

Calm down. Breathe. Find the space between the voices. Enter into that space.

I crawl into a corner with my blanket and swaddle myself. I rock and weep, rock and weep, rock and weep.

Suddenly something shifts and my psyche begins to tumble.

I resist for a second, then let go.

I don't care what happens anymore. Fuck it.

I plummet into a free fall down a dark and tight hole. I'm being shoved from above and sucked by some sort of vacuum from below.

I see her when I finally land in the basement of me. She's huddled under what looks like a collapsed staircase. She's young. No, youthful. Her eyes are the color of jade and pulsing like a strobe light. Her hair is long and wavy, the color of sand.

She looks right into me.

I surrender to the vision, deciding to fully engage it, because my *normal* mind is completely worthless right now.

"Who are you?" I manage to ask.

I am you.

Oh great. Another one.

"And which me are you?" I ask, rolling my eyes.

I'm the one you've been searching for.

"Oh please," I say. "I don't know if I can take another one who claims to be the real one or the one who knows. I'm sick and tired of all of you."

Tell me about it.

"Okay. I will! It's complete chaos in here. I feel hopeless because I haven't been able to discipline myself and successfully stabilize in my center."

So stop trying.

"Huh?"

Stop trying to silence the many selves, make them leave, or control them in any way.

"What? And let them continue to drive me crazy?"

They're not driving you crazy, dear one. You are driving you crazy.

Which *you* is she speaking to?

My psyche spins and I lose sight of her. I beg her to return. I'm afraid if I lose her I'll never find my way.

I'm still here.

Her voice is soothing. She's still shimmering before me.

I'm just about to ask her a very important question when my solar plexus snaps, slinging my bodiless self across the room. I'm now *inside* her, looking back at my body. This lasts for a second and then I'm pulled back into me, looking at her.

"Whoa," I say to her. "What just happened?"

You let yourself come into yourself.

I look around to see if this is a trick. She sits calmly, watching me. Her presence is steadfast. Trustworthy.

"Are you my center?" I whisper.

I am.

We make eye contact. But I can't hold her gaze. She smiles, then turns a bit fuzzy around the edges. Her chest emits fractured light in warm shades of blue, like a laser show.

She stands.

I hear the voices ranting upstairs in my psyche. I feel scared they will soon descend down here and ruin everything. But she is untouched by their existence. I admire her cool demeanor and attempt to imitate her.

We make eye contact again.

I'm staring so hard, my skin begins to melt.

I wonder what's happening.

You're dissolving.

"What?" I am screaming.

Relax. Let it happen.

But what if this is a trap?

It's not.

I choose to trust her and let myself melt like a snowman in the desert.

I must be dying.

Finally, an end to my suffering.

But no such luck.

I'm still here.

So is she, now sitting behind glass.

The glass shimmers and I notice an intricately carved wooden frame holding it in place. The impression of her morphs into waves of light. Then back into a human form again. I realize she actually looks a lot like me.

"Oh my God!" I shriek. "You're a mirror."

Suddenly the glass shatters and I am unzipped.

My cells, like popping corn, scatter kernels all over the floor.

12

I'm in a fetal position, the blanket covering me loosely and a pillow resting under my head. I open my eyes as the daylight appears. I lie motionless for some time. I can practically feel my cells reconfiguring and I know they're not done yet. I'm in no rush.

As I'm able to stand, I walk slowly to the window. A foggy mist rests in the hills and the shallow creek below my cottage is flowing, filled to its banks.

I know what must be done in order stabilize myself. I must ground my experience into my waking state.

I prepare for a ceremony.

I walk out to the woodpile charged with purpose. The ground is spongy. Under the tarp, near the center of the pile, I find some dry wood and kindling. I grab as much as I can hold and take it down to the creek to my favorite spot under the two grandmother pines. They stand more than eighty feet tall and most of their branches are located near the top, so their long trunks stand side by side like pillars. I hug them both and prepare a small fire pit in the ground at their feet.

I return to my cabin to prepare the offering.

Using the fabric of an old t-shirt and the innards of Fluffy, my childhood stuffed animal, I start creating a doll. I go outside to gather moss for her hair and twigs for her arms and legs.

I'll take all day to build her, then burn her at dawn. Tomorrow is also the day I had originally scheduled to break my fast. I'm weak, but no longer ravaged by my hunger. I'll make it through all five days.

The doll represents my past. She symbolizes all of my selves. She is the innocent child raised by well-meaning parents weighted with their own ignorance, the young woman navigating adult life without proper moorings, and the passionate seeker who said yes to Sam and these past seven years of monk-like existence. I stitch a red button onto her chest to represent a heart that holds the beliefs handed down my ancestral line. I sew the moss onto her head, the wild green mass depicting the insanity I've often experienced.

My doll emanates the entire spectrum of life, from beauty to horror. She's stamped with countless impressions and filled with remarkable experiences. I love her. I love her more than I can ever understand.

And I know it's time for her to burn.

I bless her.

"Sweet one, I honor every step you have walked, every breath you have breathed. I bow to your struggles and your victories. I forgive you for making choices that hurt us, knowing your intentions were always good, and I celebrate the decisions that brought us here. I honor your courage, your resilience, your intelligence, and your heart. I love you forever."

I wrap her in a worn washcloth, close my eyes, and lift her to my chest. Then I kiss her all over.

"And now, sweet one," I continue, "it's time for you to die. Your job is complete. I'll take over from here. Tonight we will sleep together for the last time."

"I'm ready," she softly speaks.

"I'm glad," I tell her.

I'm ready, too.

13

I take my seat in front of the fire pit. The morning is quiet. The sky, clear. I cradle the doll on my lap in a basket. I close my eyes to concentrate, letting the sound of the creek remind me that where there is movement there is change.

I am changed.

I take the doll from the basket, press her against my chest, and take ten long deep breaths.

I feel all my selves gathered around me now. Some are cautious, skeptical. Others, grateful and excited. Many are prepared to burn in the fire, to be washed by the creek, to be swallowed by the earth. Others are holding out. They are the ones who have no intention of giving their power over to a self only recently discovered in the basement of my fragile psyche.

Holding all my selves close, I rest in the silence for a while. Then I open my eyes, set the basket on the ground and strike a match.

The fire takes.

I tend it until it's strong.

I hold the doll up to the sky as I bless her, tears rolling down my cheeks.

I ask her one final time if she's willing to die for something new to be born.

She says yes.

I lay her on the fire.

I sing to her as she burns, Cherokee and Hebrew songs.

"*Shehecheyanu, v'kiyamanu, v'higiyanu, lazman hazeh...*"

I pray for a merciful dissolution, for her and all suffering sentient beings.

I sit in stillness, watching the flames transform the doll into ash.

Death is such a weird thing. The doll is gone, but also not gone.

Just like me.

I spoon the ashes into a ceramic bowl. I hold the bowl against my belly as I weep, squeezing lifetimes of grief from my bones and letting it mix with my tears in the bowl. I pour the paste into the creek and watch it float away.

It is done.

A ripe banana and a bowl of plain yogurt sit on the porch of my cottage. Sam must have delivered them while I was down by the creek. They are covered with a note.

"I assume you made it. Congratulations."

I take the tray inside and sit at the table. I slice the banana into bite-size pieces and pause. After five days of fasting, I can't believe that I'm not even hungry. Though my body is weak, I hesitate to eat, not wanting calories to negatively impact my new state of being.

I stare at the banana rounds. Gentle shivers of energy travel through my body as my brain registers the fact that there is actual food in front of me. I take one small spoonful. Then another. I wait between bites, savoring the symphony of flavors and textures exploding in my mouth. Sour and sweet. Cool and warm. Smooth and soft.

After breakfast, I dress to walk in the woods.

I stop at the ceremonial site and place a strand of my hair at the base of each grandmother pine as a gesture of gratitude. I gently kick fresh dirt over the depression in the ground where the fire burned. I follow the path along the creek into the forest.

As I walk, I imagine the molten core of the earth beneath my feet. Squish. Squish. Hot, but not too hot. Soft, but not too soft. Buoyant, the earth pushes back.

The air is crystal clear. The wind is calm. Periodic rustling of leaves interrupts the quiet and two turkey vultures circle overhead. This chorus of life sings to me.

We are alive!

So obvious.

We are a mystery.

So true.

We are not separate.

I am the same as you.

The rhythm of my boots vibrates into the universe: "I am here!"

Finally, I am.

Here.

awake

1

My future self has finally arrived. The doll burning ceremony marked a significant shift in me. I haven't completely stabilized yet, but I note the trending metamorphosis when I wake up in the morning. I feel at ease and curious about the day ahead. One morning I even border on cheerful.

I wonder if as a child I ever felt this way and at some point lost the feeling. As far back as I can remember, getting out of bed has been difficult, like crawling out from under a dead body.

I decide that my happiness is entirely dependent on my next breath. This is all I need to focus on right now. Breathe and be present. The simplicity of my daily routine will carry me through the rest of my retreat.

Nothing is lacking.

Except for a bath, now and then.

To satisfy my bath craving, I lie on my bed and imagine I'm soaking in a tub of steaming silence.

I draw a picture of a turtle with eight sections on its shell in the design of a mandala. Within each section I sketch an image to represent eight distinct spiritual paths: Judaism, Christianity, Buddhism, Hinduism,

Islam, Taoism, Native American spirituality, and Egyptian wisdom teachings. In the center of the shell I draw a spiral. After years of study and
contemplation, I'm convinced all religions originate from the same truth
and then spiral out into their unique creation stories and belief systems.
The center of the spiral symbolizes the center of everything. After years of
devoted practice, I suspect I've finally found my way to this center inside
myself. I'm embodying this truth and memorializing my experience as I
create this piece of art.

I transfer the drawing onto a blank needlepoint canvas and stitch
it to life with colored wool. The rhythm of needlework is like the turning
of mala beads or handling of a rosary, each bead a prayer. In needlepoint,
each stitch is like a breath. Each breath a point of contact with what is.

The smell of the earth after the winter rain is like sweet sweat. The
spring equinox is near. New life appears in nature all around me, mirror-
ing the renewal I feel inside. Wild purple orchids poke through the brush
and tiny leaf buds are forming on the oak trees. Everywhere I look, colors
are bolder and, after months of being silent, sounds are heightened. I can
hear the incessant buzz of a fly out my window and the drone of traffic on
a freeway miles away.

There's no such thing as silence in the natural world.

The silence I know is not of this world.

Today I'm walking in the forest when a breeze kicks up out of
nowhere and circles me. As I wipe the dust from my eyes, I imagine the
wind speaking to me. She tells me it's time for a new name.

The wind's advice makes sense, but I've never seriously considered a
name change. I've been called Detroit for so long, I barely remember what
it feels like to be called Lisa.

I imagine the name Lisa being called to me now.

No self in me answers to the call.

Lisa is gone.

The doll burning ritual underscored this.

I listen for a new name.

I stop walking, close my eyes, and let the wind continue to whip. I feel excited, remembering the way in which the name Turtle Dreamer came to me. This next name will arrive powerfully, too. I can feel it.

I consider some of the names I've always liked. Samantha. Isabelle. Lily. A loud whooshing sound pulls me back from my daydreaming. I look up to see a turkey vulture circling overhead, its wings like giant black sails.

My new name presents itself two weeks later. I'm walking along the same trail when the name lands in my belly like a clear bell. I've spent one entire week ruminating on names, writing lists, trying them on, and dreaming about them at night. I've contemplated pros and cons of each one based upon how they sound, what they mean, and how easy they are to say and spell. This week I stopped searching and invited the right name to arise out of the silence. I've been patiently waiting. Trusting.

When I return to my cottage I write my name in my journal. There is no hesitation. No doubt.

My name is Sarah. With an H.

In Hebrew, the word Sarah has multiple layers of meaning. It translates as "one who wrestles or is stubborn with God" *and* "one who serves God."

In Arabic, Sarah means happy.

In Sanskrit it means essence.

I'm studying Neoplatonism, a philosophical tradition attributed to Plotinus, one of Plato's students. Though not a religion, Neoplatonism *is* theological and provides a systematic description of how "reality" emerged from a single unknowable principle. Neoplatonists call this originating principle the One. As I contemplate the imagery in Neoplatonist cosmology, a clarity crystalizes inside of me.

There is only the One.

I contemplate this age-old assertion of Oneness for the millionth time.

The Jewish version, "Hear oh Israel the Lord our God the Lord is One," swirls in my head.

Shema Yisrael Adonai Elohenu Adonai Echad.

As I needlepoint, I embed my contemplation into each stitch.

Yesterday Sam left me a spiral notebook containing a sixty-page handwritten summation of his philosophy/theology. While I've been wrestling my demons, he's been writing. I spent all day today reading it from start to finish. His treatise is concise, like Sam himself. His disagreement with Neoplatonism, and with many other traditions, is repeated numerous times in various ways. His bottom line: "There are two: form and Emptiness. Emptiness did not create this world. Emptiness is totally separate from anything manifest."

In Sam's philosophy Emptiness is the same as Stillness, Silence, the Absolute, Formlessness, and the Void.

I consider how I used to argue with Sam on this point, unable to grok how the universe could exist without having *some* origin, even if it were an empty one. Over time I came face to face with the part of me simply *unwilling* to accept such a truth. Sam said, "Once you're able to overcome your resistance, you'll be able to see the validity of my position." He said my personal defense mechanism, protecting me from facing "no inherent meaning in life," was blinding me from seeing the truth.

Still, even after removing my defensiveness, setting aside my unwillingness, *and* facing my fear, I continue to grapple with an underlying uncertainty regarding Sam's position.

You're not the only person to chew on this issue, ya know.

Knowing I have company doesn't help.

You must resolve it on your own.

Over weeks of stitching and wrestling with the Neoplatonists' paradigm versus Sam's, I take my stand: It doesn't matter to me *where* creation comes from.

Who cares if Emptiness is connected to creation or not? Whether or not the former birthed the latter is irrelevant, because nothing in the entire universe is capable of changing my mind about where my devotion lies.

I am devoted to the stillness. I am in love with the silence.

My goal is to reside in the silence forever.

Nothing can change this certainty in me.

"The goal is Emptiness," Sam writes. "Freedom or enlightenment means becoming still, dying into Emptiness, jumping into the Abyss."

On this Sam and I can agree.

With this clarity regarding my goal, I'm reassured about any lingering questions I still have about Sam and me. This three-month retreat has confirmed our bond. We're still on the same path. The Abyss is our shared true north.

It's only a matter of time until I physically die and fully dissolve into the silence. Until then, I can live with Sam and all the things that bug me about him. I feel an extraordinary sense of relief. No more wondering if I should be somewhere other than right here.

2

It's the final ten days of my retreat and a feeling of dread rises in my chest. I don't want my solitude to end. I perform my equinox ritual, hoping it will help me prepare for the change. During the closing portion of the ceremony, I speak out loud so I can be the first person to hear my voice. Sound comes in a whisper, then a soft chant, followed by a melodic prayer. At the very end, I voice my intentions for the coming three months.

I will fully claim Sarah as the center of my being.

I will maintain my groundedness in truth and my commitment to the silence by enacting the following intentions:

I will sit twice daily for ninety minutes.

I will fast with only water for 36 hours every week and completely eliminate sugar from my diet.

I will walk in silence outside every day.

I will reach out to make contact with my blood family.

On a clear morning in April, I wake up with the sun, feeling calm. I sit, then fold my blanket as I've done for the past three months. I walk through the cottage one last time, thanking it for supporting me, for being the perfect cocoon for my transformation. I place a strand of my hair as a gift in the four corners of each room. I stand at the threshold of the front door, anticipating stepping over it to enter the world out there.

I slowly traverse the path between my cottage and the main house. Though the distance between the two is quite short by measure, energetically they feel worlds apart. When I reach the front door, the wind dies down and my courage stalls. I take a deep breath to ground myself.

Sam opens the door and smiles. We hug.

So far, so good.

"You okay?" Sam says.

When he speaks, I recoil.

I'm not ready. I want to go back.

"What do you have to say for yourself?" he asks merrily.

Sam is obviously happy to see me, yet his question feels abrasive. I adjust my posture and let the sound of his voice hit me. His words are like rubber bullets bouncing off my head. I pull my hair out of its ponytail to cover my ears and soften the onslaught. I keep telling myself I will be okay.

Not the end of the world.

"Let's take a walk," Sam suggests, sensing my discomfort.

Walking together will help.

I'm relieved to remain outside. Stepping off the porch, I immediately sense the wind at my back. I'm grateful to have nature as my consistent ally and touchstone.

We head towards the forest. After walking a while in silence, I speak first. I describe what happened the night I descended into the basement of my psyche. I tell Sam about my subsequent rebirth as Sarah, and how the weeks of settling into this new *me* have been exceptionally powerful.

"This one really feels like the me I've been searching for all along," I tell Sam. "I know I've said so before. But this time, it's different."

I smile and feel my center.

"Great," Sam says. I wonder if he even understands what I'm talking about.

What if he doesn't understand?

I won't defend myself. I trust my knowing.

Finally.

"I've also decided to contact my family."

"What for?"

"It's time to share with them what I've experienced. I've written a letter explaining everything: the reasons I moved to Oregon, what I've been doing for the last seven years, and what's crystallized in me during this retreat. I've let go of the past and I want them to know I'm ready to meet them fresh. Plus, I want them to know I've changed my name."

"Why do you care if they know?" Sam asks skeptically.

I consider how offended my father might feel about my name change.

"Since I plan on legally changing it, I want my family to be able to find me if they ever want to. More importantly, I want them to know *why* I've changed it. I don't want them to take my new name as a personal offense. I don't want them to take *anything* I've done personally."

"You don't really believe they're capable of not taking things personally, do you?"

"I'm sure I want to find out."

I'm reminded that Sam has absolutely no interest in relating with people who aren't on his same path. I suddenly experience Sam's position as a personal affront. I notice my chest begin to tighten and I want to move physically away from him. Instead of yielding to this impulse, I drop deeper into my own knowing.

Sam shrugs his shoulders. "Suit yourself."

We proceed in silence until we reach the boulders. As we turn around to walk back to the house, I notice our years together reflected in Sam's hair. He's now more salt than pepper.

Sam interrupts my thoughts. "What about us?"

"What *about* us?"

Sam takes my hand in his. "Are we still on the same page?"

Sam's hand in mine feels like home.

"More so than ever," I assure him, visualizing our dissolution into the silence together.

As I speak these words, I catch myself wondering if they are true.

3

Two months after my retreat ends, Sam and I trade places. Sam will be in retreat for the next ten months and I'll care for him in the same way he cared for me. I'll manage the finances, do the household chores, and bring him food on the days he's eating. The timing of Sam's retreat creates the perfect extension of my solitude. I'll have loads more time to myself.

During the first week I gather the rest of Lisa's personal belongings. I place her journals, photographs, and a favorite dress into a pile in front of the wood stove. Even though it's summer, I start a fire. I spend the evening slowly feeding the fire with the items in the pile until all that remains is ash. The house is like a sauna. The next morning I shovel the ashes into a bucket and spread them around the base of my favorite redbud tree.

Three months later, I begin to host mini retreats in the main house for our friends. Alice, Sonia's friend, comes for a ten-day period. Robert and Sonia each stay for a week. I feed my guests and make sure they have what they need to be alone and silent and to do their practices. Sam and I observe silence with one another, but with the others I spend time each evening talking to them about their personal challenges and offering guidance.

After five months I start to feel annoyed by the increasing noise in the neighborhood. After seven months, I'm so aggravated that I'm feeling ready to move. Our house is simply too close to the road. There's more traffic than ever and I can't stand the way the sound travels right onto our porch. Plus, we now have neighbors who like to play horrible loud music on the weekends.

While Sam hunkers down in the cottage, presumably edging towards the Abyss, I hunt for a new home. I read an ad in the local newspaper for forty acres surrounded by National Forest. The property includes a ten-year-old house, a pond, a large barn, and a one-acre garden. The first time I visit the land, I'm struck with how quiet it is. I make the hour-long drive to walk on the property four more times before I decide the house is perfect for us. When Sam finishes his retreat, I convince him we should buy it.

Within two years of changing my name, Sam and I have moved into our new home. Bordered by forest on three sides, with the closest neighbor a quarter of a mile down the road, my intimacy with silence and nature deepens. I sync up with the rhythms of the plants and animals around me and live through the seasons feeling deeply content.

I hike often, sometimes bushwhacking far into the hills, challenging myself not to get lost. I heighten my senses to the sights and sounds in the wilderness by experimenting with Castenada's energy practice. I close my eyes, then curl my fingers while running on the deer trails. I learn to use my energy body to see.

During our first winter, I cross country ski from our doorstep. I carve fresh trails in the snow on one of the old logging roads. This road leads to a ridge where I can see the snowcapped peak of Mount Shasta a hundred miles away. In spring I hike up to the same ridge and practice Castenada's gazing technique. I sit still on the ridge for about an hour, softening my eyes and staring at the mountain. I allow for a different sort of "seeing" to arise.

One morning after breakfast I grab the binoculars in time to look directly into the eyes of a bobcat sitting in the meadow. I move slowly towards the window so as not to startle him. He looks right at me, his green eyes conspicuously human. I could swear he sees me. He's so close, I want to reach out and touch him.

In the spring, while sitting alone on our deck, I hear a tree fall in the forest. At first I'm not sure what I'm hearing. The initial noise is an eerie moaning sound. It lasts a few minutes. Next is one long groan, followed by a thrashing, then a crashing thud. Then silence again.

If a tree falls in the forest and no one is around to hear it, does it make a sound?

The following day I hike until I find the fallen tree. Surrounding the giant pine tree are torn-off limbs from trees and bushes in the path of its descent. Beneath it lie flattened ferns and decimated mushrooms.

I lie on the enormous trunk, nearly double the width of my body, and rest. Everything is so still. I wonder about the tree's long life and all that it witnessed. I kiss it. Though I know the tree is dead, I know it is also alive.

At the corner of our four-acre meadow is a pond. Sam's building a bridge from the island in the center of the pond to the shore. It's the most ambitious building project he's ever undertaken. I can hardly wait to stand on the bridge and watch the wild turtles swim beneath me. I also intend to plant water lilies.

While Sam's strategizing how to empty the pond so he can pour concrete forms for the bridge, I'm drawing plant maps for the garden. Already fully fenced to keep out deer and bears, the garden is a sanctuary. It's filled with fruit trees, blueberry bushes, and raised beds for vegetables. I'm learning how to prune, to apply organic pesticides, and to build a compost pile. I enroll in the local Master Gardener program.

Nature is a steadying force, helping me remain stable in my relationship with Sam. He and I begin each morning together with meditation and yoga. After breakfast, we're both busy with solo projects until dinner. After dinner we study together, most recently listening to cassette recordings of talks by Ram Dass. Two nights a week we spend on the phone with Alice, Sonia, Robert, or Barb, supporting them in their ongoing evolution.

It's been almost three years since I ended my solo retreat and sent my letter to my family. I haven't heard back from any of them. Though tempted, I don't try to explain their actions. I'm surprised not to have received even a simple note. Perhaps even something like, "Have a good life." But at this point I'm at peace with the way it is.

It's been more than six years since I've spoken with my mom. Other than Jacob, it's been even longer since I've talked with any of my siblings. I sometimes wonder what they're doing with their lives, but I don't feel moved to reach out again.

My dad hasn't called in more than a year.

It's the end of summer. Sam and I are nailing up sheetrock in the unfinished guest bedroom when the phone rings. It's Jacob.

"Dad's having open-heart surgery tomorrow. I thought you might want to know." Jacob is short, like this call is next on his to-do list.

"Tomorrow?" I'm startled by the news. Sensing Jacob's distance, I wonder how we have drifted so far apart?

I thought it was different between Jacob and me.

"The surgery's been scheduled for months," Jacob reports. "It's been twenty years since his first bypass and his veins are blocked again."

I remember my dad's first surgery. Triple bypass. He was only forty-eight.

"Will he die?" I ask.

I might need to prepare if he's going to die.

"He's in pretty good shape, but you never know," Jacob answers.

"Is he scared?" I ask.

"Probably. But he doesn't show it. You know Dad. If something needs to be done, he just does it."

I admire this about my dad. But I also wonder how he determines what "needs to be done."

Jacob tells me about work and his new girlfriend. I tell Jacob about my new home and the mountain lion I saw while driving home just the other night. I describe the copious grapevines winding onto the deck and tell him how Sam and I joke about opening a winery.

"Instead we make raisins," I laugh.

Jacob laughs, too.

"Sam and I are hosting a retreat during the summer," I tell him. "You should come."

"Maybe I will," Jacob says unconvincingly.

I remember when Jacob was curious about what Sam and I were doing. He used to meditate, read nonfiction, and write poetry. Now, he seems content to bake bagels and ride his motorcycle.

I ask Jacob how the rest of the family is doing. He tells me David still lives in Florida and is finally completing his undergrad degree. Ellen has finished graduate school and lives in DC. Adam passed the bar in Michigan and got married last summer.

"Married?" I'm shocked.

Did my invitation get lost in the mail?

"Was I invited?" I ask.

"No." Jacob says. "You weren't. You know Adam. He didn't want any family drama. He wanted his wedding to be about *him,* not about *you* showing up after so many years."

News of Adam's marriage confirms how distant I am from my family. I thought I'd at least be invited to weddings and funerals.

Jacob is silent. In the background I hear his employee shouting something about sacks of flour.

My brother is married and I didn't even know he was engaged.

I wrestle with this news.

"You okay?" Jacob finally asks.

"I'm not sure," I admit. "I'm relieved that I didn't have to make the decision whether or not to go to Adam's wedding because I'm not sure I would've gone. But I'm also bummed I didn't get the opportunity to choose."

"Adam has written you off," Jacob says flatly.

"Oh," I say, not completely surprised.

What did you expect after all these years?

"I guess I wish he'd have told me himself," I say.

"Adam thinks *you* wrote *him* off long ago," Jacob says. "Why would he bother to tell you anything?"

What about the letter I wrote?

"I get it," I say. "It just sucks that Adam can't speak his truth directly."

"I know," Jacob replies and then yells something at his employee.

"Sounds busy there. You'd better go," I say. "Thanks for letting me know about Dad."

"Yeah…all right…" Jacob stumbles. "I'll call you if Dad doesn't make it."

I hang up and return to sheetrocking alongside Sam.

"I feel privileged to be living life on my own terms," I say, holding a board for Sam to nail. "I grant Adam the same right. I wish the same for everybody. If Adam didn't want me at his wedding, for whatever reason, I'm glad he chose to act on what *he* wanted."

Sam measures the next board.

"And I'm feeling…something else." I consider what the feeling might be. "I'm not sure if I feel nostalgic, or disappointed, or just left out."

Maybe sad.

Sam nods with disinterest and grabs another nail.

I shut up and silently wonder about Adam and his new wife.

Then I wonder about Jacob.

I watch Sam masterfully sink one nail then another and decide to save my wondering for later.

4

I'm asleep in the loft when the phone rings. I wake up, startled. I glance at the clock next to my bed. The glowing red numbers read 6:21. Downstairs I hear Sam fumble to grab the phone next to his bed. I can't quite make out what he's saying, so I roll out of bed and make my way gingerly down the spiral staircase. It's still dark when I walk into Sam's bedroom.

"I'll turn on the radio now," Sam says. "Talk to you later."

He hangs up the phone and turns to face me.

"Two passenger airplanes flew into the Twin Towers in New York City a few minutes ago," Sam says to me. "That was my father who called. He said the crash was intentional. They think it's a terrorist attack."

"What?" I shake myself to wake up more.

The decade of the nineties has passed. It barely registered in my peripheral vision. Occasionally, I'd glance at the headlines on the newspaper in the grocery store. But they read like background muzak. Headlines sensationalizing president Clinton's blow job and the cloning of some sheep named Dolly came and went without catching my attention for more than a few minutes.

The nineties was my dead-to-the-world decade.

But now, this news, invading our oasis, *is* capturing my attention.

I'm curious to know more but also cautious about getting drawn into the chaos of the outside world.

"I can't believe it," I blurt out as Sam and I walk into the living room to get our portable radio. Sam tunes the dial to NPR. We sit on the couch and listen as the first signs of daylight appear in the sky outside the picture window.

I start to cry, feeling surprised by this unprecedented event. My tears, not the attack.

My chest starts to itch from the inside out.

I'm good at witnessing my emotions and not getting caught up in them. Same with my thoughts. What I feel now isn't like any emotional response I can remember ever having. This feeling is deeper, as if originating at the base of me, coiled up there for a long time patiently awaiting its release.

The report of a woman hurling herself out of a window on the hundredth floor comes through a voice in the plastic box on our coffee table. The whole thing is surreal. I begin to sketch pictures of the jumping woman in my mind, fending off a morbid desire to see her leap with my own eyes.

Waves of energy begin to vibrate in my solar plexus, intermingling with the energy rising from my base. I carefully track the moving energies with my awareness. The waves cascade outward, dislodging what feels like old sludge in my chest. The whole experience is accompanied by a steady pressure at the base of my skull.

Later that afternoon I convince Sam to drive with me to a hotel for the night.

I want to get to a television.

I'm compelled to be part of this historical event.

Watching it on TV is the only way I know how to participate.

I'm sitting in the hot tub on our deck. It's been three weeks since 9/11 and I'm still feeling unsettled. I haven't been able to determine exactly what's going on inside of me. But I know I don't like feeling this way. There's a growing pressure in my body and my mind, like the force of a powerful river pushing on an equally formidable dam. I thought I was finished with internal disruptions of this intensity.

As the hot tub's heater cycles, I slow my breathing and lean back. I close my eyes and try to relax.

My imagination is pulled back to my first vision quest. I see myself on the ridge staring out at the horizon as the turtle entered my belly. I sit up straight in the tub as I feel the turtle moving in my belly now, and then crawling up into my throat. I open my mouth to release her. She flies towards the sun in the form of a hummingbird, holding a silk cord in her mouth. It's attached to my center. As she flies away from me, I orgasm.

The orgasm creates ripples in the hot water.

Stunned, I sit perfectly still. I let my awareness settle into my chest. My diaphragm feels stuck. I do some gentle yogic breathing to loosen it. Then I pray.

"Oh Sacred Ones, what's happening? Am I being tested? Guided? Please help me see clearly so that I might continue to walk with integrity."

For the past nine years I've contained my sexual energy within my own skin. After completing my year-long self-pleasuring practice, learning about the sexual energy in my own body, I transitioned into a fulfilling celibacy. The amount of tactile contact I've had with Sam through holding hands and spooning has satisfied my need for human touch. When I've felt pulled outwards sexually, I learned to successfully recycle the urge inwards through meditation, yoga, and *pranayama*. Within the first full year of my celibacy I stopped craving sex altogether. Though occasionally I'd climax in a dream, I haven't had an orgasm since 1992.

Until now.

I slide off the hot tub seat and submerge my entire body. I undulate like a mermaid, guiding the aftermath of the orgasm to spread itself throughout my entire body.

When I surface, I see Sam watching me from the upstairs window.

I feel suddenly shy.

Two weeks later I'm hiking in the forest on an overgrown logging road. I'm watching the ground, lost in my thoughts, when I hear a loud rustling on the trail ahead of me. I look up into the face of a large brown bear. Three cubs scramble up trees behind her as the momma stands rooted, protecting what is hers. I freeze. I soften my stance and whisper "Hello." Momma bear stares at me without moving. Our eyes stay locked for some time.

When the cubs are high in the trees, the momma bear shifts her body ever so slightly. I bow and slowly back away from her. She releases me without harm.

I take a shorter route home, stopping to sit under my favorite pine tree at the edge of our meadow. I lean against the trunk and close my eyes to recapitulate my encounter with the bear. I know it was significant, so I listen for the meaning. I wonder if I'm being told to become a mother and chuckle at the ridiculousness of this thought. I'm nearing forty and have no intention of bearing a child. The motherhood window feels closed and, though I always thought I'd have kids, clearly life had another plan for me. Lisa may have been destined to be a mom, but Sarah clearly is not.

What was the bear telling me?

It's time to take better care of yourself.

"In what way?" I ask, bewildered.

I continue to be still.

In my mind's eye the momma bear lifts her front paws to the sky, balances on her hind paws, and smiles.

"You're standing?" I state the obvious, trying to figure out if this is a clue.

I am taking a stand.

My body freezes. I'm weighted down by an invisible force and can't move.

I wait, listening.

The invisible force releases in super slow motion, one cell at a time, allowing me to track the dis-ease embedded in my body. I see a pasty white film encasing my red blood cells and a cloudy syrup-like substance covering the inside walls of my intestines.

I stand.

Sam and I are sitting on the hanging swing inside the screened porch. It's cool outside and we snuggle under a wool blanket. I tell Sam about my meeting with the bear.

"I think it's time for me to find a doctor."

"A doctor?" Sam is confused. "What does a doctor have to do with the bear?"

"The bear showed me how she protects her cubs. Keeps them safe. Healthy. Alive. Then, while considering her message to me, I'm immobilized and shown the inside of my body. What's the meaning? For as long as I can remember, I've felt like shit," I remind Sam. "I've been taking care of myself spiritually all of these years, but not physically. And, truth is, even though I eat well and get a lot of exercise, as I age, my symptoms are getting worse."

When I arrived in Oregon, I'd been subsisting for years on a lifestyle that included alcohol, tobacco, and caffeine. After about a year of simple living, I experienced a physiological "base point" free of all drugs, stimulants, and most processed foods. Still, I felt a persistent fatigue, dull sore throat, and mild headache—the same symptoms I still experience every day and have chosen to ignore.

"I've been *watching* my symptoms for all these years," I tell Sam, "same as I've been observing my thoughts and feelings. But I'm tired of not feeling well. Before I die I'd like to experience what it feels like to be physically well."

This is the first time I've acknowledged to Sam the truth about how I feel. For years I've been powering through a rigorous meditation practice, long periods of silence, and regular water fasts. When I'm meditating, doing yoga, or studying, I don't consider how awful I feel because my attention is focused elsewhere. But ever since we moved to this beautiful land and I'm physically more active, I notice my body struggling to keep up. I no longer wish to focus my attention elsewhere when I feel so awful.

I want to experience a healthy body.

I've been operating under the premise that it doesn't matter what condition my physical body is in, in order to do my spiritual practice. I don't need a healthy body to be enlightened.

It's true, you don't.

I've asked myself, "If the goal is to die into the silence, wouldn't it be harder to disentangle from a healthy body? It might actually be easier to let go of a sick body. So who cares if I have a healthy body?"

Maybe you care.

I'm leaning on Sam's chest and listening to his heart beat. He doesn't see my tears.

"Well," Sam says, "you need a certain degree of physical health in order to sustain your spiritual practice. So if seeing a doctor would help you in your practice, then I'm all for it."

The next morning I scour the yellow pages and call six doctors' offices to inquire about their methods and philosophy. I want someone who values Western *and* Eastern medical systems. I need a champion.

You need a momma bear.

I make an appointment with a doctor of alternative medicine in Ashland, a small town an hour away.

The doctor's name is Gina. She specializes in hard-to-treat cases, using a combination of chiropractic adjustments, applied kinesiology, herbs, and massage therapy. She has me visit a traditional medical clinic for a comprehensive physical, including a complete blood work-up, a gynecological exam, and an EKG. She has all of the test results sent to her.

Gina is smart, attentive, and kind. She's also beautiful. She's tall and thin with long dark hair and radiant skin. Gina's office is decorated with large colorful paintings of flowers. On the shelf behind her desk, sitting between stacks of medical journals, are a tiny Buddha statue and a bear totem carved out of stone.

On a warm autumn afternoon, I begin my journey with Gina. I take a stand for my health. Gina views me as a complex puzzle waiting to be put back together. But she treats me like a friend.

5

I meet Joanne in my Master Gardener's course. At first we share notes on local seeds and where to buy iris bulbs. Eventually we begin to talk about our lives. Joanne is in her late fifties, grew up in Medford, and lives with her husband and their twenty-year-old daughter. She spends most of her time gardening and reading books on philosophy and spirituality.

In the spring, I invite Joanne to visit my garden and to meet Sam. I've decided it's time to share my life with somebody new, a complete outsider, and I'm curious how it will go. I'm excited to be in a position to introduce another person into our small circle of practitioners, but not so sure how she will react to Sam. After all, he remains cold, harsh, and aloof. Joanne doesn't seem to be put off. Or at least she doesn't say so. Instead, she begins to visit frequently. Together we meditate, do yoga, and talk about her views on God. Joanne easily discusses what's on her mind, but when it comes to her personal life and growth process, she's guarded.

I sense Joanne's deep-seated hatred of her body and decide to broach the subject gently. Joanne is five-foot two and more than thirty pounds overweight. With deep brown eyes and dark graying hair to her shoulders,

Joanne is naturally quite pretty. Her contempt for her body shows in how she moves. She shuffles as if she's trying to be invisible.

One day, drinking iced tea in her backyard garden, Joanne finally opens up. She reluctantly admits she hasn't been sexual with her husband in almost five years. When Joanne describes her mounting feelings of shame, I suggest she go to one of the Sex, Love, and Intimacy workshops I attended back in my twenties.

"It could really help," I tell her.

"I couldn't do it," Joanne says to me. "Too scary. A room full of strangers. I think I would freak out."

Joanne is an introvert. A loner.

"What if I went with you?" I ask impulsively.

"You?" she says.

"Yes, me!"

"Why would you do that?"

"Why *wouldn't* I?"

That evening I present my idea to Sam.

"I think it would be great for Joanne to do the workshop, but why would you want to go with her?" Sam asks.

"Because Joanne's terrified," I say. "She won't even consider going without me."

I want to support Joanne.

"Well, if you feel that strongly, go ahead."

I call the next day and register us for the workshop. Three weeks later, Joanne and I load her car with suitcases, snacks, and sleeping bags. We get on the road and head south to California for the weekend.

"I can't believe I'm doing this," Joanne says to me, two hours into our five-hour drive.

"I can't believe I'm doing this either," I say.

"Why?"

"Because I never imagined I'd be going to this workshop again. I'm curious how I'll feel being there."

I share with Joanne some of my experiences at the workshops. I tell her about the time I was in a group with six other women. We each told our personal stories of sexual abuse. Simply the act of speaking and being witnessed healed something for each one of us. I also tell Joanne about the evening talent shows and how singing in front of the whole group was one of the biggest stretches of my life. Then, in between snacking on pretzels and stopping to pee, Joanne and I talk about Plato and the One.

It's late afternoon when we arrive at Harbin Hot Springs. Joanne and I unload our stuff and stake out a spot on the deck. We tuck our suitcases against the railing and lay our sleeping bags next to each other. Joanne fumbles with the zipper on her down bag. She seems untethered.

The workshop begins with dinner. Nearly sixty men and women of various ages, colors, and sizes gather together to eat. I tolerate the awkward hellos and where-are-you-froms. These are precisely the kinds of conversations that, in the not-so-distant past, would have made me cringe because of their superficiality.

After dinner, I'm leaning on a backjack scanning the crowd when the two facilitators, a moderately attractive middle-aged white man and a younger, dark-skinned woman, enter and welcome us. They sit on plush oversized chairs at the head of the large meeting room and begin outlining the agreements and logistics for the weekend. Then they instruct us to stand and find a partner. Joanne is sweating profusely and looking like she wants to bolt. I choose her as my partner.

The group forms two large circles facing each other. I'm approximately two feet away from Joanne and we're looking directly into each other's eyes. Soft music plays in the background as the female facilitator talks us through the choreography of this exercise.

"Greet this person by looking deeply into their eyes," she says. "Breathe and allow yourself to feel whatever you're feeling. Maintain eye contact without speaking."

We move in a circle that snakes around itself until each of us has greeted every other person in the room. I remember doing this exercise at my first Sex, Love, and Intimacy workshop. It's a dance of intimate connection. Except for Sam, I haven't looked into anybody's eyes in this way for almost a decade. By the time I get to the eighth pair of eyes, tears are streaming down my face. I'm not sure exactly what's happening. All I know is, this is intense.

Soon my body begins to shake. I'm scared. I take a deep breath and consider stepping out of the circle. But I don't want to disrupt the program. I'm sobbing, wondering if maybe, somehow, I can shut off my tears. Detach. Center myself.

But, it's too late. I can't.

And I don't want to.

Later that evening, the tears stop all by themselves, but I can't sleep. I lie on my sleeping bag observing the energy coursing through my body. It circulates in the path of a figure-eight extending from the top of my head to the base of my vagina.

At breakfast the following morning I'm unable to eat. Food is completely unappealing to me. I sit at the table and watch everybody else eat, listening to them share their experiences from last night.

Later, I let one of the workshop assistants know what's happening with me.

"If fatigue hits me at some point today, I may need to excuse myself from the program and lie down," I tell the assistant.

"Not a problem," he says. "You seem to have things under control. Just let me know if you need any other support."

"I will," I reply.

But I don't need anything.

I never tire.

And I never eat.

Not for three whole days.

Jason is twenty-nine, with dark curly hair and deep green eyes. He works for a non-profit organization in San Francisco. Jason has been my buddy for the entire workshop. This means we keep an eye on each other, sharing our internal processes and offering support and encouragement when needed. Jason wants to kiss me, he tells me. But he knows I'm celibate and doesn't press. I want to kiss Jason, too. I want my tongue in his mouth so badly I ache. Instead of yielding to the sexual desire, I pull the energy into my body and hope I can contain it.

6

I return to Oregon still buzzing. In order to integrate what's happened, I focus on finalizing my presentation for the upcoming retreat Sam and I are hosting. There'll be seven of us gathering on the land, including our newest companions, Joanne and Alice. Barb will be traveling from Michigan and Robert and Sonia will be driving up from California. Jacob won't be joining us, citing the expansion of his business as his reason.

As in the past, our retreat schedule is highly structured with practices and activities designed to push the growth of each member of the group. This year we've each been assigned the task of sharing an updated articulation of our spiritual views.

It's day three of the retreat when the presentations begin.

It's a hot afternoon. Because there's no central air conditioning in this house, we lower the window shades and turn on the ceiling fan.

Sonia goes first. She stands in front of the group, lecturing on Ouspensky's *In Search of the Miraculous*, sharing a superficial understanding of what she's read. Ouspensky, a student of Gurdjieff's, left Gurdjieff's school to become a teacher himself. Though I love Gurdjieff and Ouspensky,

I'm completely bored with Sonia's talk. I'm not interested in hearing her regurgitate the ideas of a dead person. I want to hear Sonia's own knowing.

After all, sharing our personal views *was* the assignment.

She doesn't have her own knowing.

Robert is next. He stays seated for his presentation and doesn't speak for very long. He restates Sam's position on complete annihilation of self and removal of all desires. Robert has taken on Sam's view as his own. His iteration of Sam's paradigm is thorough and his argument is sound. I trust his sincerity and believe that Robert is truly aligned with Sam.

At one time, you were aligned with Sam, too.

When it's my turn to speak, I tape a long piece of butcher paper on the wall and lay a pile of colored markers on the stool next to me. I'm sweating as I turn to face my audience.

Sam sits in his brown wingback chair, nestled in the far corner.

His gaze is severe.

Trust yourself.

Sam leans forward, presses his elbow on the arm of his chair, and sets his chin into his hand. He strokes his beard.

I take a sip of water, pick up a green marker and draw a diagram on the wall behind me. I begin with a basketball-sized circle. On the inside of the circle I draw numerous different colored lines of various lengths. I then draw an especially thick line halfway in the circle and halfway out.

"This is me," I point to the circle. "The lines inside me represent the many voices or selves within me. Each one carries its own unique self-interest and has a need for control or expression. All together, they make up the dynamic complexity of humanness I call *me*."

Robert nods. Sam remains perfectly still.

I point to the thick line. "This particular self represents what we call the witness. This is the self who sees all the other selves objectively, plus has a view of what exists outside the circle of me. Once stable, the witness can take control and help guide all of our actions."

I pause. Barb smiles at me.

I take the purple marker and draw more circles, filling up the whole sheet of paper with them.

"These circles represent all humans. I can't fit six billion on this page, but you get the idea. Are you with me?"

Joanne leans forward in her chair nodding. She and I discussed our presentations on the drive home from the workshop, so she already knows where I'm going with this.

Sonia looks confused.

I don't care.

I place my hand on the bare wall next to my drawing and take a deep breath.

Stay on point.

"This wall represents Emptiness." I knock on it. "The presumption within this community of practitioners is, in order to end suffering, we must somehow get ourselves out of this universe," I point to the butcher paper as the universe's representative, "and dissolve into Emptiness or the Abyss." I knock on the wall again.

I watch Sam adjust in his seat. It's a squirm of discontent. I can tell by the way his eyes get small.

"In Sam's view," I say, looking right at Sam, "Emptiness exists outside of or beyond the universe and has nothing to do with the universe, or anything in it."

Years of conversations with Sam flood into my head. I'm wanting this explanation to be an elegant encapsulation of Sam's theory, simple enough that even a complete beginner can understand it. I look to Alice for signs of comprehension, as she's newest to the group. Based upon the glazed look in her eyes, I fear I am failing miserably.

Maybe it's just the heat.

I wonder what a *complete* stranger would think of my diagram. I consider myself to be intelligent and articulate. I'm offering a synthesis of some very wise lineages: Theravaden Buddhism, Zoroastrianism, and the teaching of Carlos Castenada among them. Still, a stranger might wonder if I'm of sound mind. Who walks around saying the point of life is to annihilate one's self?

I look at the people sitting around me.

I love them.

Half of them have been my family for more than a decade.

I feel suddenly alone.

Breathe. Stay in your body.

I take the markers off the stool to sit on it. I slide closer to the group.

"After years of practicing, I'm able to hold steady as the witness," I say. "I've deconstructed or destroyed many of the voices and beliefs that have been with me since childhood. I've managed to disassemble a good portion of my conditioning, enough to stabilize as Sarah. Plus, I can successfully bring a focused concentration to my sitting practice, to the point where I'm able to rest into the silence for long periods of time."

Suddenly, my ears pop and my voice sounds like it belongs to somebody else.

I continue. "My relationship with Emptiness is well established. I should therefore be committed to dying fully into It. However, I've come to realize that Emptiness is not asking me to dissolve into It forever. Only Sam is. The Emptiness and I are actually having a different kind of relationship. I'm therefore not committed to my extinction in the way Sam is committed to his."

There. I said it.

I hope Sam's open to what I'm about to say. I want him to accept my realization as true. I don't want to be cast out.

Sam's already taken his position.

Robert sits up straighter in his chair.

"At times I've questioned whether my experience of Emptiness was authentic," I explain. "This questioning inspired me to go back to the cushion again and again, sitting quietly and with renewed tenacity. Over and over, I've listened and inquired. Though Sam has been telling me the endpoint is complete dissolution, the deepest place I access in the silence has *never* told me to annihilate myself. The silence has never asked me to stay inside of her forever."

I pause briefly to give my words an opportunity to land.

"Annihilation, or jumping into the Abyss, as Sam refers to it, is not what my realization of Emptiness is revealing to me."

Did they hear this?

Whether they agree with you or not doesn't matter.

"What if the experience of Emptiness is not what leads us to a spiritual death, but is actually the source of our capacity to truly meet life?" I propose.

I feel suddenly proud of myself, confidently expressing the certainty I've worked so hard for.

I look directly into Sam. I let my eyes speak to him: Don't dismiss me, Sam. From the very beginning you always said I should validate everything for myself. Try to prove you wrong. Well, here I am, challenging you now. Will you accept the challenge?

"What do you mean by 'truly meeting life'?" Barb asks.

I'm glad to have the opportunity to explain.

"It's my experience that the whole point is not to radically self-destruct, but to gradually re-construct. Freedom from suffering happens when we remove our unconscious conditioning and live in conscious alignment *with* the Emptiness. Not by dying into It. By accepting this distinction, then..."

"You're wrong, Detroit," Sam interrupts from his corner. His words, like darts, head straight for my heart.

I brace myself, ready to take on the challenge. I know sparring with Sam can only strengthen me.

"I know you believe you've had an authentic realization." Sam's voice is steady. "But it's your ego, tricking you again. As usual, it's doing an excellent job, presenting its most enlightened argument yet."

Sam's making an example of me in front of the whole group.

"I know this is a possibility, Sam," I say with conviction. "Of course, I know this. Look who you're talking to."

I stand up.

"I think *you're* wrong." I'm feeling bold. "And I'm asking for you to give your view another serious look. If you're totally convinced you're right, fine. Don't question it for yourself if you're so fucking certain. Question it for me. For us. Your sincere involvement in the discourse will help all of us be clear."

Robert's face is contorted, as if he's wondering whether I realize what I'm saying. I sense Robert preparing to take a side. I don't want there to be sides.

Nobody speaks.

Give them time.

I sit down.

"You've been working on deconstructing yourself for years," Barb finally speaks. "You've been such a help and model for me. Are you saying that everything you've done up to this point has been wasted?"

"It's a good question," I reply, grateful we might have a conversation rather than an inquisition. "I don't believe anything I've chosen to do up to this point has been wasted. Having the goal of radical annihilation, even if it's not the true endpoint, has motivated me to examine and remove a lot of habitual beliefs and behaviors, making room for what I'm now calling my 'authentic self' or 'center' to emerge and stabilize. Grounding into this center is what has forged my stable relationship with stillness and silence, leading me directly to my own knowing of what Emptiness is asking of me. I don't know that I would have found my center or accessed this realization without all these years of practice, contemplation, and solitude. I see now how essential these disciplines have been in making way for this deeper knowing."

"And," I continue, looking at Sam, "I'm hoping that together we can explore my discovery as an alternative, or possibly an addition to, Sam's experience and point of view."

I feel nauseous.

You're trying to convince yourself as much as them.

Shit.

This is okay.

I don't need convincing.

Apparently you do.

I realize there's some part of me hoping the group will set me straight, stand behind Sam and the paradigm we've been working with for years, and put me in my place. I don't want to blow up my life. To lose my community. To lose Sam.

I feel dizzy.

Stay present.

I'm committed to truth as much as Sam is. He's always said so. He married me, after all. Therefore, if my realization is *more* true than his, Sam will come around. He'll have to.

And I'm willing to be wrong. If my view isn't true, then I'll change course.

Sam poses a question. "Does this mean you want to go out in the world and become a normal person, get married, find a job, reunite with your family?"

Sam's question brings me pause. Put this way, all those things sound completely unappealing.

I take a sip of water.

"I don't know, Sam," I answer honestly. "I'm not sure how this will impact my life. I'm not trying to figure that out. I just know I'm being influenced by a deep certainty inside me to begin to explore being alive in a new way, to be in my body in a different way, to engage with life *while* remaining rooted in the silence."

"You're caught in your delusion," Sam interjects, standing up now. He's done with this ridiculous conversation and is leaving. "You'd be best served by deepening your relationship with the cushion, not some untrustworthy voice you call your center."

Your relationship with Sam is over. Can't you see?

I shake off Sam's judgment and put my hands on my hips. Like an advancing force field, he walks over to me. Someone once told us that we form an impenetrable energetic spiral when we are in a room together. As Sam approaches me I pull away from our energy vortex. I already know the strength of our bond, and right now I need to trust *my* bond with silence.

Sam's proximity pulls at me like iron to a magnet.

He walks past me to my drawing on the wall and rips it down.

Joanne gasps.

Having made his point, Sam leaves the room.

I gather my markers. Barb and Joanne help me roll up my drawing.

I am stunned.

Over the past couple of years my knowing has surfaced like a slowly maturing fetus.

I now feel a sudden growth spurt.

I make room for it.

7

In my dream, I'm sliding down a mountain that just gave way from an earthquake. I dig my heels in, trying to slow my descent, reaching for something to grab hold of. If I can stop my fall, eventually the earth will stop moving and I can crawl back up to the top.

Where it's safe.

Instead the mountain refuses me and I tumble into a free fall.

But I never hit bottom.

Sam and I have drifted apart. I keep hoping he'll take a more serious look at my view, but he is immovable. We've had a few unemotional theoretical conversations since the retreat, but his stance is intractable. He still encourages me to focus primarily on my sitting practice. He advises me to test the waters of my realization carefully if I must, but only with matters of little consequence. He's certain I'll see the fault in my view any day now.

With Gina's guidance, I'm doing a series of cleanses to remove the residue of having taken antibiotics daily for so many years. Gina's plan is to help my body eventually ignite a fever, signaling its ability to fight off any viruses still lingering in my system. I'm feeling drained from the process, but I also sense some vitality returning. Gina says this is how it'll be for a while. "As toxins surface for release, you're going to feel yucky," she told me. "But you'll also start to experience a hint of your natural health long buried underneath."

This inkling of renewed energy, combined with my spontaneous orgasm in the hot tub, inspires me to consider exploring sex again. Sex is certainly a worthy testing ground for bridging my rootedness in stillness to life. After all, sexual energy is a primal life force. The experiment will be low risk, contained in my own body, and, if I choose to recruit a partner, I can always invite Sam or somebody else from our group.

"I'm not exactly sure the best way to go about this," I say to Sam one night after dinner when I tell him of my plans to begin having sex.

"I'm not sure sex is the best choice to begin with," Sam says.

"Why not?" I say gently, anticipating his resistance.

"I think you should choose a less dangerous desire to play with," Sam cautions.

"Like what?"

"I dunno. Like getting a part time job or buying new clothes?" He is sarcastic. Angry.

"I'm not genuinely *moved* to do either of those things, Sam. And I'm not interested in testing my realization by doing something insincerely. It would skew the data. If I'm going to be honest, I need to follow where life is calling to me. And life appears to be placing sex in my path."

"Why can't you just sit quietly with the movement to have sex, Detroit, instead of acting on it? Like you've been sitting with it for the past nine years. Why must you move so fast?" I sense Sam's discomfort and wonder if it's hitting too close to home for him, challenging his nearly twenty years of celibacy.

"I'm not moving too fast for me, Sam," I say calmly, being sensitive to his underlying distress. "I'm trusting what's happening through me instead of suppressing it."

I pause.

"I was actually wondering if you might be interested in joining me," I daringly propose. "Maybe you would like to be my partner for this."

I know it's highly unlikely he'll say yes, but it feels important to ask. Over the years we've discussed the possibility of having sex together. We've never been against being sexual per se. We just haven't felt guided to go there.

"I'll have to spend some time considering this, Detroit," Sam says. "I wouldn't count on it."

Sam gets up from the table, turns away from me, and walks into the kitchen to make tea.

"And in the meantime?" I ask to his back.

"In the meantime, let's rent you an apartment in Medford where you can do whatever you want with whomever you want."

"All right," I say. And the discussion is over.

It takes a month to find an affordable apartment in a decent part of town. This is more than enough time for Sam to respond to my invitation to be my first sex partner. His answer is no. He's not feeling guided to end his celibacy.

I call Robert and tell him I'm ready to explore my sexuality again. I ask if he'd be willing to be my partner. He says yes. Since he lives in California, we can meet only every four to six weeks, a weekend at a time.

Robert is the perfect first partner after such a long abstinence. Since I'm not overly attracted to him and feel no romantic involvement, I won't be distracted by either of those variables. We've already been sexual with one another, so I'm acquainted with his body and he with mine.

We'll stay focused purely on the sexual energy and I'll likely be able to stay connected to the stillness throughout my experience. Robert will support my intention.

I feel like a virgin again.

When Robert and I meet for the first time, we discuss the specifics of how I want to proceed. He's completely willing to be of service to me in any way. I choose to activate my sexuality by simply sitting together and feeling the sexual energy in my body. I want to take this process slowly.

Robert and I are both clothed and I'm in his lap, my back to his chest. He wraps himself around me as if I'm an extension of his body, and places his hands in mine. Then we breathe, tracking the energy in our bodies. During my years of celibacy I would track energy moving in the center of my body, as if it climbed up and down an invisible elevator at the front of my spine. I notice the energy oozing out of the central elevator shaft and spreading to other areas in my body—my belly, my shoulder blades, and my forehead most notably. Robert and I change positions and watch the energy while seated, standing, and lying down.

At our sixth session, we sit together naked. Then through deep controlled breathing we expand the energy and ignite excitation in our genitals. We explore the sensation of arousal without touching our genitals or achieving orgasm. The energy moves within and around my uterus in waves that don't crest or crash, but instead undulate for a long time.

Robert is well practiced in restraining his ejaculation and doesn't push any agenda other than caring for me. I appreciate the gentleness of his touch, the potency of our two bodies breathing together, and the sweetness of feeling turned on. For many sessions we meet in this way, reserving our orgasms for a later date.

I engage in sex in the way I practice yoga. Yoga postures are body movements and shapes that arise from within the silence and stillness. Sex has the same quality of arising. If I remain connected to the stillness through my breath while Robert and I engage sexually, the stillness does not leave me. On the contrary, it informs my engagement with the sexual energy, and with Robert. My body's excitation seems to be enhanced through my sustained connection to the silence.

Note to self: Life appears to be enhanced by the silence, not diminished.

Practicing with Robert is satisfying but not frequent enough. After a few months I decide to locate someone closer who can meet more often. Though this means going outside our group, I feel it's the right thing to do. Robert suggests I place an on-line personal ad, recommending a site devoted to sacred sexuality. Robert gives me his old laptop, teaches me how to use it, and helps me set up my ad on Tantra.com.

I craft my ad with a clear intent: "I'm looking for a male sexual partner to explore the practice of sacred sex. I'm available to explore all practices short of sexual intercourse. I'm not looking for a romantic long-term relationship. Only serious practitioners need reply."

Joseph answers my ad the following day. He's twenty-seven years old, a graduate student living in Portland.

We arrange to meet midway at a hotel in Eugene.

As I drive to meet Joseph, I remember my days as an escort. Though I will not receive money from Joseph, my intention feels similar to when I'd meet a client: I'm driving to meet a stranger with whom I plan to engage sexually. We have an agreement around the purpose of our encounter.

The difference is that tonight I will enjoy giving to another person *and* take satisfaction in asking for what I want.

Simple.

Joseph and I meet in the lobby of the hotel. He's my height, balding, and slightly overweight. We sit in the lobby and drink tea while going over our plans for the evening. We establish our ground rules and clear the way for a mutually beneficial experience. When I acknowledge there's not much physical attraction on my part, Joseph doesn't flinch. But when he admits to not having any experience with sacred sex, I want to smack him.

"I was extremely clear in my ad," I say forcefully. "What the hell?"

I don't have time or energy to waste.

Joseph confesses that he was just very curious to meet me. He's been meditating every day for more than a year now, reading a lot about sacred sexuality, and wanting to gain experience.

"I figured I could learn by being with you," he explains. "I'm willing to do whatever you want."

I'm annoyed he lied to me. At the same time, I can understand the temptation.

I tell him I need a moment to myself.

I go into the bathroom and consider my options. Since I traveled three hours to get here, I want to take advantage of this opportunity to practice.

Even though it's not what I had originally planned, I decide I'll stay, teach Joseph some basic sacred sex practices, and see what happens.

We spend a couple of hours working with some fundamentals. We meditate together and practice tracking the energy while seated back to back, then lying naked in various positions. We go over certain breathing techniques and discuss the relationship between breath and sexual arousal. Then I teach him about female anatomy and how to pleasure a woman. I give him some general communication tips any young man would want to know when talking with a woman.

Joseph's an adept and eager student. We have fun. He leaves more prepared for his next lover, and I feel rejuvenated from the exchange.

Note to self: Experience is not the most essential quality in a sacred sex partner.

Joseph drives back to Portland.

I spend the night in the hotel room.

Soon after, two other men answer my ad. Neither lives locally, but they're closer than Robert. Now I have practice sessions scheduled once every two or three weeks. Sam wants me to share about the sex I'm experiencing, but our conversations don't last very long. Since he's never experienced anything like this, it's not long before his input feels wholly theoretical and not based in reality at all.

Sam and I drift farther apart.

I spend more time at the apartment alone and Sam begins to resent my absences from home. Caring for the property starts to feel like a strain on him. We discuss downsizing. In the early spring, we put our beloved property on the market in order to both move into town.

I'm heartbroken around leaving the land. It's an important anchor and sanctuary for me. As Sam and I pack up the house, I realize my relationship with Sam may also get left behind. I'm afraid that losing both Sam and the land will be too much for me to handle at once.

Our property sells within two months and Sam and I purchase a home in Medford just a few miles from the apartment. Because the sale happened so smoothly and the new house is so perfect for us, I consider that my relationship with Sam may not be crumbling. I prefer to believe that we are "reorganizing."

A week after my spring equinox ceremony a guy named Steven answers my ad. He lives in Ashland. We arrange to meet on a Sunday afternoon.

While driving to Steven's house, I'm strangely inspired to stop at a flower shop to buy an arrangement for him.

I flash back to Ani, the Armenian florist in Michigan, and recall the bouquet I bought on the Sabbath that Jeremy and I spent together. I wonder how Ani is.

I wonder how Jeremy is.

Steven greets me with a warm smile and a solid hug. I hand him the bouquet. He's fifty-two but looks ten years younger, and has the energy of a teenager. He has rich brown eyes and dark hair with one wisp of silver at the hairline above his right eye.

I like him immediately.

We take a hike in the woods behind his home to discuss our intentions regarding sex. He found my ad surfing Internet sites while doing research for a client. Steven says that his client is developing a proposal to "improve the adult television industry by creating conscious and mindful pornography."

Steven recently ended a relationship and is enjoying his autonomy. He's not looking for a long-term partner either. He's been studying sacred sexual practices from two different teachers over the past three years.

After our hike, we get naked and breathe together.

8

I can't stand wearing a bike helmet because it impedes my sense of wildness, so I leave mine on the front porch. I'm pedaling wicked fast, letting the wind whip hard against my face. I stay fiercely focused on the road.

I speak out loud to Sam as if he's actually on this bike with me. I pretend he's behind me and we're pedaling in tandem.

"We always agreed we would trust one another's inner guidance no matter what. Right?"

The wind pushes my tears sideways along my cheeks.

I lean forward, causing the bike to accelerate.

"Yes!" His imaginary voice blows into the back of my head. "I want your freedom more than I want your love or companionship. I do!"

I reach back to grab his invisible hand and squeeze it.

"I know, Sam. I know you do," I say.

But I don't believe him.

I open my mouth to the sky, letting the wind plunge down my throat as I push it back out with a scream.

Aaaaaaaaaaaahhhhhhhhhhhhhhhh!

It's the autumnal equinox. Tonight I will prepare for my ritual and, in the morning, I will perform my ceremony. For fifteen years I've been enacting this process on solstices and equinoxes. Tomorrow will be my sixtieth ceremony. I can hardly believe it. Throughout all these years, it seems that my time alone, my time in nature, and this Native American practice have kept me close to the holy and connected to my Self.

I thank the ancestors for this gift.

I know tonight's ceremony will be one of the most significant ever.

I build the altar. I place objects to anchor the four directions. In the north, a quartz crystal I found on the property where Sam and I first lived together. In the west, an arrowhead I found in the meadow on the forty acres of land we just sold. In the south, the ceramic bowl I used for grinding the ashes in the doll ceremony. And in the east, a chunky red candle Steven gave me.

I take a long hot bath. Though the tub is tiny, I'm able to adjust my frame and completely submerge my belly while resting my feet on the tile wall. I can see the lavender twilight through the open window.

I remember sitting in this tub with Steven the day he brought me the candle. It felt especially cozy in here with two of us. He was leaning against this wall and I was resting into him. I close my eyes and call up the scent of him: agreeable, with a hint of vanilla. I can feel my back against his soft skin and his strong arms wrapped around me. My legs are crossed, his stretched out. I feel his breath again in my ear. And then his voice.

"I've been wondering, Sarah," Steven says. "We haven't talked a lot about our views on spirituality, but I was thinking of you yesterday."

"Yeah?" I let him continue, wishing I had never told him anything at all about my personal life. Our agreement was simply to be sexual practice partners.

But you did tell him.

"I was reading about transcendence," Steven continues, "and how getting lost in experiences of Emptiness is the result of an unbalanced masculine approach to the spiritual path. Without the feminine approach along for balance, it's easy to slip into an unhealthy detachment from life."

He pauses.

I wait.

"It's like trying to fly with only one wing. You never take off," he adds.

"What if flying's not the point?" I say, humoring him.

"What if it is?" he says calmly, sowing something sacred between us.

I dismiss him through my silence. He carries on.

"I think, Sarah, you may be suffering from a case of a nipped wing," he declares as he tickles my left scapula.

My body twitches.

"If you really want to be enlightened, you might want to consider giving this wing," he says as he kisses my left shoulder blade, "as much time and attention as you've given the other one."

I turn around to get a good look at his face. I need to make sure he's real.

Based upon the little I've shared, I have no reason to believe Steven has any idea of how I've spent the last ten years or any comprehension of what I've discovered. I've always presumed nobody will ever understand.

Steven and I are nose to nose when I see a twinkle in his eyes.

"Who *are* you?" I finally ask.

Who indeed!

9

I curl up in the center of my altar. Sleep comes easily. Followed by the dream.

I'm in a tent. There are women all around, preparing for some sort of ceremony. We don't speak, but they're giggling and lovingly playing together. One woman is washing my feet in a giant earthen tub of warm water while another is combing my long hair. I'm sitting on a plush red sofa. There's a fire in the center of the tent.

The women leave and I'm alone. There are silver bells on my ankles and purple scarves draped over my shoulders. I'm wearing a long crimson gown. I hear music in another tent. I look into the fire and begin to chant.

Now I'm lucid.

An elder approaches me. I recognize her as a Sacred Mother. She is regal and earthy. Her shiny silver hair lies in a braid along her spine. She takes my hand and we walk in silence to another tent where the entire community has gathered. The men play music on strings and drums as the women sing softly. The children are latched onto their mother's breasts or quietly playing games. The Mother leads me through the crowd to the front of the tent where I see two oversized chairs. On the left sits Sam and, on the right, Steven. They don't look like themselves, but I recognize them. I stand in front of them, between them. The Mother lets go of my hand and steps behind me.

I respect these two male beings. Each strong in body and mind, loved and revered by his family, a pillar for his people. I also feel sad, confused, and disoriented.

A gray-haired elder approaches from behind them and places a hand on each man's head. He says a blessing as they close their eyes. I wait. Then, as if already choreographed and rehearsed by all of us, both men stand. Sam walks towards me and bows, touching my feet. He lifts me into his arms and cradles me as if I were a child, looks into my eyes, and says something I can't make out. I put my ear close to his mouth, reaching desperately for his voice. I hear only a melody without lyrics. The sound coming out of him feels like warm milk.

I can't speak. First my eyes respond to him, then my whole body. Waves of energy pour from my skin like light beams through a prism.

In slow motion, Sam carries me over to Steven. I look into Steven's face, then back at Sam. Sam's face morphs. I can't tell if he's Sam or Steven. I look back at Steven and his face is now Sam's. Then it becomes mine. I feel disoriented. Dizzy. I close my eyes and bring my attention into my chest. This is what the Mother told me to do at this point in the ritual. I'm relieved that I remember. I'm supposed to close my eyes, stay centered in my heart. Relax. Surrender.

I see the Sacred Mother's face. I hear her eyes say to me, "It's time."

I feel my body being passed into Steven's arms. Sam retreats to his chair, where he sits again, staring blankly at the crowd. He is empty.

Steven touches his lips to my forehead, jostling my pineal gland, causing me to blink. He then sets me on my feet and leads me to the far side of the enormous tent, where our community is celebrating with wine and sweets. I stay for a while, then leave Steven behind as I walk into the night alone.

I never turn back.

I'm awake at dawn, half expecting to find myself in a tent. I check my ankles for bangles. I sit up and wrap myself in a purple shawl. I light the red candle to begin my ceremony. I offer the dream to the southwest, the direction that holds our personal stories. I set my intention to receive guidance. I do this by getting still, leaning into the Emptiness I now know as my home.

First, I offer my gratitude.

"Oh Sacred Ones, I give thanks for your grace and guidance and support. I ask that I continue to be worthy as I walk forward on this sacred journey."

I begin to cry.

Something in me is breaking wide open.

I remain perfectly still, conscious of the silence, my sobbing, and my awareness of both.

I feel split *and* whole.

Don't try to understand what's happening. Expand your awareness to embrace it.

I feel my skin molting. But the old skin snags in some places.

Breathe.

I stand up and face north. At my feet is a wooden turtle. I pick it up and hold it to my chest.

"Keep going," I hear my inner turtle say.

You're on track.

I take a step forward.

You are whole.

10

It's a hot Indian summer morning. Now that most of the other tenants have gone to work, the apartment complex is quiet. I'm lounging alone on a green inflatable floaty in the pool, contemplating what I'll say to Sam about "us" when, unexpectedly, he shows up. He leans on the fence surrounding the pool area, slides his aviator sunglasses on top of his head, and nods hello.

I wish he had called first. We haven't spoken in ten days.

"How did your ceremony go?" he asks.

"It was good," I say, reluctant to offer much.

"Want to talk about it?"

Not really.

It's not fair to make him wait.

"Sure. I'll come over to the house later," I answer. "How about dinner?"

"Five o'clock?" he suggests.

"Five is good," I say.

Sam lets his glasses drop back onto his nose, turns his back to me, and leaves.

I close my eyes and float until I feel my nose getting sunburned. I flip into the pool and swim a few laps.

I arrive at our new home for dinner. The house feels vacant, like neither of us has landed. Sam chose the master bedroom downstairs for himself and I took the two bedrooms and the bathroom upstairs. I have a mattress and my meditation cushion in one room, and a desk and reading chair in the other. Unpacked boxes of books and art supplies are stacked in the walk-in closet. Sam is unpacked and settled in. He's been busy working on the screened porch, turning it into a yoga room. He's putting in walls and laying a hardwood floor.

Sam is setting food on the dining table when I sit down. I fill my bowl with brown rice and steamed vegetables, then bow my head in silence before I eat.

After a few bites, I speak.

"I had a powerful dream last night. By the time I finished the ritual this morning, it was perfectly clear to me what needs to happen regarding us. We're finished with the way it was, Sam. If we're to remain connected, I need to do this relationship in a new way."

This has been obvious for months.

"What does that mean?" he asks, his voice verging on cold, harsh, and aloof.

"It means I can't live here with you as partners, spend time at an apartment you never visit, and live the way I need to live," I say calmly, tracking the sweat gathering under my arms.

"Why not? You can do whatever you want," he protests.

"Sam. Come on. It's clear. We're moving in different directions. My path is taking me into life in ways that don't interest you."

"So what?" Sam says. "If we still share the same commitment to truth, which you keep assuring me we do, then do whatever you feel you need to do. I don't really care."

"Even though you *say* you don't care," I say confidently, "you obviously do. My actions affect you. Your desire that we share the same daily practices and your preference that I return to being solely focused on dissolution are in the way of you truly supporting me."

Sam puts his fork down and glares at me.

"My desires are *my* problem," he says. "I'll deal with them. I'm clear enough to prevent my personal preferences from influencing how I treat you."

"No, honey, you're not," I say.

"And," I add, "your desires are not just your problem. In this case, they're *ours*."

I feel deeply rooted in my center. Sam sits with his hands gripped tightly on the table as if he wants to jump up and flip it over.

"Well, Detroit," he says slowly. "You know me. Either you're in or you're out. If you don't feel supported by me, then that's *your* issue. Sounds like *your* preference is for things to be a certain way. So I guess we're finished."

His body is rigid. His jaw is tight.

"Well, Sam," I say tenderly, "I was hoping there might be another way."

I push my chair back from the table.

"I'm hoping you love me enough to find a way for us to continue being in some sort of a relationship," I offer.

"Love has nothing to do with this," Sam barks.

"You have no idea what love is, Sam."

He'll let his heart break before he'll change his ways.

"Your commitment to truth is being compromised by your recent engagement with worldly things." Sam's voice is loud. "Why don't you just admit it?"

"No, Sam," I say with certainty. "My commitment to truth is intact."

"We'll see."

"I guess we will."

I knew this conversation would be challenging but, until now, I haven't realized how invested I am in Sam being willing to move forward with me. He's clearly not interested.

Turns out you're not so special.

I quickly strategize. Knowing there's no turning back, I decide to press further. Before Sam's anger escalates, I broach the topic I never imagined I would have to bring up because I never imagined we would ever break up. It's the topic I've been thinking about all afternoon.

"What about money?" I say.

This might send him over the edge.

I watch Sam's agitation increase as he stands and begins pacing the room. I want to talk this through with him, just as we have for the past twelve years. I want to help him sort through his feelings, explore his anger, and get to a clear place.

A wave of sadness moves through me and I want to cry for what we're losing. But I don't. Not here. Not yet.

I take a deep breath and stand waiting for his answer to my question.

Sam stops pacing and stares at me in disbelief. Then he says coolly, "I'll cover the rent on the apartment for six months. You can take the car and I'll give you some spending money to cover yourself until you get back on your feet."

I'm speechless.

Just like that. I am excommunicated.

I feel suddenly enraged. I want to run to him and shake him, remind him who I am to him, how much he loves me. I want the "generous Sam" to show up and find a way for *us* to navigate this transition together.

But CHA Sam has already cut me off.

"Sam!" I shout. "We've been essentially married for over a decade. Ours isn't like any of your other relationships. You can't just turn away from me so quickly."

"I'm not doing the turning, Detroit." He faces me. "*You*'re leaving."

"So that's how you're going to twist this? All these years you've treated me as an equal. And now because I want to shift the form of our partnership into something new, you're going to blame me and just walk away? You're going to claim that you have nothing to do with the condition of our relationship?"

"Yes." He's cold. "I'm not interested in changing our relationship in any way. I want it to remain the same as it's been."

"That's insane!" I yell at him. "You're making a huge mistake."

"I'll take my chances." He stacks our bowls and walks into the kitchen.

Fuck him. You don't need Sam or his money. You can take care of yourself.

I consider all the ways I've supported Sam over the years, with his health, managing the finances, encouraging the investment in the property we just sold and made a profit on.

Surely you're entitled to half of that!

I follow Sam into the kitchen.

"Maybe we should sit down with Robert and get his input," I suggest. "Maybe he could help us navigate this transition."

"I don't want anybody's input," Sam says. "Take my offer or leave it."

"Fine," I say and leave the room.

I feel so far away from him.

I can't believe this is happening.

I take an empty cardboard box from the garage and carry it upstairs to my bedroom. I begin to repack the few things I've already unpacked. I'll soon be erased from here. Sam won't want any trace of me.

I look around. The bedroom has lots of light and views of the tree-tops outside.

It's so peaceful here.

I collapse onto the bed and begin to cry.

I hear Sam coming up the stairs. He joins me on the bed. Laying his tense body next to mine, he carefully embraces me. The familiarity of him sends me over the edge. I weep uncontrollably into his chest.

"I wish you would change with me," I say as I soak his shirt with snot. "I wish we weren't moving in different directions."

Sam's crying now.

But he doesn't speak.

We just hold each other.

11

Steven and I are lying in bed resting after a session. My head is on his chest. His heartbeat is steady. In a calm voice Steven suggests I meet his friend Jun Po.

"I'm not interested in meeting any of your friends, Steven," I tell him.

"I know," he says, unruffled by my stance. "But this is not an ordinary friend. He's a Zen Roshi."

"Zen?" I say, feeling slightly intrigued.

"Yeah. I've known him for twenty-five years. He's a good friend and a powerful teacher. Being from the Zen tradition he has a deep understanding of the Emptiness you're so enamored with." Steven smiles and tickles me.

"Why would I want to talk to him?"

"To see if he has a similar perspective on Emptiness. Besides, I doubt he's ever met somebody who's been sitting outside of a zendo for as long as you have. I'm sure he'd be interested in hearing what *you* have to say from your perspective. Plus, you may want to sit with him sometime."

"Well…maybe." My curiosity is piqued. "I'll think about it."

I wonder if Sam would consider talking with Steven's friend.

Sam and I haven't spoken in weeks. We're at a stalemate regarding a financial arrangement, and I've contacted a lawyer for advice. Emotionally, I feel bereft, robbed of my best friend. There's an inconsolable ache in my heart. I let the ache live in me without trying to fix it. I know my grief will eventually pass.

In the meantime, I deepen my sitting practice, work more closely with Gina on my physical healing process, and search for a job. But Steven's invitation has my interest. The next time we meet for sex I tell him to arrange a visit with the Roshi.

The Roshi opens the door before Steven or I touch the bell. I'm so startled I practically fall into him head first. I look up at blue eyes that exactly match the color of his shirt. The smile that follows is warm but fierce.

"Hi," I say, "I'm Sarah."

"Welcome, Miss Sarah, " he chuckles. "Jun Po, here."

We shake hands.

He and Steven embrace. Then we follow Jun Po into the living room.

The room is tidy, tastefully decorated in earth tones, a little more urban than Zen. Jun Po sits in an armchair, Steven on a wooden stool in the corner, and I sit on the edge of a couch directly across from the Roshi. Large purple pillows are scattered on the couch. I lean into one for support.

"Tell me about yourself," Jun Po begins.

I decide to go for it. Test him. If he's an authentic Zen Roshi, he'll know all about Emptiness and understand radical annihilation. He'll be able to have an intelligent conversation with me and speak to my realization with some authority.

I look into his eyes as I speak. His gaze penetrates and tugs at the center of my chest.

Jun Po sits perfectly still, listening attentively as I tell him about my years of sitting practice, yoga, silence, and fasting. Then I tell him about the three-month retreat and the breakthrough I experienced at that time. I also tell him about Sam's insistence that annihilation is the endpoint and my questioning of this truth. As Steven sits quietly on his stool, he is hearing all this for the first time.

Jun Po asks a few clarifying questions about the specific type of meditation I've practiced and what I hoped to gain from it.

We then sit quietly together. I sense the Roshi looking *into* me and I feel suddenly exposed.

I shouldn't have told him *everything*.

"Stand up," Jun Po says, after a while.

I stand.

He places his hands together and bows to me. I can see the stubble breaking through on his shaved head.

"Your realization is genuine," he says to me, "but incomplete."

The pores on my skin open.

"I want you to try something with me," Jun Po says as he, too, stands.

"Pretend I'm Emptiness for a moment," he suggests.

He waits while I get very still and successfully shift my awareness to reorganize around him as a representative of Emptiness.

"Got it?" he asks.

I nod.

"Now, without losing contact with me as Emptiness, I want you to turn around and face Steven."

I hear Steven stand up behind me.

I start to turn, but feel the contact with Jun Po falter.

"Take your time," he says. "There's no rush."

I root my feet, soften my knees, and close my eyes to regroup.

"Eyes open!" Jun Po shouts.

I jump, feeling poked by his command.

I open my eyes.

Jun Po is smiling.

I make solid contact with him again. He starts to turn fuzzy. I imagine him dissolving into light. I imagine Emptiness as light, too. I let it penetrate me. As I merge with the Emptiness, I freeze, feeling one with the Emptiness, but also still feeling myself distinct as Sarah. I'm reminded that the Emptiness is not outside me. It's inside me. It's what I am.

The Sarahness is also what I am.

It's not either/or. It's both/and.

Yes!

I slowly turn my body to face Steven.

Don't blow this.

Steven's eyes are looking right at me. They appear to slant like a samurai's and his creamy brown skin turns a shade darker. I feel drawn into him, but I hesitate.

My body wobbles and I feel strongly pulled towards Jun Po.

What's happening?

I feel stuck, trapped in the Emptiness.

You can't ever be separate from it.

But I clearly have a preference. My love of Emptiness seems to be greater than my love of Sarah.

Only if you decide it is.

Jun Po steps towards me, standing right behind me. I feel him towering over me. My body wants to fall backwards into him. I struggle to remain anchored.

I feel Jun Po's breath on the back of my neck. "It's time for you to sustain your contact with Emptiness *while* being fully in the world."

Jun Po's words land in my heart. I gasp.

This is the same realization I shared at the retreat last summer.

"Know that the Emptiness is holding you. It's always here," he promises.

I feel Jun Po's body right behind mine. So close.

"For the full realization, Miss Sarah," his voice is now loud but tender, "you must go live it in the marketplace. Leave the mountaintop!"

Then Jun Po gently, but firmly, pushes me towards Steven.

His palm hits the spot right between my shoulder blades.

alive

1

It's been five months since Jun Po pushed me, encouraging me to trust my inner knowing and to fully participate in "normal" life. I'm managing by taking baby steps. I'm also struggling. I feel apprehensive and abandoned. Except for Joanne, almost everybody in our community wants nothing more to do with me. I have no friends remaining from my life as Lisa and no contact with my blood family. Not even Jacob, at this point.

After a brutal negotiation process, Sam and I worked out a financial agreement. On the last day I see him, Sam writes me a check for exactly half the profit from the forty-acre property sale. We drive in separate cars to the bank where I sign a document promising never again to ask Sam for money. He thrusts this on me at the last minute.

How insulting.

He's so paranoid.

He has no idea who you are.

I had no idea who he would become.

I sign the document, feeling sorry for Sam and distraught by the condition of our relationship. It's the first time I sign "Sarah" on a legal document.

"Sam," I say as we walk out to the parking lot, "I want to talk to you again some day. I don't feel complete with our relationship ending like this."

"You'll have to get complete on your own," Sam retorts. "Don't contact me under any circumstances. If I change my mind, I'll contact you."

Sam's surgical cutting away of "us" has its value. Like ripping off a Band-Aid, the experience is swift and clean. But it also hurts like hell. The grief from the loss of my friendship with Sam erodes my vitality like another systemic infection. On days when my melancholy sets in, I reconsider whether the path of radical dissolution is where I belong. I crave a heart-to-heart encounter with Sam. I yearn for the kind of talks we had in the early days when we were exploring our spirituality together.

I regularly meditate with Jun Po in the early mornings. Some days, after sitting practice, Jun Po brews me a cappuccino and we sit down at his kitchen table to talk. Jun Po kindly and fiercely helps pull me out of my melancholy. He reminds me that I'm not abandoning the stillness for the messiness of life; I'm taking stillness with me.

"Radical dissolution is *not* the way," he stresses. "Your friend Sam is wrong. Annihilation is a half-baked understanding of the teachings and the distorted conclusion of a potential sociopath."

I work three days a week as a massage therapist at a recently opened Aveda spa in town. One of the job requirements is to exchange treatments with other practitioners. I'm scheduled to receive a haircut and color next week.

I'm nervously excited.

Not caring what I look like has kept things simple for so many years, allowing me to devote my attention inward rather than outward. Spending months never looking in a mirror taught me that my sense of self is not dependent on what I look like. If I start caring about how I look now, will I be distracted by the belief that looks actually matter?

What if it's not about looks mattering, but more about the joy of expressing beauty?

I decide to find out.

My hair turns out looking refreshed, with soft golden highlights and no more split ends. I like it. But so what?

What good is beautiful hair if there is suffering inside?

Note to self: Outer beauty is not a substitute for inner peace. Ever.

Note to Sam: Inner peace is not compromised by mindful appreciation of external beauty.

Ever.

Steven and I spend more time together. I'm cautious about jumping into another relationship so soon after Sam, yet I recognize my connection with Steven is more than just sexual. He has become my friend.

We continue to practice sacred sex, honoring our agreement to keep the intention pure and our ground rules in place. But lately we've begun to follow our sessions with dinner or a walk. These simple encounters with life initiate me into the joys of being a sensual human in a material world. We sometimes talk for hours, sharing details of our pasts, our present, and our futures. Steven tells me about his history with Transcendental Meditation, Trungpa Rinpoche, the Arica School, and Swami Muktananda. Along with two profound near-death experiences, Steven has forged his own ever evolving way of being mindful and awake to life. When we discuss the theoretical underpinnings of what Sam and I were exploring, the depth and clarity of Steven's insight begins to impact me and I continue to soften. I feel as though I'm coming alive in Steven's presence, like waking up after a long coma.

Plus, we laugh a lot, which Steven says is good medicine for me.

"You're way too serious," he says one day as we lie in bed. "Serious Sarah, that's what I'm going to call you from now on."

I roll over to face him and say, very seriously, "Y'know it's *not* funny. I was actually born with a defect."

"Oh. What kind?" he asks cautiously.

"I was born without a funny bone," I smile.

We crack up, then agree to pitch in together for a bone graft.

This is how it is with Steven. Deep but light.

In the fall, after knowing each other for nine months, I ask Steven if he'll take me along the next time he travels abroad. I feel ready to have a substantial change of scenery. I want to shake things up a bit. See how I do.

In December, I travel with Steven and his eight-year-old daughter Alexandra to Thailand for a two-week vacation. We spend one week visiting ornate Buddhist temples, eating unfamiliar spicy food, and bargaining for wares with Thai shopkeepers at a giant outdoor market. I'm captivated by the sights, sounds, and smells. At the same time I find all of it exhausting and overly stimulating. When we finally board a boat for an island in the Adaman Sea, I am so ready. On the water I feel myself relax.

My relaxation is short lived when I realize our room has no flush toilet, just a hole in the ground. When I express my minor distress to Steven, we decide to change accommodations and move farther down the beach. A longboat is scheduled to transport us in the morning.

After breakfast I'm standing on our balcony gazing at the sea when I feel the air pressure shift. A strange wind enters my lungs and I catch my breath.

Something's wrong.

The air feels dense. Though there's not much humidity, I feel pressure on my skin.

I assume I'm suffering from a bad night's sleep and shrug it off. I scan the room to make sure we haven't left anything behind. Then I walk to the dining room for tea.

I turn a corner and crash into an attendant. He apologizes in broken English and tells me that our boat has arrived early. We'll have to hurry to catch it. Steven, Alex, and I rendezvous at the dining room, then head to the dock.

As I step into our water-taxi, I feel excited. I love the feeling of being on the water. Sitting in this small boat brings back childhood memories of being on my grandfather's boat and the numerous fishing excursions we shared on Lake Huron. I snuggle up against Steven.

Something's still not right.

"Something seems weird today," I say to Steven, as Alex nestles into his other side. "I can't shake the feeling. Is it me? Or do you sense something off about the weather today?"

"I do," Steven says, "like the tide is stuck or something."

Or something.

The boatman's long oar slices through the water. We arrive at our destination in less than twenty minutes. We wade waist-deep in the water to get to shore as the attendants carry our suitcases on their heads. The sea feels cool on my legs. I want to swim.

Steven and Alex unpack while I go to the office to lock our passports in a safe. On the way back to our bungalow, I meet them on the path.

"What's going on?" Steven asks.

"What do you mean?" I answer.

We walk towards the water.

"I think some sort of weird wave hit the island," Steven says as we watch people gathering their belongings. Alex bends down to play with sea foam.

That's when I see it.

Right beyond her little body.

"Look!" I gasp, pointing at the sea.

What I see isn't a wave. It's a *wall* of water. Ten feet tall and moving steadily towards us. It's only a few boat lengths offshore.

Leaving their beach bags and books behind, people begin to run frantically in all directions. Steven grabs Alex's hand and runs with her towards higher ground. I take a few steps back and then freeze, mesmerized. My brain hasn't yet communicated to my body that running would be a good idea. I'm transfixed, watching the water rush towards me. I stand ready to greet it.

Now the water is waist high. My knees buckle under the force and, when a wooden beach chair slams into my shin, I shudder awake. I stumble. I feel the undertow pulling me out to sea.

The force grips my thighs, tugging me under. I'm being given the opportunity to end it. Right here. If I consent, I won't have to struggle with life ever again.

Let's just die into the Emptiness right here. Right now.

It would be so easy.

From somewhere behind me I hear a shout, "SAAARAAAAHHHHH!"

Steven's cry lands in my belly with a thud, like a fastball hitting the catcher's mitt. It helps me relocate my center. I take a deep breath as I see a third wave approaching off shore. If I stay here, my life will surely be over.

I turn my back to the sea and run towards Steven's voice.

This is a conscious choice.

The three of us are standing together when the final wave hits. We watch from above as the water lifts a twenty-foot anchored longboat and throw it upside down into a tree. Then the water floods the grass beneath us, taking the wooden deck chair out to sea.

My whole body is alert.

I feel alive.

Ready.

Steven pulls his daughter and me closer in. His stance is solid. Just ten days ago, the three of us were crammed in the coach section aboard the longest flight of my life. Now a bond has formed between us.

I'm not sure if I want this.

Steven pulls out his cell phone and calls Alex's mother in Oregon.

"We're fine," he says calmly.

"What?" I hear her groggy voice coming through his phone.

"Something big has happened here. Not sure what exactly, but I just wanted you to know we are fine, in case communications go down."

Is this really happening?

"You okay?" Steven kisses my forehead.

"Yeah. Wow. What *was* that?"

"I imagine it was a tidal wave," he says. "My guess is there was a big earthquake somewhere. Let's go see if we can find out anything on the news."

I look down at my shin where blood trickles slowly from a gash. I'll have a scar for sure. I walk with Steven and Alex to the office. I need a bandage.

An old TV hangs from the ceiling in the corner of the resort office. Thirty of us have gathered here. We are a group of strangers fast becoming friends under the circumstances. We are the people staying on site, those who work here, plus a family of castaways who were on a boat offshore when the first wave hit. The BBC reports start streaming in.

We learn that a 9.2 magnitude earthquake has rocked the Asian continent, triggering a tsunami unlike any experienced in modern history. Hundreds, presumably thousands, of bodies washed into the sea, wiped away by the tsunami as easily as I might rinse an invasion of ants off the kitchen counter.

As the story develops, more facts emerge.

Waves measuring up to one hundred feet high.

Entire planet vibrates one centimeter.

Longest duration of faulting ever observed.

Energy released measures more than fifteen Hiroshimas.

Fifteen Hiroshimas!

Cell phone cameras and videos document the disaster on shorelines along the coasts of Sri Lanka, Indonesia, and Phuket, only fifty miles north of us. I'm fascinated by the monster wall of water uprooting trees, crumbling buildings, and dragging people to their certain deaths.

So many missing people. Piles of dead bodies.

They're so close, I can practically smell them.

I could easily have been one of them.

In another room, three outdated computers with weak Internet access share popularity with the television. People frantic to contact loved ones clamor for a turn to email their families.

I stand at the back of the room watching.

No one on earth even knows I'm here.

I have no loved ones wondering about my fate.

I'm free from the tethering of family ties, allowing me to be fully present right here.

I'm reminded of 9/11 and how I felt transfixed on that day, pulled out of my monk-like existence and drawn into the stories of New Yorkers and their loved ones. I recall how much I yearned to help. Now I'm in the heart of a disaster. Ready.

In my search for a first-aid kit, I find the manager near the beach, leaning against a tree, barely able to hold herself up. She must be in shock. I gently touch her shoulder. Her long black hair is matted to her face and mascara has left dark circles under her bloodshot eyes. When she sees me, she falls into my arms. We sway and sob together.

My tears are laced with lifetimes of grief, but also unexpected relief, maybe even joy.

As I hold this Asian woman, I feel my heart, my belonging. She is my sister, my mother, my daughter, my friend.

And I am hers.

That night, lying in bed with Steven, sleep comes slowly. The light of the full moon fills our bungalow. I see the sculpted lines on Steven's face and this comforts me.

I watch Alexandra asleep in the bed next to us. I'm moved by her innocence and wonder what impact this event will have on her.

Steven's whispering breaks the silence, "You know, if we had boarded our water-taxi at the originally scheduled time, we'd have been on the water when those waves came."

I nod. Unable to speak.

Visions of our boat twisting around a tree rush into my imagination. I push them away and move closer to Steven, letting him pull me all the way in. Like a turtle rests into her shell, recognizing it as home, I acknowledge somewhere in my deep unconscious that I, too, am home.

I lie there listening to small waves lapping onto the shore, feeling the rhythm of my breath in sync with the sea.

2

I wake abruptly before dawn with a busy mind. I question my decision to walk away from that third wave. I wonder whether I really want to live in a world where death strikes so indiscriminately. I'm not sure if I can stomach it.

Stirred up, I crawl out of bed quietly while Steven and Alex still sleep. I need to be by myself. I head to the sea.

I walk along the edge of the shore. The sand between my toes is cool and soft. The beach is ravaged. It smells like an overdose of seaweed. The air is lighter than it was yesterday, and the quiet is thick.

I slow my gait and stare at the debris left behind from the disaster. The beach is sprinkled with particles of shredded sea plants. A child's shoe peeks out from under a mound of sand. I pick up a seashell, palming it in my hand.

A rush of insight pours through me.

Death and life live in tandem.

Emptiness holds them both.

I feel my chest as if it's literally splitting open. I feel it's too much for any one person to hold, the beauty and the horror of life. Surely death is better than grappling with such extremes.

There is no such thing as death. Only change.

I get down on my knees, scoop the salty water into my cupped hands and pour it over my head. I let it burn my eyes and mix with the salt of my tears.

"I know you," I whisper now to an invisible force. "You, death."

"I see you," I say out loud. "Hovering. Inevitable."

I stand up and walk into the ocean. The current is strong.

If death is a part of life, then there's no shame in choosing it.

I walk farther out, feeling the undertow.

"Why did you spare *me*?" I cry out, imagining all the children swallowed by this sea. "Surely it would've been a more compassionate choice to have taken me. Think of all the mothers now childless and shattered."

Death is silent. Determined. Relentless.

It reminds me of Sam.

I submerge my whole body into the holy *mikvah* of the sea, descend into her sacred womb. I hold my breath and swim. I dare death to take me now. But, instead of pulling me out, the current pushes me back to shore.

Death will not take me.

Not yet.

It's not your time.

I turn away from the water, from death, and crawl onto shore, into life.

"I'm not sure I can do this," I say to the earth as I lie with my face in the sand. "Living in this world feels like too much to handle."

"You can handle it," life whispers directly into my heart. "You must."

It's time.

Death will have to wait.

I lie on the beach for some time absorbing my fate. The rising sun bakes the wet sand into my soft skin.

For years I imagined I'd eventually dissolve completely into Emptiness. I believed dissolution naturally happened to anyone brave enough to cross the threshold into its realm. I was willing. Ready. But Emptiness would not take me. Instead, it nudged me out.

I see clearly the source from which the flow of life and death emerge.

Emptiness and I are not separate.

Sam was so wrong.

Life and death live in tandem.

Life and death are inseparable from the Emptiness.

Emptiness holds them both as love.

I walk back to the bungalow and sit down to write my mother a letter.

I haven't seen or spoken with her for more than eight years.

It's time.

3

I'm anxiously waiting in the terminal where my mother will arrive any minute now. She's flying into Portland from Detroit. We decided to have our reunion on neutral ground in order to transition gently into our new relationship. I've rented a house on the Oregon Coast for two nights. My mother loves the beach as much as I do.

I see her before she sees me. She looks mostly the same, her hair still short and dyed blonde in the front. Her body is trim and agile for her nearly seventy years. She walks towards me without recognizing me.

I'm nervous.

Does she hate me?

I wave to her.

She's sobbing, almost howling when we finally hug. I'm not sure if it's grief or joy escaping her broken heart. I cry with her, barely containing myself. We hold our embrace for a long time amidst the rush of travelers. We could be any mother and daughter reuniting.

But we aren't.

"Let's just pick up from here. I'm so happy to be with you," my mother says, as we load her suitcase into my car. "We don't need to talk about anything from the past."

How can we not talk about *anything?* It's been almost ten years. Don't you want to understand where I've been, what I've been doing, how I ended up here?

I say nothing and keep loading her stuff.

"I'm just happy to see you," she says again as she takes a cell phone out of her purse. "Let me call your father and let him know I landed safely."

I walk to the side of the car, out of view, and throw my purse in the back seat. I let out a deep sigh. I don't know if I can do this. I don't know how to be a normal daughter.

There is no such thing.

What will we talk about? What will we do?

Talk about the weather. Play Scrabble. Go shopping. Watch TV.

I knew this was a big mistake.

Stop thinking you need to act any certain way. Just be with her.

Just be.

With.

Her.

I stretch my arms over my head and take a deep inhale. I look over at my mother and see a tender little girl in an aging woman's body. I stare at her.

I have no idea who she is.

You can do this.

I realize that my whole life I've wanted my mom to be somebody different. It's time to meet her as she is.

Just be real.

What if real means I want to punch her?

Real from your center. Not from your fear.

I breathe into my center.

We begin our drive.

"Tell me how you are, Mom," I say. "I want to know everything."

4

One month later Steven invites me to attend a weekend workshop on conscious relationships. I agree to go, imagining it will be a good opportunity to reflect on our connection, to have a lot of sex, and to impress upon him my unwillingness to lose myself in a man. I'm testing how fully he supports my autonomy. And how willing I am to support his.

It's the final night. We're lying side by side in bed.

"Steven?" I say, looking at the ceiling.

"Yeah."

"This weekend has been amazing. I've learned new things about intimacy, transparency, and longevity in relationships. You know how much I love being with you. But, I'm beginning to feel nervous about going any deeper.

"Why? What do you mean?" he asks.

"Well, I trust that I'm where I'm supposed to be in life. It's been more than a year and, though I still miss Sam at moments, I feel pretty solid. And even though I know it annoys you at times, how I could ever question leaving Sam, the truth is that what I'm really afraid of is losing my connection to the sweet quiet source of stillness within. I'm concerned a more serious and involved relationship with you might pull me away from my center."

Steven rolls onto his side and looks at me.

"The Stillness, the Emptiness, the Source, whatever you want to call it, is always here, Sarah," Steven answers. "I suggest you stop worrying about the future and simply trust yourself and the solidity of your bond with it, like Jun Po told you. Relax. Let yourself live and love and serve and play in life with abandon."

He smiles, looks directly into my eyes, and adds, "With me."

"Abandon?" I say as I sit up. "I don't know about abandon. That feels *way* too out of control for me."

"Precisely, Serious Sarah!" Steven laughs.

His wildness excites me and scares me.

"Let your humanness be a little bit out of control, Sarah, because the truth is that it *is*. And trust the stillness as the ground of you, because the truth is that it *is*."

Steven pulls me back down next to him, then slides me closer as we tuck our bodies into each other like stacked spoons. His breath is in my ear.

"Then ask yourself the question: Why *not* let me be a part of your life, your stability in an out-of-control world? Embracing your autonomy doesn't mean you have to do life alone. You just have to be sovereign in your relationship with yourself. Same as I am. We could make a great team, the two of us. We'd be alone together."

Is this even possible?

"I know I want to continue to move into life," I respond. "But I'm in no hurry. I just don't know about a serious relationship right now. It might be too soon."

"Remember," Steven cautions me, "to live with abandon doesn't mean to be reckless. The right relationship will only support your blossoming.

What's unfolding between us is so rich. Neither you *nor* I were looking for this, but it's happening. We can't deny this. So why not embrace it?"

Now Steven's tickling me, kissing me all over.

I try laughing with abandon since the tickling has got me started. At first I hold back, feel phony. But then I let go. And it feels okay. Safe. I'm hysterically laughing, until I'm crying, practically peeing my pants.

Maybe I *can* do this.

"Falling in love" is a romantic affair, filled with all kinds of fantasies about what the person and the relationship should look like. Romance begins with a whirlwind of oxytocin and all danger signs hidden. Reasonable people wait for the romantic wave to pass before they commit long term.

Since Thailand, I've actually considered asking Steven many times to disappear for a while, but the tsunami sealed something between us, as if our fate were somehow consummated on that beach. I see this more clearly now and feel us being drawn into a future together. And yet I remain cautious. I want to ask him to call me in ten years after his daughter has grown up because I don't feel up for step-parenting. I want a simple life. A tidy life. A manageable life.

There is no such thing.

One year later Steven and I move in together. Holding sacred our fierce commitment to supporting one another's individual path, we create a relationship grounded in mutual respect and love. We remain autonomous and interdependent.

I open my own massage therapy practice, teach mindful movement classes in town, and gingerly build a relationship with Steven's daughter, Alex. I spend many hours in conversation with Jun Po and other teachers and practitioners, discussing the relationship between form and Emptiness, grounding myself in a philosophical understanding that supports my evolution.

In December, Steven and I are traveling to the Dominican Republic for a holiday. On layover in Miami I impulsively purchase a paperback from the bookstore. I haven't read anything other than spiritual and philosophical texts in more than twelve years. I tuck *Eat Pray Love* into my carry-on bag.

On the last day of our holiday, Steven and I take a walk on the beach. I tell him I'd like to talk about marriage. He abruptly stops walking and sits down in the sand. He's clearly in shock.

"Marriage?" he repeats, looking up at me softly.

I lean over and kiss him tenderly on the lips.

"Yes, marriage." I repeat. "We've been together long enough that I don't see us as a passing thing. And, you know me, I don't generally do things half assed." Steven smiles. "So, if we're going to do life together I want a ceremonial process to seal our intention and declare our commitment. It doesn't have to be anything fancy, it just has to be real."

Steven pulls me down into the sand and wraps his strong arms around me.

"Okay, Serious Sarah," he whispers in my ear, "I'll consider it."

Steven and I spend six months learning about the purpose, value, and meaning of marriage in various traditions throughout history. We discuss the value and meaning of what marriage might mean for us. Soon, I find myself planning three weddings. Each ceremony has its own purpose, setting, dress, and cake.

The first wedding is with Steven's family in California. His mother no longer travels, so we take the wedding to her backyard. Joining us are Steven's brother and sister-in-law, Steven's son Jordan and his fiancée Melissa, and, of course, Steven's daughter Alex. My mother and father fly in from Detroit. A close friend and Buddhist teacher officiates. This intimate ceremony initiates us into sacred relationship. I wear a simple white linen dress. We order a cake from Whole Foods.

That night when we crawl into bed and make love, I feel the countless sexual experiences in my body coalescing into unanticipated wholeness. It's like the eight masks on the Wheel of Sexuality are finally fusing into one single mask. Ready to weave my sexuality, emotional intimacy, and spirituality into one relationship, I wrap myself around my husband and squeeze.

"Two wings, my love," I whisper into his ear, in between nibbles. "I now fly with two wings. Right next to you."

The second ceremony is in Ashland with our community at a beautiful private home overlooking the valley where we live. Dear friends officiate. She is the personification of the grandmother in my dream in the sacred tent. He is like the Jewish uncle I never had. I wear a designer dress from Paris that looks like a Monét painting. It's strapless and long with soft pastel flowers woven into the fabric. The stylist from the Aveda spa does my hair in an up-do and a local baker makes an organic cake with frosting the same colors as my dress.

The third wedding is with my family in Michigan. Steven and I are fortunate to actually find a rabbi with strong Buddhist leanings to marry us. I buy a traditional white wedding dress for $25 at Goodwill and have it cleaned and tailored to fit.

In the morning before the wedding, my father pulls me aside and asks if I will allow the rabbi to "officially" change my name from Lisa to Sarah. When I was born, my father's rabbi blessed me with the name Lisa, the one my father chose for me. Rabbis' blessings have always been important to my dad.

I agree to allow this rabbi bless my new name.

As my father holds my hand, the rabbi places a prayer shawl over our heads and recites a prayer blessing me as Sarah, the daughter of Eliyahu.

With this ritual act, my father and I complete something. Nothing from the past is ever discussed again as we step across the threshold into the present.

During the wedding ceremony, my four siblings hold the *chupah*, the traditional canopy under which a Jewish bride and groom are bound. My three nieces and two nephews carry my train. After the ceremony, we eat bagels and lox while the rabbi tells stories of how Judaism and Buddhism are actually not as different as one might imagine.

5

I'm driving in a rainstorm when I get the call. It's my youngest brother Adam. I let it go to voice mail. After pulling over to park, I listen.

"Dad has taken a fall and is in the hospital. Call when you can." Adam's voice quivers.

A golden maple leaf hits the windshield and sticks.

My skin ripples, sensing something ominous.

I dial Adam's number. He answers. He's with Mom and Dad at the hospital.

"They've done a CT scan," he tells me. "There's bleeding on his brain."

"They're waiting to see if the bleeding will stop by itself," he continues. "They're giving him blood thickeners."

I wonder what "they" look like.

Adam hands the phone to my dad.

"Hello," a shallow and quivering voice says.

"Hi Dad." I try to sound cheerful. "How ya doing?"

"Not so good, baby."

I'm learning to love it again when he calls me this.

"I'm so sorry," I say.

Silence.

"Hang in there," I add.

"Okay," he whispers.

"I'll come soon," I promise.

"Good."

Silence.

"I love you, Dad."

This time the words don't catch in my throat.

"I love you, too, baby."

That night the phone wakes me from a deep sleep.

"Hello?" I'm groggy.

"Sarah? It's Ellen."

I hear the panic in my sister's voice.

"What's up?" I sit up in the bed.

"It's Dad. We just got a call from the hospital. He's gotten worse. They're taking him in for emergency brain surgery."

Ellen is sobbing uncontrollably.

"I'll get there as soon as I can," I say.

I hang up, wondering if, after so many years of being estranged from her, my sister can feel me now. If she is willing to. To let me show up. To help. And to do my best at loving her.

I call United and ask the airline agent to help me arrange for an immediate departure. I tell her that my father is in surgery. They're cutting open his skull.

What kind of tool do they use for that?

They're sopping up the bleeding on his brain. Left brain. I need to get there.

Can the brain think while it bleeds?

Will he ever be able to tell us?

I arrive on a Tuesday afternoon. A vigil has already begun in the ICU waiting room. Our family has taken over. We settle ourselves into uncomfortable chairs that look like they should recline, but don't. My mother and I bring our knitting. We talk patterns, wool, and missed stitches. She taught me how to knit when I was young and, now, like lost members of an ancient sisterhood, we've found our way back here, to this familiar place, where stitch-by-stitch we weave the tapestry of our incomprehensible connection.

My father survives the surgery and is in recovery. The extent of the brain damage is unknown because he's still unconscious and intubated.

He's a fighter, we all agree. He's tough, we all know too well. He could make it, we say. But none of us are sure we believe it this time.

I was in eleventh grade when I came home from school to find my father lying flat-out on his bed suffering from an acute angina attack. He could barely speak. He said I should call Mom.

"Call Mom?" I said. "Screw that!"

I called 9-1-1.

At the time, my dad was only two years older than I am now. He was in surgery within forty-eight hours to replumb his heart with veins taken from his legs.

My dad said the worst part of that surgery was being intubated. He hated the feeling of having a tube down his throat, unable to communicate, to swallow, to breathe on his own. They tied his arms to the bed like they do in the psych ward so he wouldn't rip out the tube.

It was a control thing.

For fifty years my father has sat in the same seat in his synagogue every week. His spot was on the end of the very last pew on the left. You could find him there every Saturday. One might presume he chose that seat so he could greet people as they arrived. But that wasn't so.

It was a control thing.

My father didn't want anybody sitting behind him. He did the same in movie theaters. Sat in the last row. My brothers think his behavior had to do with something traumatic that happened to him during the Korean war. They never told me the story.

Now, as I see my dad lying on the hospital bed with a tube down his throat again, I think, Oh God, please let them take that tube out soon. His bleeding brain may not kill him, but having to deal with being intubated might.

He looks like a Halloween ghoul.

I stare at him and cry.

Days and nights fold in on each other as we wait for a sign.

It's late in the evening on the fourth day. My brothers have gone home with their families and my mom is in the hospital room with my dad. She thinks he's aware of her presence, so she sits next to him and, in her distress, incessantly rubs his hand. My sister and I are alone in the waiting room.

"I'm sorry," I blurt out of nowhere.

Death is hovering. The tan walls of the hospital feel like sandpaper against my skin. The only thing holding my sister and me together is our shared blood. And it's thin.

"I wish I could have done things differently," I say to her.

I wish we could rewind.

I'm not even sure she hears me. She's texting.

"It's okay," she finally responds, still staring at her phone.

Then she looks up. I stand before my baby sister flooded with love. Unguarded. Vulnerable. She says nothing, but offers me a glimpse of her heart through her moist eyes. I can see where her heart's been broken, cracked by my obscene selfishness, my inability to connect with her, my lack of receptivity to our sisterhood. I don't blame her for never reaching out. I had no idea how to receive her love. Or to love her.

Ellen takes a step towards me. We hug.

I sob.

She holds me.

This says everything.

6

Finally my father's condition stabilizes enough to breathe on his own. Our family stands around his bed, optimistic that he's still in there somewhere, as the tube is removed. He goes in and out of consciousness. The doctors still can't determine the extent of his brain damage.

My dad's breathing is raspy but even. When he opens his eyes and turns his head towards us, he appears to see us. But he doesn't speak.

My mother is certain my father recognizes her, but my siblings and I are doubtful. I feel my father's gaze on us like a newborn's. It's as if he's comforted by our familiarity, but has no clue who we really are. He follows commands to close his mouth, but within minutes his jaw drops open again like a broken hinge. He's able to squeeze our fingers, but only with his left hand, as he manages to growl in a desperate attempt to say something.

Every now and then his body lurches and he opens his eyes wide as if trying to escape through them. He then peers into us, through us, as if to say, "Whoa, what a trip this is. Get me outta here, will ya?"

It's weird and scary and uncomfortable to be with my dad in this way. Not knowing what he's registering makes communication awkward. I chuckle to myself. This is how it's often felt between my dad and me.

The doctor reminds us that neurological recovery is slow. Just because he hasn't spoken yet doesn't mean he'll never speak. These things can take time.

As my siblings and I leave the hospital that evening, we start a new topic of conversation. Today our father's breathing on his own. Now we have to talk about rehab centers. We wonder where we'll put him and how we'll pay for it.

I place sheets on the couch for myself as my mother crawls into the left side of the double bed she's shared with my father for almost fifty years. My mom likes to remind us kids that it's the same bed *she* was conceived in, twenty-three years before she met my father. She's proud of that. I think it's a tad creepy. My parents had their sleeping configuration down to a science. The way they conformed their bodies, each to their side of the bed. Never touching.

I marvel at how they never upgraded to a queen.

The call comes at 3:30 am. My sister answers it. Dad's brain has hemorrhaged again. They intubated him and the doctor has sent him down for another CT scan. We should come to the hospital immediately.

The scan reveals another hemorrhage. This one has displaced his midbrain. My father's body is no longer viable.

We each take a few moments alone with my father. Then we gather around his bed like a sacred posse, each of us holding a hand or a leg or his cheek as we sing the *Shema,* the holiest prayer of the Jewish people. *Shema Yisrael...* My dad sang it every day of his adult life. *Adoniai Elohenu...* If recited when you take your final breath, it assures the soul an elevation to holy status. *Adonai Echad...* Since he can't do it himself, we recite it for him, trusting that God will understand. I'm so happy to do this for my father. The prayer floats into his ears from our familiar voices. We sing as we cry, not knowing what's registering in his broken brain. Knowing we'll never know.

The doctor says that, once they take him off the ventilator, it might be hours until he is gone.

It takes six minutes.

The harvest full moon has just set in the west. The sun rises crimson in the eastern sky just as my father takes his final breath. It's the dawn of All Saints Day on the Gregorian calendar.

This is a good day to die.

My family stays huddled together around my father's body. I stare at his withered face and wonder where he is.

Right here. He is right here.

The torment has left my father's beaten body and his skin looks smooth. I know his life is over, but I sense something about him still here.

Still.

Here.

Nothing dies. Everything changes.

I can't shake the feeling that my father orchestrated this whole ordeal. The vigil in ICU was for us. While he tinkered with death from his hospital bed, my family was forced to enter a timeless zone together, where we could only reminisce, share, laugh, and take care of one another. Like we used to when we were growing up. I can't help but think my dad did all this for me. So I can be a part of the family again.

My father always said that family was the most important thing to him. He would do anything to keep us together.

It was a control thing.

7

She's barely the length of my forearm. I carefully cradle our little bundle of newborn. Her breath is like a purr. I'm captivated by her tiny face and pursed lips, the one perfect hand reaching out of her swaddling. Her long fingers remind me of an old person's, wrinkled and wise. I could stare at Edie all day and not get bored.

I imagine what it would have been like to have birthed a child of my own.

Edie is our first granddaughter. The first child of Steven's son Jordan and his wife Melissa. Steven is so excited with his new role as Grandpa he can hardly stand it. Edie calls forth a side of him I've never seen. With Edie, Steven is softly playful and deeply tender-hearted. He melts easily around her. I'm charmed by the way he shows up as grandfather, equally at home with soothing her cries as he is changing her teensy diapers.

Married for more than three years, I'm in love with Steven on an even deeper level now.

I want to have a child with him.

Steven is clear. He doesn't want more children. Having two kids nineteen years apart, he's already devoted almost thirty years to parenting. Plus, he's twelve years older than I am. He's looking forward to having time and energy for other things once Alex is grown, such as being a grandpa and doing fun stuff with me. Besides, he says, "I don't think I could graciously handle parenting a teenager when I'm in my seventies."

I'm forced to examine where my desire to have a child is arising from. Is it coming from the ground of Emptiness, or is it left over from my life as Lisa, coming back now to haunt, possibly torment, me?

I want to give birth so I can feel the primal thrust of a fully formed baby emerge from my body. I didn't give myself the opportunity to do that twenty years ago when I had the two abortions, but I could still do it now. Something feels incomplete in the core of my female self.

A couple of months ago, my close friend Debra asked me to be at her first child's birth. I took it as an opportunity to show up for her, but also for me to give birth vicariously. As she surfed the waves of pain, I squatted and breathed with her, sensing an ache in me much deeper than merely physical. When the final push came, Debra's son ripped her open, announcing his entry into this breathing world. I sobbed uncontrollably. Gabriel's entry was intense like a raging fire, alive and messy and out of control. Completely miraculous. My awe was ecstatic. All I could do was laugh and cry simultaneously.

For me, this urge to birth is body based. I want the birthing experience. It's not about raising a child. After Debra's baby made it safely through the birth canal, I watched his papa cut the umbilical cord and lay Gabriel on Debra's chest. The look between Debra and her husband caught my attention. The intimacy between them touched me deeply. Together they had created a miracle and they knew it. I saw the power of love in that single glance. I want to feel *that*.

I ache to co-create something with Steven, and what's more co-creative than making a child?

You're creating a life together instead of a baby. This is enough.

Since the tsunami I've sat many hours in meditation and prayed, asking for guidance about whether my full immersion into life requires the birthing of a child. Do I need that experience in order to be whole, to be human, to be fully woman, to embody the complete experience of inhabiting the form side of the Emptiness-and-form equation? Because if I do need to have a baby, I'll find a way. It just won't be with Steven.

I always get the same answer.

No.

You were not meant to have children of your own.

I'm consistently relieved by this answer.

And stricken with grief.

I track these two waves in my body now. First the grief. It originates and terminates in the cells of my physical body. My ovaries shout about their holy responsibility to produce eggs for successful fertilization and production of more humans. "How could you deprive us of fulfilling our purpose?" they scream.

As if it's my job to make sure their purpose is fulfilled. What about *my* purpose?

"Come on, Sarah," cries my body, "there are a few more eggs left in here! It's not too late. We can still do it! Lots of women are having babies in their forties."

I listen. I understand. I let my body grieve.

Then I trace the relief. It originates deep inside, and spreads out farther than the grief. The relief belongs to my soul and it embraces my heart. I'm charged to Love, capital L. Period. Having a child of my own would limit my ability to Love in the way that Love wants to express itself through me.

I surrender to this truth as I stare at Edie. She's nestled in the hollow of my lap.

I Love her.

That night, lying in bed, I snuggle into Steven's arms to weep. I'm sad to have missed the experience of creating a child with him.

No one gets to experience everything. The secret to a happy life isn't found in any particular experience, it's hidden in the quality of how we live the experiences we have.

Steven doesn't try to take away my grief or to fix it. He doesn't offer to reverse his vasectomy and impregnate me. He simply holds me in my grief. He pours his Love for me directly into my heart.

I melt.

We *are* creating a beautiful life.

Early the next morning I sit rocking Edie in her nursery. The sun casts an easy glow through the thick curtains and the light is perfect. She is awake in my arms. The house is quiet.

"I feel so lucky," I say to her, "to be intimately involved in your life from the moment you were born. I haven't done that with anybody before."

I sway in this revelation and let my Love for this innocent being flood the landscape of our future. "My granddaughter, Edith." I love the way that sounds. Through some ironic synchronicity, she bears my maternal grandmother's name. I hold her as if she is of my flesh and blood and bone. Because, in a way, she is.

"You know, sweetheart," I continue, "a girl can never have too many grandmothers."

She coos as if she's hearing me.

Softly weeping, I lift her up on my shoulder and rest my cheek on her head. I close my eyes and sense my grandmother's presence in the room with us. Then I'm aware of my entire ancestral bloodline, back, back, back towards the beginning of time. I see an infinite pyramid of souls. There is no beginning.

There's only now.

Here I sit, a truly unfathomable mystery, alive in the nexus between no beginning and no end, holding a miracle named Edie.

"I'm just so happy to be here," I say to Edie. "I want to harvest everything I've learned in my life's journey, squeeze it into a single point of light and give it to you right now. Something you can keep in your back pocket forever."

I missed not having a grandmother who was truly wise and able to guide me. I never realized how much I needed one. Until now.

I rock Edie as we walk around the room.

"If you ever feel lost and wonder which way to go," I whisper, "try going inside. Go in and down, in and down, until you find the deepest knowing of who you are. Your essence. You don't have to retreat from the world, digging through a broken life to find your Self, like I did. There's a better way, an easier way."

I continue walking as I bring my lips to Edie's tiny ear.

"I know you already know what I'm talking about," I continue. "You still embody so much Emptiness. You're *made* of Emptiness-dust!" I giggle.

Her soft skin against my lips is like a gentle kiss from life itself.

I chuckle at our secret conversation, at the preciousness of it. I wonder how my own life story might have unfolded if I'd had a grandmother like me.

"I'll help you as much as I can, Edie," I tell her.

I was born, and broken, for this.

I lift her off my shoulder and hold her out in front of me.

Her eyes are wide open.

Now

Steven and I continue to deepen in our love. We walk steadily through life together, nurturing our individual selfhood while weaving our separateness into an exquisite partnership. We're passionately engaged in our work as agents of change in a complex evolving world, answering the call to elder. The process of reconciling with death has us wandering into the final chapters of our lives tenderheartedly, delighting in being friends, lovers, parents, and grandparents.

While writing this book, I founded *Selfistry*, a school for mastering the art of being human, offering simple and elegant methods for self-discovery. Derived from my personal experience, *Selfistry* maps three essential elements of the journey to radical self-knowledge and authentic selfhood. Through *Selfistry* I offer a way into the depths of stillness and silence without needing to retreat from the world. I show the value of cultivating solitude alongside a capacity to objectively witness both internal and external influences. I teach the difference between facing one's self and trying to fix one's self. *Selfistry* harvests many tools and teachings from spiritual traditions throughout history, but strips them of dogma, rhetoric, and ritual, making them accessible and effective for these times.

I teach *Selfistry* worldwide and am an embodied ambassador for a healthy selfishness. When not teaching or blogging or podcasting or engaging in rich conversations through various platforms, I enjoy traveling and exploring other lands and cultures, eating locally sourced sustainable delicious food, reading a wide range of fabulous writers and bloggers, being in the magnificence of nature, resting in the arms of my beloved, and appreciating the remarkable creativity emerging in our world.